OSHA PSM COMPLIANCE WITHOUT GOING BANKRUPT

Other books by **Max Ansari** available from Washington Industrial Management Books (425-771-5928):

1. **Zero-Base™ Industrial Maintainer Training** - Unleashing of the Maintainer Power. $29.99
2. **Zero-Base™ Industrial Operator Training** - Unleashing of the Operator Power. $29.99

OSHA PSM COMPLIANCE WITHOUT GOING BANKRUPT

The Zero-Base™ Strategy That Works And Saves Money

Max Ansari

WASHINGTON INDUSTRIAL MANAGEMENT BOOKS
13619 Mukilteo Speedway D-5; Suite 1175
Lynnwood, Washington 98037-1606
Phone: (425) 771-5928; FAX: (425) 771-6439

This text is printed on acid-free paper.

Published by Washington Industrial Management Books

Technical Editor: Tom Burke
General Editor: Richard Johnson Jr.
Line Editor: Kathleen Masurak
Technical Drafting: Dylan Miller
Typesetting: Amy Liu

Library of Congress Catalog Card Number: 97-60911

Publisher's Cataloging-in-Publication
(Provided by Quality Books, Inc.)

Gold, Max, 1947-
OSHA PSM compliance without going bankrupt: the Zero-base strategy for compliance at 75% savings / Max Ansari – Ist ed.
p. cm.
Includes bibliographical references and index.
ISBN: 0-9656888-1-X

1. Industrial safety--Standard--Management--United States. 2. Industrial safety--Law and legislation--United States. 3. United States. Occupational Safety and Health Administration. I. Title.

T55.G65 1997 363.11'0681'0973
QBI97-40608

ISBN: 0-9656888-1-X
Printed and bound by Thomson Shore Inc, Dexter, Michigan 48130

This book is dedicated to the line managers everywhere, for having the patience and fortitude to live in the downsized world of ours.

Contents

PREFACE

My experience is that most maintenance improvement efforts focus more on reducing the cost of maintenance than producing the overall results. In mills with low maintenance productivity, a reactive mode of maintenance exists. When there is little planning and scheduling, the organization itself is often unaware of its absence or lack of emphasis on it. They might even think they do a great job.

CHRISTER IDHAMMAR

PRESIDENT AND CEO IDCON INC.

PULP AND PAPER, MAY 1997.

Most of what we do is fundamentally driven by our need to achieve something, which is governed by the following three factors:

- The nature of an advantage we tend to accrue from a given action. Or conversely, the nature of some undesirable situation we want to avoid
- The magnitude of the potential advantage or the undesirable situation
- The probability of occurrence for the desired or the undesired situation.

If an error is made in evaluation of any one of the above factors, then we are not likely to achieve what we were hoping to achieve.

If we focus only on avoidance of unpleasant or dangerous situations then this exercise is called **Risk Management.**

By extending the argument a little further, we can safely say that if we do not seem to have a good handle on the risk management aspects of our business, we must not be managing one or more of the three elements appropriately.

Going a little further we can also say that our management decision-making processes would be easy if we had a good grip on these three factors.

In a report (April 1997), the inspector general of the Transportation Department found the Federal Aviation Administration (FAA) to have exercised inadequate managerial functions as far as equipment maintenance is concerned, resulting in numerous failures of electric power systems. The FAA put the blame on old equipment and errors by technicians. But the report found that the administration had lost track of what was happening on the shop floor and ignored problems such as equipment obsolescence and technician training. It was not due to laziness; for many years the management and the technicians had put in long hours and were overworked in many cases. All of them did do something with their time, but apparently they did not know the difference between the important and not so important.

This scene is played out every day on most of the US industrial stage. The only difference is that there is no inspector general to write a report about it. The reality check is provided by the fact that the safety and the process reliability are still hot issues in our industrial world.

These days the US industry is faced with making tough decisions on the following fronts:

- How to make the plant operation safer for the employees and other stakeholders. This aspect is primarily driven by a multitude of regulations
- How to make the facilities more productive. This objective is driven by intense international competition.

A wrong decision on either one of the above challenges is likely to exact a steep price.

To look into such matters, in May of 1994 a group, **The Presidential/Congressional Commission on Risk Assessment and Risk Management,** was assembled. One of the goals of the commission was to *assess the uses and limitations of* ***risk assessment***. Though the focus of the commission was health and environmental problems, it took a comprehensive look at the general practice of risk assessment. It published its final report in 1997 and provided excellent guidelines called Risk Management Framework – which is likely to become a template for future state and federal policies on this subject. A few of the commission's findings are quoted below:

- Despite many years of managing risks, however, there have been few systematic attempts to examine the role of risk assessment itself in risk management and health and environmental protection. No generally accepted framework or principles for making risk management decisions has emerged
- A clear need to modify the traditional approaches used to assess and reduce risks emerged as a major theme from our deliberations. These approaches rely on a chemical-by-chemical, risk-by-risk strategy. They tend to focus attention on refining assumption-laden mathematical estimates of the small risks associated with exposures to individual chemicals, rather than on the overall goal of reducing risk and improving health status.

The report says that the traditional approaches are "often either too simplistic or too complex to be effective and relevant." (Reported by Chemical Process Safety Report, May 1977.)

Now going back to the point which was being made earlier, it is essential to have tools that can be used to assess risks in proper contextual and relevant manner. The tools must also be practical – without being too simplistic or cumbersome. Otherwise, given the challenges of real life, appropriate decisions cannot be made.

Unfortunately, the industry (as borne out to some degree by the Presidential/Congressional Commission) lacks such tools.

This book is an attempt to partially fulfill this need by providing a practical tool which is highly effective, practical and inexpensive: Zero-Base™ Methodology. This tool can be used to present a properly weighted picture based on the following components:

- Practical assessment of risk of failure for a piece of equipment
- Practical application of failure modes
- Impact of failure on safety, environment and revenue.

Finally, the tool produces, for each piece of equipment, a numerical value representing the threat posed by it to the operation. The idea being that if you control the most threatful situations, you are likely to end up with a highly safe and productive plant.

Acknowledgements

*F*or many years I've badgered hundreds of industrial technicians, engineers and line management personnel for informal interview sessions. In some cases, for some particular individuals and groups, I was forewarned to expect a difficult time and less than perfect cooperation. I am happy to report that I did not come across a single instance where people refused to open their heart and share their innermost feelings with me. Why? I am no Barbara Walters. Perhaps because the issues we explored weigh heavy on the mind of people who seek innovative solutions and know that we can do better. To all those people I am indebted and wish to express my deep appreciation.

Tom Burke, a senior production manager with Boise Cascade, went over the draft of this book in his own unique way: word by word and sentence by sentence. Few people know thermal power and pulp production better than Tom. I am grateful for his incisive reviews and comments.

I am also thankful to Dick Johnson and Kathleen Masurak for rendering an outstanding editing job.

Les Wittenberg and Joe Mettalia of Center for Chemical Process Safety (The American Institute of Chemical Engineers) shared valuable practical nuggets of wisdom with me, for which I am grateful. I strongly recommend all major chemical and petrochemical companies to join in on their new reliability data project (212-705-7673).

Finally, I owe it all to my wife Ismat, who did not know what she was getting into when she made the covenant of staying by my side through thick and thin. I'm thankful to her and our daughters Sophia and Nadia for having the patience and tolerance to live with me and give me their love and support, as I do what I have to do.

1

Introduction: A Magic Bullet?

It all depends on how we look at things, and not on how they are in themselves.

–CARL JUNG

What Carl Jung had to say applies only to humans. Unfortunately, we tend to apply the same to things mechanical. Industrial equipment is what it is–no more, no less. If you take care of it, it'll last a long long time. And, if you know what among your equipment is important and take care of it preferentially, you'll achieve unprecedented safety levels and process reliability. It's as simple as that.

The purpose of this book is to present a maintenance management philosophy and a system, which will enable any organization to comply with the ***mechanical integrity*** aspects of OSHA's PSM Rule and EPA's RMP Rule. The system being presented will help the users to do so at a cost saving of approximately 75% of what it would be if they did not use this system. Although the book emphasizes the safety aspects, the system is designed to be applied to all maintenance functions, and will yield unprecedented levels of system reliability and profitability.

This book does not present a fad. You will not find any "one-minute" solutions. Instead, the maintenance management issues are looked at in a holistic sense. If you need to bring about a change in a department as embattled and over-committed as the maintenance departments are in the large organizations, you need to look at many internal and external forces. What role does the corporate vision play in all this? How do people respond to risky situations, and why? What are the strengths and weaknesses of current maintenance practices? What are the strengths and weaknesses of desk-based analytical methods? This book explores all these questions and provides practical solutions that reflect real life and accepts the shop floor people as equal partners in this giant step forward.

This is a very difficult book to write – it has no natural constituency. Two of the subjects I feel passionately about are the free enterprise system and worker safety. Sometimes, at least on the surface, these two are looked at as fundamentally incompatible to each other, and this makes the writing of this book rather difficult. I envy the people who write books on one-sided issues, where the readers know where it stands before they pick up the book. But if you want to write a practical book relating to a contentious issue, you need to zero in on and build upon the strengths of both sides without compromising the fundamental *raison de etre* of either side. And that is not easy. The difficulty arises in finding your constituency, because as you wax eloquently on one set of issues, which may be close to the heart of one side, you run the risk of alienating the other side. Of course, a few pages later you change course and lose the rest. Having said that, I'm sure I'll end up with some open-minded readers who will take the agreeable, and not so agreeable and go through the whole book; so much for writing a best seller.

In this book I present a very effective and inexpensive system, which I refer to as Zero-Base™ Compliance (ZBC™) methodology or the ZBC™ method, which is guaranteed to enable you to start and complete your compliance journey very effectively in a cost-effective manner. The strategy presented here addresses only the equipment and system mechanical integrity aspects of the **PSM and RMP** requirements – which are likely to be the most cost-intensive of all, especially if handled improperly.

Some time back, I was reviewing the PSM compliance related activities of a client, an interesting exchange took place, which went something like:

> Max: ***So, how many people do you have working on the PSM compliance project?***

Client: Well, let's see. We have a Project Manager for this job. We've hired XYZ Corporation to help us out, it has three people on site, who are doing a wonderful job, I might add. Other than that we have put six of our own hourly people full time on this project. You should count me as well, after all I'm the PSM Coordinator – it's my full time job. Mind you, I'm not doing much developmental work, so maybe you should not count me.

Max: ***It's a lot of people, isn't it?***

Client: Yes, it sure is. We've postponed many of our other projects to get the PSM and RMP stuff out of the way. Our management has asked us to make sure there are violations. Money is difficult to come by, but we are postponing some of our other projects to get the money.

Max: ***What is your measure of success for this project?***

Client: (Pointing to some empty shelving) I want to see those shelves filled up with manuals. When the auditors come, I'll dump everything in their laps. Last time all they wanted to see was manuals and documentation.

Max: ***So management is really committed to PSM and RMP?***

Client: Absolutely.

Max: ***How often do you review your progress with the steering committee or members of senior management?***

Client: There is no steering committee. To tell you the truth, management is really not interested in the details. All I have to say is "Everything is coming along fine", and they leave me alone. But they do want to know about cost estimates and expenses.

Sound familiar? Actually the above discussion was spread over several hours, I've paraphrased only the interesting parts.

What was really happening there? Let me give you my assessment.

- Senior management was treating PSM as a necessary evil, and wanted to get over it somehow. In one case (somewhere else) I noticed that most of members of senior management were more concerned about their personal liability under the PSM legislation than anything else. Some of them were trying to find some sort of personal insurance to protect themselves. I've not seen this phenomenon in too many other places but I did find it interesting.

- There was no desire or evidence to internalize the intent of the PSM legislation. Most of the documentation, such as Process Safety Information, was being designed as a shelf ornament. Other information, such as the operating procedures, were being prepared in a manner, which rendered them useless for actual field application.
- Middle management had blown the PSM regulation completely out of proportion, and scared senior management out of its wits. Consequently, senior management had allowed diversion of human and financial resources from other projects to the PSM related activities. This was a classical "throw money at the problem" approach.
- The PSM Compliance Team was completely divorced from the intent of the legislation. The only intent was to please the auditors. Apparently, the auditors (these were internal auditors, by the way) left you alone if you had mounds of paperwork.

However, in some cases, the PSM-related activities were not really so much out of synchronism with the real world. As time goes by, most companies are trying to build up on the value-added aspects of the PSM/RMP regulations.

Then I asked my client another question:

Max: ***Do you think all this PSM related work that you're doing would make your plant safer than what it is today?***

Client (after thinking about it for a few minutes): Not really. Let's put it this way – it won't be any more hazardous than what it is today. But, there will be fewer environmental incidents.

What does this mean? How can one be forced into spending enormous amounts of money and expect nothing in return? There is something wrong here.

Some companies, on the other hand, do not go all out to comply with the legislation. They continuously deploy a small token amount of resources. However, most of the time they go about it the wrong way. A lot of marching-in-place goes on, without really achieving anything. Wasting a small amount of money in comparison to others does not really make it right or a better strategy.

Try an experiment at your plant: Ask first line supervision and the technicians the last of my questions stated above. You may be surprised at the response.

Now ask yourself, why you'd want to invest money in activities that don't really improve safety and have a questionable ROI. I realize that some companies are resigned to do so since they do not know any better. Most people think there is no way out of it – there seems to be no win-win solution.

This is where this book comes in.

As you go through this book I'll convince you that there is a better way to go about all of this, which also happens to cost much less. Since you are required to comply with the PSM/RMP legislation anyway, why not make the most of it and make some real improvements in your operation to boot.

This book demonstrates a system through which you can meet the intent of the legislation by focusing on real issues in a relatively inexpensive manner.

There are many ways to handle complex problems such as what we are talking about here:

- Very expensive ways which get the results
- Very expensive ways which don't get any results
- Inexpensive ways which don't get any results
- And inexpensive ways which are highly effective.

The method, which I am proposing, happens to fall into the last category. And since solutions of this sort are such a rarity, I intend to repeat this contention again and again. Many times, I've seen millions of dollars being squandered away on ideas which did not get anyone anywhere, so I'm sensitive to the cost and effectiveness aspects of any proposed initiative. It is very easy to create work, which looks impressive and keeps many people busy, and results in mounds of reports and paper work, without adding anything to the bottom line of the operation. This is exactly what is happening in most of the compliance-related activities in the industrial world today. I do have to admit that in at least some of the plants, management has selected qualified and prudent people to head the compliance effort. In these cases, not much money or time is being wasted, but neither is the compliance effort meeting the deadlines.

In this book we will be looking at some regulation language in detail and find some curious aspects about it. The regulation language (like elements of any other complex piece of legislation) can be dissected and studied ad infinitum, until it ceases to make sense. This is not the objective here. The goal is to review some curious usage of words and phrases. ***The ultimate aim of this book is to make a case for the intent of the regulation, and not against it.*** I am painfully aware of the fact that some would like help in finding loopholes in the regulations. It would be highly inadvisable to do so. Contrary to the present day conventional wisdom, OSHA regulations are as necessary as, say, traffic laws. They are restrictive but good for us in the long run. You see, the cautious car drivers have to obey the laws written for not so cautious drivers. Most people agree with this assertion in principle. Still some, for good reason, would argue with some of the logic behind the legislation language. I agree with that, some of the language is counter-productive. In some facilities, the challenge is how to comply completely with the legislation without going under. (OSHA having very little to do with the how's of the compliance – though at the time of writing it was becoming more participative in the solution development aspects.) The purpose of this book is not to find loopholes in the legislation, especially since there are none (the General Duty clause has taken care of it). Even if there were some, it would be foolhardy to make use of them. Doing so would be similar to driving at 100 mph in a school zone, just because you found a loophole in the traffic laws.

OSHA LANGUAGE AND COMPLIANCE

I deal at length with this subject later on in this book. However let me state at the outset that you have a choice of delivering compliance in one of two ways: compliance with the letter or with the spirit of the legislation. Both of these ways of doing business are mutually exclusive – you cannot have it both ways.

Thus my contention: You cannot really comply with the regulations, because OSHA and EPA would really like you to meet the intent as well as demonstrate literal compliance. It does not really matter whether you agree with my contention or not, this issue is not central to the message being delivered in this book. This book explores ways to achieve high levels of compliance through inexpensive means.

The intent of the regulation is to enhance worker and public safety by protecting them from catastrophic events. This is very clear and laudable (and very much needed, I might add). However, the regulation language requires that you create documentation and procedures for all of the covered "systems" and "equipment". Furthermore you are required to train operators and maintainers in the proper use of these systems and equipment. Taken literally, this requirement translates into hundreds of thousands of documents, which can cost millions of dollars to prepare and implement. Irrespective of how many people you throw at the job, it is impossible to maintain and update hundreds of thousands of documents in a timely fashion, especially if they cover both the banal and the critical. Leaving the money issue aside, such schemes are simply not desirable since they are likely to jeopardize worker safety instead of enhancing it. In the practical world, no tradesman will pay attention to the paperwork if it takes him hours to find the right one, especially if it deals with the equipment which he considers to be rather routine. It is a fool's dream to think workers will take the time to find procedures for every little thing they do. Also it creates a new danger, the workers, being saddled with the onerous paperwork, may ignore some of the really critical procedures along with the routine stuff. I realize computerized systems can play a big role in alleviation of these problems, but unless we delineate the important from the trivial this problem is likely to persist.

So ask yourself: are your current activities addressing the regulations in the literal sense or are you addressing the intent of the legislation? This book presents you with a method, which not only caters to the intent of the legislation, but also nudges you toward a situation where you may be able to seek and get the blessing of the enforcers of the regulations.

PRIORITIZATION OF EQUIPMENT

We do not know how to prioritize our work. I'm sure at this point most readers will disagree with me. In this book I intend to demonstrate this fact and explain why it is crucial to our safety and productivity.

I have yet to see an industrial plant where they prioritize their equipment correctly. I am sure that there are some exceptions, but I've not seen any. For the day to day business, we can intuitively prioritize our activities fairly accurately. That is, however, not the case when you have an enormous amount of equipment to do something with and limited resources to do so.

I used to manage the operation and maintenance of a major part of a very large plant. In the context of priority setting I used to notice a few curious things. There were hundreds of operators and maintainers. All of them were kept busy doing something, apparently important stuff, in the eyes of their bosses. The operators were continuously griping that the maintainers were ignoring the important tasks and were doing things, which were sometimes of no value (and at times detrimental, it was claimed). And maintainers, on the other hand, had exactly the same concerns about what the operators were doing. The important thing to remember in this context is competent people, who prioritized their work on some kind of analysis, headed both of the groups. The priority of a task, it seemed, depended solely on the view of the beholder (actually the background of the beholder). To make it more interesting, both of the groups (operators and maintainers) thought exactly the same way about the technical service people (i.e. not knowing what was important and doing useless things, which were at times silly – it was claimed). Later on I found similar problems in scores of other plants. An interesting thing in this context was how corporate management solved the problem. Instead of creating some initiatives, which would determine what was important and what was not, it handled this issue as a bouncing ball or a monkey on one's shoulder. The monkey was put on different shoulders, but the underlying problem was never solved. At different times, different solutions to these problems prevailed. Some of them are listed below.

- The operators were ordained as the "owners" of the equipment. The maintainers were asked to abide by the priorities set by the operators. However, the maintainers were still held responsible for reliability of the equipment. Instead of designing work, which made sense, a political battlefield was created. I only saw one senior manager, Floyd Mulligan, who rose above the battlefield problems and focused on real work issues.
- The maintainers were upgraded from second class citizens to a level where they could select what they wanted to do. They were allowed to select the important equipment and do appropriate things to keep the reliability up.

- The operators and maintainers were deemed to be co-owners of the equipment. They were supposed to work together in close cooperation with each other. The operators and maintainers made their own individual wish lists and then organized horse-trading sessions. In this scheme of things the group with stronger personalities came up ahead.

Curiously, management and the technical service engineers were never consistently involved in such exercises. So my contention is that when you say that your people have prioritized their work, all you are saying is that you have a priority list which reflects someone's opinion. There may be a lot of backup analytical paper work, but it is still an opinion, and does not necessarily reflect the needs of management and the shareholders.

Ask yourself: Do you really know what is important and what is not important in your plant? Or is it someone's guestimate, which is driving the work processes.

WHAT IS THIS ALL ABOUT, ANYWAY?

We should not lose sight of the two fundamental laws of nature.

- Most work puts our health and well being at risk
- Most work alters the environment.

It's as simple as that.

The redeeming factors are that even when we don't work our life and limb are at risk due to commonplace ambient happenings (slipping in the washroom, traffic accidents, etc.) around us. Let's call this our base-line risk.

Also, even if we don't work, many natural agents (Mt. St. Helens, etc.) continuously modify the environment, which is sometimes permanently altered and sometimes repairs itself to an earlier status. Let's refer to this as the capacity of the environment to maintain itself as a life-sustaining ambiance.

So the issue at hand can be transformed to the resolution of the following questions:

- How can we work while maintaining the risk to our health as close to the base line as possible?
- Secondly, how can we design our production processes so that we do not cause damage to the environment, which is beyond its

natural capacity to handle, and is likely to deplete its life-sustaining capability?

The trick is to somehow, **without spending too much money**, develop and implement management systems which:

- Maintain worker safety
- Preserve the environment
- Increase worker productivity.

It sounds like a tall order, but it can be done.

My journey into this realm of business management started in the late eighties. During an assignment as a Maintenance Manager, I (among thousands of others across North America) confronted a stark choice: Either come up with innovative ideas to do more with less money or become a statistic in front of the downsizing steam roller. Having written a few papers on equipment reliability – as a part of my master's degree in engineering – I had some background in applied statistics. I was able to come up with a system, which separated the essential from the non-essential – after that, all we had to do was develop some hard-nosed implementation plans. As a result I was able to deliver the highest reliability and availability at the lowest cost for the system under my custodianship – in comparison to all similar systems across North America.

Since then the system has gone through some radical changes and has successfully been applied on equipment relating to gigantic oil pipelines as well as smaller enterprises such as bleach plants in pulp mills.

After many years of trial and error the system was radically changed in late 1996 to reflect the needs of the emerging industrial world.

It is certain that industrial development and creation of wealth could not be where it is today, were it not for the aggressive initiatives taken by the earlier entrepreneurs. Sure, it took an enormous human toll. But was it worth it? This question has no answer. A society determines its own course, and whatever course it chooses is right for it at that time in history. Sometimes the society errs and consequently pays a heavy price. As a matter of fact *vox populi* is never perfect or totally reasonable, the agents of change it responds to make it swing like a pendulum – but it is the voice of the owners and must be heeded. This brings me to one of my fundamental beliefs: There is no such thing as a precise and static definition for **adequate safety** or **good enough environmental**

conditions. The quality of industrial safety and the environment is determined by the prevalent societal values, which are constantly changing and are shaped by the diametrically opposite influence of the wealth creators (the entrepreneurs) and the wealth-creation-platform owners (the public). This tussle has been going for hundreds of years and will continue to do so for many more centuries to come. I do not pretend to be qualified to judge either party, and in this book I do not make any attempt to do so. My purpose is to help deliver whatever society has deemed to be necessary in an economical and expedient manner.

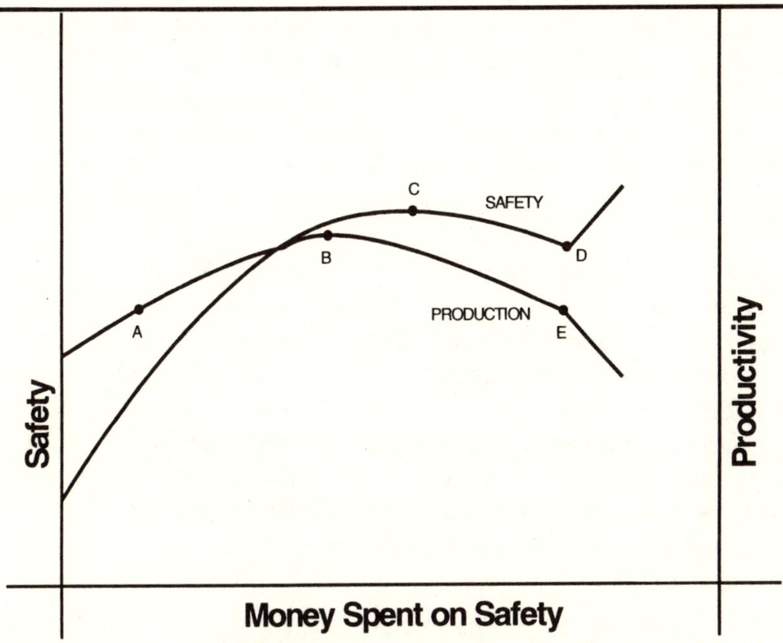

FIGURE 1 This figure shows the effect on safety and productivity as a function of money and effort spent on safety.

SAFETY VERSUS PRODUCTIVITY

Intuitively, we know there is a relationship between worker safety and industrial productivity. At this time we lack the scientific research and data covering the whole range of relationships between the expenditure on worker safety, and worker productivity. In my estimation the relationship is somewhat as indicated by the curves shown here. The figure shows two curves, one showing the worker safety versus the expenditure on safety, the other showing worker productivity versus the expenditure on safety. Let's start at the beginning of the curves, on the left-hand side – near region A. As you increase expenditure on safety, worker safety increases as well as productivity. It is a no-brainer to spend money on safety if your plant happens to be operating in this region. Do not consider this region to be of theoretical interest only – I know of many plants that operate in this region.

As you spend more money on safety, productivity and worker safety eventually level off (not necessarily at the same point). Productivity peaks at region B, and safety at region C. The relative location of regions B and C is determined by individual plant conditions. Later on, I will explain why worker safety levels off. Eventually the safety systems become so cumbersome that they create additional safety hazards – this is a real-life phenomenon, also explained later. As plant personnel get bogged down with safety, productivity suffers – this explains the peaking of the productivity curve. It is folly to think productivity will always increase if you spend money on safety. Theoretically it is possible to place a large amount of protective armor on people and systems to attain almost complete safety, however it is likely to slow down your production processes, which will actually increase safety even further, since fewer pieces of equipment would be operating. I must admit, that I've never seen a plant so bogged down with industrial safety systems that the production lines came to a halt. However, it remains a distinct possibility, but my guess is that long before that would happen, the plant would be moved to Mexico or elsewhere.

I've had the opportunity of looking closely at the shutdown of a few plants. In all cases I found the root cause to be the failure of management to rise to the challenge and delineate between the important and the frivolous. Also at play was the ignorance of management as to what was really happening or not happening on the production floor.

Getting back to our curve, the trick is to somehow find point C and operate there. The Zero-Base™ system, explained in this book, if followed, will nudge you closer to region C.

Frequently we talk about how much time and money is wasted in improving worker safety and the environment. The investment in safety or the environment has nothing to do with its utility, it largely depends upon the maturity level of society. I've heard many entrepreneurs say that the regulators will come to their senses when most of industry moves offshore and people take to the streets in protest against the high unemployment. I don't think it will ever happen in any meaningful degree. My bet is that a mature society, unfettered from external threats, will prefer a safer environment over affluence. So let's stop pretending that anyone will be able to move back the hands of time. Of course, the zeal and support of regulators will go up and down, and regulations will go through a continuous cycle of approval and repeal, but the underlying direction will always be toward better safety standards and a better environment. Incidentally, some of the other countries will go for the same goal but will follow a different route – being forced into remedial actions, rather than development and acceptance of pro-active plans. India, for example, lacking the foresight and will of the western group-think, is likely to pay a heavy toll in public health before it turns to better safety and environment standards – by that time it will be a no-brainer. So let's accept reality, but let's go about the rectification plans in a rational manner.

During an interview, a senior petrochemical production manager commented: "OSHA's regulations are a manifestation of natural evolution in social values. They are neither right nor wrong. They just simply are. And we simply must comply. I keep on telling my bosses: Let's stop fighting it and look for cheap compliance solutions."

This book explores many facets of PSM and RMP regulation application, and it can be very easily rejected as pro-OSHA or pro-business – depending upon the chapters you read – if you do indeed read only a few. Unfortunately I do not have the luxury of expounding on a one-dimensional philosophy. I deal with a fairly complex subject, where, unfortunately, there is no black or white, but numerous shades of gray. Furthermore, most of the shades of gray are irrelevant, meaningless and sometimes detrimental, leaving only, a few which make sense and need to be sought out. That is what we do in this book – find the shades of gray which make the most sense.

Having stated the main objective for this book, in the following sections, we'll briefly introduce the components of the problem definition and the proposed solutions.

COMPONENTS OF THE PROBLEM DEFINITION

Benign Neglect By The Industry

Most of the OSHA's edicts are based upon sound principles. Somehow, in the industry, people have no idea about the intent or the background of the regulations. With the exception of senior OSHA officials, no one ***ever*** talks about them – either on the side of industry or the OSHA's enforcers. Consequently, what is left on the table is a set of narrowly interpreted regulations. An unintended consequence of this is the default mode of industry's response – benign negligence: *Let's throw money at the problem and hope it goes away.*

Peripheralization of PSM/RMP Regulations

Having accepted OSHA's and EPA's presence as a necessary evil and having money to throw at it, in general, industrial management fails to tackle the compliance issue as a business objective. It is rather handled as an essential project on which some progress must be shown. With that mindset, the whole ball of wax is put it under the wings of a project manager, who is left to define the philosophy, objectives, and tactical plans. In such cases the project manager, and rightly so, focuses on the deliverables which look least contentious and self-blessed – thereby needing little additional justification, rather than the confirmation of validity of the goals, and the necessity of exploring the alternatives. Mind you, this happens because the project manager responds to the regulations and interpretations by lawyers who tend not to be business managers. The missing element is the managerial insight and intervention. Please note that approval of a budget or an occasional progress review by a steering committee does not qualify as managerial input.

Lack of Prioritization of Regulation Elements

Not much effort is put in determining the elements or sub-elements that yield the biggest bang for the buck in the form of real ROI, or *most compliance* per dollar spent. It is not done, probably because it is difficult to do so. This is a key issue in the sense that you cannot really ever have a state of perfect compliance. All you can hope for is a demonstration of due diligence while garnering the maximum compliance achievement for the money you want to spend. If this aspect of the business is not looked at carefully then it becomes highly probable that you may not have much to show for the money being spent. It makes no sense to spend the money and have nothing to show for it. Demonstration of actual expenditure and effort to the regulators, if substantial, gets positive results – but with a very short half-life. At the first violation or accident you'll probably need to demonstrate the soundness of your compliance strategy and prove that the shortcoming, which caused the incident, was indeed one of low probability instead of an accident of a reasonable probability that was just waiting to happen. My guess is that a situation where a lot of money is spent, but is found to be devoid of an overall strategy, may not look very impressive under adverse conditions.

To summarize, the net result of a peripheral approach to PSM/RMP compliance is:

- A large expenditure which does not add much value to the business. All you get in return for this expenditure is a myriad of internal hand-tying regulations, instruction manuals by the yard which no one uses, and a definite loss of productivity which only a few have the courage to talk about
- A transient improvement in relationship with the regulators, which quickly vaporizes when the first violation comes about, and the newly developed procedures are found to be wanting or do not exist
- Loss of an opportunity to really improve process safety, and add something of perpetual value to the bottom-line. You see, it is very difficult to fund safety-related projects, so it is heart-wrenching to see good money being squandered away on non-issues while real safety issues stare you in the face every day.

Inconsistent Use Of Terminology

During the last ten years or so I've been mystified at the different meanings and nuances being ascribed to the terms "critical equipment, or criticality". To be honest, for decades I participated in use of this meaningless jargon. Like others, I used it to indicate what I considered to be important at that point in time. Usually a critical piece of equipment was the one that caused last week's incident, which somehow got the attention of senior management. On the subject of criticality, I've a large collection of definitions given to me by various technicians, engineers and managers. Most of these definitions differ from each other. Are they wrong? No, certainly not. They represent personal points of view of what is meant by "criticality", and from that perspective it is probably all right. But, what we really need is an interpretation of this term that reflects the needs and aspirations of the management and the shareholders.

Since the application of such terms is inconsistent, usually no one pays much attention to them or to the equipment deemed to belong to such a category.

Absence Of Meaningful And Consistent Failure Rate Data

The cornerstone of any program designed to increase the reliability of a system depends upon knowing the expected failure rate of the major components of the system. Contrary to common belief, such reliable data, for the general smokestack industry, does not exist. Some data vendors do supply some numbers, which in most cases do not reflect real life in a specific plant and are practically useless. Sometimes the range of the numbers is so wide that it is very difficult to apply them. For example, the probable rate of failure for a differential pressure transmitter may be given as something between 1 and 250 per million hours of service. Now what do you do with this number? Actually these numbers are saying that the transmitter can be fairly reliable or completely unreliable, or something in-between! The only advantage it does give one is an ability to cook the end-result in any fashion one wants.

Again, I realize that it is hard to believe, but this situation is true for over 95% of industrial equipment. (To be generous I picked this number of 95% – in real life I've experienced this number to be as high 99%).

The bottom line is GIGO: Garbage In-Garbage Out. If your primary data is not valid, how can you expect the outcome to be to of any good?

Another problem with present day practices is the failure rate data is always backward looking. In these days of rapid technology advancements, it is simply imprudent to take this stance. The failure rate, say for a pump, as experienced today will have no relevance ten years from now because during this period we may make improvements on the pump seals, impeller material, cooling water flow rate, lubrication oil quality and filtration system, lubrication oil inspection regimen, etc. As a matter of fact, usually the equipment which is most troublesome in its early life is given extra attention and made much more reliable than a piece of equipment which is occasionally troublesome for reasons not fully understood. However, if you decide to use the backward-looking reliability data, your actions will be exactly the opposite of what they should be. This is because you'll be designing baby-sitting systems for something, which has become reliable over time, and you will be ignoring something, which has a potential to bite you at an inopportune time.

Insulation Of Human Aspects From Technical Processes

It has been proven time and again that human error plays a major role in a large percentage of accidents. Therefore you can make your equipment as robust as you want, but as long as humans are involved in the business, some accidents will occur. This also says that when you are evaluating the overall reliability of a process you must look at the human element as well. Before OSHA's crackdown, in most of the reliability or safety-related initiatives, the human element was ignored. This should explain why the new legislation puts so much emphasis on personnel-related requirements.

In spite of the above, in most places when the overall risk posed by a process is studied, the human element is generally ignored. This certainly does not represent real life, as we know it.

Limitations On The Depth Of Analysis

A hazard can be created by a particular piece of equipment in many ways:

- Failure of the equipment itself
- Failure of the equipment of interest while some other system is not functional
- Failure of the equipment of interest while two other systems are out of order.

And so on.

In the above, each additional element (variable) reduces the probability of occurrence of an undesirable event in a dramatic manner. In real life, a failure is usually caused by series of mistakes or problems. Yet most practical analysis is limited to two variables.

Inability To Study Different Types Of Impacts From The Same Root Cause

We are generally interested in three categories of outcomes:

- human safety
- environmental impact
- loss of revenue.

I commonly refer to these as the impacts of interest. As managers, we really need to know the impact of our actions and the reliability of our equipment on any one of these three aspects, separately or collectively according to our needs. At different times we have different needs, we may emphasize one aspect or another.

At the present time, most of the practical analytical methods cannot clearly delineate between the three aspects of interest.

Absence Of An Overall Strategy

This is probably the most prevalent and significant shortcoming of all. In most places the strategy is missing, thereby an atmosphere of directionless effort is created. As an old saying goes: If you do not know where you are going, you'll certainly end up somewhere, which will definitely not be to your liking. In some places the following slogans are thought of as strategy:

- Safety is our number 1 goal
- Our people are our most valuable resource.

These slogans and others like this have become common for over twenty years. About fifteen years ago, no one believed in them and paid them little attention. Since the early nineties I've noticed a subtle change. Now most of the employees handle these slogans in the following manner:

- Most employees **do believe** that safety is management's number one priority. They also think that management doesn't really know what to do about it. Management's sincerity is not in question any more. Also, most employees know that they have the best chance of getting something approved if somehow they can label it as a safety item.
- As to the second slogan, very few believe that. "You wouldn't lay off your best resource at the first chance you got, would you?" the employees ask.

Now we come to the good part. The system, Zero-Base™ Compliance, as presented in this book, resolves all of the above issues to a very large extent.

COMPONENTS OF THE PROPOSED SOLUTION

Development of meaningful and consistent terminology

It is absolutely essential that the definition of basic terminology be meaningful and consistent. In the Zero-Base™ method we define the two most important forms of criticality in a clear and meaningful manner. The definitions are constructed to be consistent under most circumstances and serve as benchmarks.

- Catastrophic-Criticality
- Disaster-Criticality.

Creation Of Meaningful And Consistent Failure Rate Data

We've created a new classification for failure rates: ***Zero-Base™ Failure Rate (ZBFR).*** To develop this type of rate of failure, the following information is looked at:

- Design Maturity
- Manufacturer's Reputation
- Ambient Conditions
- Application Severity
- Operational Conditions
- Operator Competence
- Maintainer Competence
- Five-year Failure History
- Published Rate of Failure.

After looking at all these factors, the expected failure rate for the future is determined by a very small group of experts. One of the advantages for using this approach is that you only look at the future and are not blind-sided by those elements of the past that are not relevant any more.

This approach combines the hard numbers with the opinion of the best available talent. There is no better way. Numerous researchers have investigated the needs of developing such a combination. A list of the few prominent works in this field is included at the end of this section.

Combination of human aspects with the technical processes in analytical work

The ZBC™ method uses a holistic approach throughout the analytical as well as the application process. The operators and maintenance technicians are considered as much part of the process as any piece of machinery. The combined operator and maintainer readiness (training and morale) plays a key role in determination of the expected failure rate. This takes care of the first part of the spectrum. On the other end of the spectrum, after the Zero-Base™ method has determined the equipment criticality for you, you are able to backtrack and reduce the criticality in a measurable sense by increasing the quality of human effort in the shape of better training or increased monitoring of the processes.

You can, of course, reduce the criticality by installing hardware solutions as well, in the form of improved ambient conditions, modifications in the operational duty of the equipment or substitution of some components with better ones.

No Limitations On Depth Of Analysis

The ZBC™ system is not limited as far as depth of analysis goes. Theoretically it is possible to construct ZBC™ analyses to look at an unlimited number of dependent variables and interdependent failures. However, for most of the applications three levels of failure modes suffice as far as sufficiency of rigor is concerned.

Ability To Distinctly Separate The Outcomes – According To The Nature Of Impact

The Zero-Base™ Compliance methodology allows you to determine **separately** the effect of failure of each piece of equipment. You can assess the impact on worker safety or environmental problems or loss of revenue. This is an important feature since it allows middle management to formulate tactical plans according to the strategy laid out by senior management. For example, management of a company may be satisfied with the safety numbers, but may decide to make improvements on the environmental front. Well, with ZBC™ you can do so, and pinpoint your actions and expenditure to bring about the most economical improvements in the environmental performance. You can similarly target improvements in worker safety area or the potential loss of revenue to the bottom line due to any issue.

The Zero-Base™ strategy depends upon a numerical calculation of threats posed by each piece of equipment. Each piece of equipment is looked at for:

- Threats to safety
- Threats to environmental damage
- Threats to loss of revenue

Each of these threats is evaluated in the form of an index. This really defines the nature of the beast. After that it's clear sailing, you can learn to kill the beast, feed it, or tame it. You cannot ignore it, since you know it exists.

Ability To Facilitate Creation Of An Overall Strategy

One would probably wonder why we did not put the strategy-related comments at the top of this list. There is a good reason for that: We needed to develop the preliminary concepts before we could get into discussions relating to strategies.

At first comes the vision. The vision is the "prime directive" – to borrow a phrase from Star Trek. It reflects your aspirations and your definition of the challenges you've decided are worth going for. This vision represents the first phase of the conceptual thinking which is commonly mistaken as the strategy. If you want to achieve something, you need to have a guiding vision to help you enunciate your desires and feelings.

The vision gives birth to strategies and tactical planning. You simply cannot hope to achieve anything unless you have vision and a desire to do so. A preliminary analysis will show that most of the compliance and productivity issues can be traced right back to a lack of vision and strategies.

The Zero-Base™ methodology helps one create strategies that can:

- Help determine what needs to be implemented
- Help implement what needs to be implemented

- Help communicate the overall strategy to the employees and others
- Help make a case to the regulators that such actions should be accepted as diligent and responsible behavior.

Having the right vision and an appropriate strategy is so important that a full chapter has been devoted to this subject.

THE ZERO-BASE™ COMPLIANCE METHODOLOGY: A MAGIC BULLET?

Some people have referred to the ZBC™ methodology as the magic bullet. I do not agree with that for many reasons, the principle of which is the expectation that one can close one's eyes and fire the bullet and all will be well. Such expectations accompany most management fads and usually end up taking one too many steps backward. Other reasons:

1. The Zero-Base™ system forces management to do its part in the development of strategic directions. Hence, this system should be considered as a tool for management to go about its business, rather than a magic bullet which anyone can fire.

2. This system yields qualitative and quantitative results and recommendations, which are based on rational analysis and assessments. These recommendations, while unquestionably among the best that anyone could practically and economically do, are not perfect – mainly because we have too many equipment and human-nature based vagaries. And since we cannot define the state of perfect compliance or the perfect operation or maintenance for that matter, we cannot have an absolutely perfect system. I tend to think (a conjecture on my part at this time of evolution of ZBC™) that if one could define the perfect compliance or the perfect operation/maintenance, the ZBC™ could easily be modified to deliver a requisite solution.

This system enables one to look at PSM/RMP compliance as a business objective in a straightforward manner. Compliance with OSHA is not always an opportunity to rake in more money like some will have you believe. For example, in the case of a mill, where the rate of undesirable incidents is already low, and where they need to spend millions of dollars to comply with OSHA, I do not see much of a business opportunity – only a business objective which needs to be met – as a cost of doing business. Let me hasten to add there are many instances where intervention from OSHA and EPA is a godsend to turn the place around and to make it profitable and fiscally sound.

The ZBC™ method is essentially a system, which seeks out the potential to make your system more efficient. It builds on principles which are generally used by OSHA and EPA to create regulations, but it certainly goes beyond that, since it is capable of considering the loss of revenue criteria on its own or in conjunction with the safety criteria. The government, however, has little interest in talking about pure loss of revenue issues.

This is a book that describes a system, which will reduce your exposure to undesirable incidents (safety, environment and loss of revenue) by a large amount and save you a huge amount of money to boot. Please consider going through the chapter THE BOTTOM LINE, which discusses what one may gain through the use of the ZBC™ method.

This book is one of a trilogy, the other two being:

1. Zero-Base™ Industrial Maintainer Training - Unleashing of the Maintainer Power
2. Zero-Base™ Industrial Operator Training - Unleashing of the Operator Power

Philosophically, these books are interdependent but each is designed to serve as a self-standing document.

References

Svenson, Ola. *On Expert Judgments in Safety Analyses in the Process Industries.* Reliability Engineering and System Safety, 1989.

Coolen, F. P. A., et. al. A Bayes-Computing Risk Model for the use of Expert Judgment in Reliability Estimation. Reliability Engineering and System Safety, 1992.

Kaplan, Stan. *"Expert Information" versus "Expert Opinions." Another Approach to the Problem of Eliciting/Combining/Using Expert Knowledge in PRA*. Reliability Engineering and System Safety, 1992.

Pulkkinen, Urho. *Methods for Combination of Expert Judgments.* Reliability Engineering and System Safety, 1993.

Chhibber, S. et. al. *A Taxonomy of Issues Related to the use of Expert Judgments in Pobabilistic Safety Studies.* Reliability Engineering and System Safety, 1992.

Mosleh, Ali. *Bayesian Modeling of Expert-to-Expert Variability and Dependence in Estimating Rare Event Frequencies*. Reliability Engineering and System Safety, 1992.

Amalberti, Rene. Safety in Process-Control: An Operator-Centered Point of View. Reliability Engineering and System Safety, 1992.
Ujita Hiroshi. *Human Characteristics of Plant Operation and Man-Machine Interface.* Reliability Engineering and System Safety, 1992.
Yoshimura, Sadanori. *Reliability Aspect of Man-Machine Interface.* Reliability Engineering and System Safety, 1992.
Hollnagel, E. *Reliability Analysis and Operator Modelling.* Reliability Engineering and System Safety, 1996.
Montmayeul, R. et. al. *The Managerial Dilemma Between the Prescribed Task and the Real Activitiy of Operators: Some Trends for Research on Human Factors.* Reliability Engineering and System Safety, 1994.
Macwan, A. et. al. *A Methodology for Modeling Operator Errors of Commission in Probabilistic Risk Assessment.* Reliability Engineering and System Safety, 1994.

2

Life Is A Risky Business

Believe me! The secret of reaping the greatest fruitfulness and greatest enjoyment from life is to live dangerously!

–NIETZSCHE, 1844-1900

Chapter Summary

This chapter provides an overview of how during the last few hundred years, modern humans have handled "risk" in business life. A summary of how "risk" evaluation became part of every day life is also discussed. Contrary to common belief, "risk" cannot be totally evaluated in objective terms. Not only does the perception of "risk" depend on the availability of evaluative tools, the psychological makeup of the effected parties and their background also have a major role to play. In this chapter some examples are provided to demonstrate how identical conditions can be perceived differently, depending upon how the facts are presented.

In the end, mathematical basis for the modern day risk evaluation techniques are discussed.

*I*n the quotation noted above, Nietzsche captures the essence of nineteenth century human enterprise. That is our heritage and the basis of the problems we face in some corners of the industrial world.

The most important issue this book deals with is risk evaluation. For this reason, it would be interesting to see how we got to where we are as far as notions about risk to human condition are concerned. As we go through this chapter I'll make an attempt to tie some esoteric concepts to what we see on the industrial shop floor.

Prior to the industrial revolution, organized saving of human lives was not an issue because injury and death were rarely accidental. The acts of getting hurt or getting killed were associated with being clumsy. It was probably reasonable since most of the injury causal factors were within one's control. Also every one believed in personal accountability – there really was no other choice, and it did make a lot of sense.

Then came the industrial revolution and life started to change. During this period human imagination was captured by the possibilities of enormous strides in productivity, as well as the likely ensuing damage to the environment. The doom and gloom stories were rampant (as they are today), some saying that all of the earth's oxygen would be eaten up by the steam engines in a period as short as ten years. At that time the stories were based on intuition and conjecture, these days they are largely based on results spewed out by supercomputers – leading one to ascribe a higher level of credibility to the present day forecasters in comparison to their nineteenth century counterparts.

Nevertheless, during the industrial revolution not much attention was paid to human condition – perhaps we were still suffering from the older mind set – personal accountability – even though the causal factors were gradually getting out of one's personal domain of control.

Most of the momentous human achievements involved individual ambition and willingness to place one's life at risk. OSHA would never have allowed the likes of Christopher Columbus to man a ship built under the auspices of unknown construction codes, manned by uncertified workers, to sail uncharted waters. Most of what we have today can be traced back to somebody who took personal risks and committed unsafe acts.

Mercifully, it does not follow, at least to any great degree, that if we cease to take personal risks, we cause the civilization to stagnate.

Gradually, the nature of new and adventurous initiatives is changing; they are being fueled more by institutional goals than by personal ones. Consequently the fruits of such labor are also harvested by the large institutions. This is a crucial new element in the whole scheme of things. That being the case, intuitively, we've come to realize that it's not fair for us to risk all we have (our lives and health) for something which we don't fully understand and which is much bigger than us. Sometimes we are a party to setting of the objectives or sharing the gains. It still doesn't seem fair. This is the essence of worker agitation for increased safety today.

The counter opinion is equally compelling: The workers' share of the booty should be seen in terms of continuity and stability of gainful employment. The process of job creation is based on someone investing money where, very frequently, no one else would. It is not unreasonable for someone, who invests most of what he has, to ask a worker to accept risks, which are not higher, hopefully, than those one experiences in other simple acts of living. The availability of jobs should not be taken as granted and must be predicated on, as one of the fundamental principles, the assumption of the newly created risks by the two parties.

The challenge is to find an equitable balance between worker safety, environmental sanctity, productivity and profitability. Unfortunately, there is no perfect point of balance; it continually shifts back and forth. However, at this point in history, the underlying trend is toward greater worker safety irrespective of the cost. When, in fifty years or so, the rest of world catches up with us in productivity, the situation may reverse.

We seem to have crossed a magical line. Now, at this time in history, we can enrich ourselves without putting human life and limb at much risk.

In the past, we made great strides in the sciences, technology and the discovery of the unknown. Other than astronomy, most of the meaningful endeavors took a great toll in human life. Also, unfortunately, most of the technological innovation (barring the industrial revolution) came as a result of war-making initiatives.
In this aspect two things are worth noting:

- We are far safer at work today than ever before
- Our environment has been at much greater risks in the past, than it is today.

Before the above statements are twisted and blown out of proportion, let me add that what I have noted here is a statement of fact. It does not, however, mean that at the present time the work place safety is adequate or the environment can indefinitely sustain the threats from the present day industrial processes. Such evaluations are made by society as it evolves and comes in better synchronism with its long term vital interests.

It is true that in earlier times we did not have some of the dangers we face today. Good examples of which are threats to human life posed by asbestos and radioactive substances. In spite of that it was not a pleasant scene. In an excellent book, *The Good Old Days - They Were Terrible* (Random House), Otto Bettman describes some of the aspects of, well, the good old days.

For ferries, before the invention of radar, river collisions were commonplace. In July 1871, the operating boiler onboard the ferry *Westfield* exploded, killing 104 people. Later on it was determined that the boiler had corroded to such an extent that a knife blade could cut through it. That was before the ASME code days. To name a few others, in June 1880 the steamer *Seewanhaka* exploded and sixty-two people were literally blown to pieces. During those days, before the establishment of boiler construction and operation codes, such disasters were the order of the day. **Curiously, the free enterprise system, on its own, could not resolve the challenges posed by explosions, fires and collisions.** It did take public ire and intervention by the government to improve the public and worker safety to an arbitrary higher level.

Same is the case with the railroad development. During the same period, wood-burning furnaces powered the locomotives. Smoke, cinders and steam engulfed the whole train as it sped along. At the end of the journey, the travelers found themselves coated with ash and grime. The train cars were heated by open iron stoves which were unstable and often overturned, especially if the train jerked to a stop or had an accident. The result, of course, was a fire and a multitude of fatalities.

Working conditions in the industrial sector were equally bad. Again, most of the problems were caused by the indifference of the entrepreneurs toward the working man. Workers were constantly exposed to toxic gases and general unhygienic conditions. An industrial worker's health was generally destroyed by the time he was forty. He had two choices: to continue to work 12-hours day at a daily wage of $1.25 in hazardous conditions or take a sweeper's job at 75 cents. Another alternative, of course, was to quit work and regress into a state of pensionless retirement.

President Harrison observed in 1892: "American workmen are subjected to peril of life and limb as great as a soldier in time of war." In 1890, about 0.3% of all railroad employees were killed in accidents and

3% were injured (which is hundreds of times greater than what we consider acceptable today). The public paid even a higher price than the railroad employees. In 1890 civilian deaths caused by the railroad were estimated at 10,000, while the number of people injured was pegged at 80,000. It was rare for a worker to round up enough money to bring a lawsuit against an employer, and when he did do so, the law usually sided with the employers. The employers refused to invest in protective equipment and rarely paid compensation for injuries on the job. The only concession was in the form of reimbursement for burial expenses.

All of the above was the good side of the industrial scene since we did not talk about the underground mines at all, where episodes of unimaginable horror took place.

I'll not go into the disgusting state of affairs as far as the environment was concerned. The industrial sites and the nearby towns were usually engulfed with toxic and odorous fumes. It was commonplace for travelers to carry smelling salts and perfumes for prompt application when they drove through certain sections of some cities, such as New York, Chicago and Pittsburgh, just to mention a few.

This certainly is a new era. It gradually came into its own after the Second World War. Today the passion for wealth creation is no longer alone at the center stage, it shares the limelight with the passion for public safety. We are no longer allowed to take unnecessary risks, nor are we allowed to put others at undue risk. This shift in values delineates this time in history from the earlier periods. This shift in values, augmented by an increasing ability to quantify risk, indicates this state of affairs is likely to be permanent.

RISK: AN HISTORICAL PERSPECTIVE

In earlier times, the quantification of risk to humans was of little interest to the philosophers and scientists. You will be hard pressed to find any reference to human safety in the classic records of human endeavor, starting from Homer's Iliad through many real wars and battles, discovery of America among other noble deeds, right down to the American civil war.

The historical development of risk quantification is narrated by Peter L. Bernstein in his excellent and highly acclaimed book *Against the Gods*, (John Wiley and Sons). The interest in understanding of probability of random events started with administrative problems' associated with gambling. During the fifteenth century a problem was posed to the monk Luca Paccioli, who taught mathematics to Leonardo da Vinci. The issue at hand was how to divide a common pot between two gamblers during an unfinished game of chance when one of them was ahead. Two hundred years of effort by many did not produce any meaningful results. In 1654, Chevalier de Mere, a French nobleman, with deep-rooted interests in mathematics and gambling decided to solve this problem. He enlisted the help of Blaise Pascal, a great French mathematician, who in turn involved Pierre de Fermat, a lawyer and a brilliant mathematician in his own right. The result of this collaboration was the discovery of the theory of probability. Immediately thereafter many mathematicians created and proposed new applications of this theory in every day life.

The British government was the first large institution to put this theory to public use. In the early eighteenth century it started to finance itself through the sale of probability-based life annuities. This instrument to raise capital played a key role in expansion and dominance of the British Empire.

As time went on Jacob Bernoulli invented the Law of Large Numbers, and Abraham Moivre determined the nature of the bell curve and how it governs our every day life.

Along the way came Harry Markowitz, a Nobel laureate, who, in 1953, mathematically demonstrated that putting all of your eggs in one basket was not a prudent thing to do. To make the most of your situation, you must diversify your exposure to risk. Although this concept was originally applied to investment portfolio management, it has, in my opinion, a direct application in the world of industrial risk management. Consider a pressure vessel containing a hazardous substance. Let's review two options to minimize the exposure risk of the toxic substance to the humans. Let's assume that for both of the options, we have a limited amount of money that can be invested to bring about an improvement in safety.

Option 1: Increase the vessel and pipe material thickness over and above what the usual codes call for, to reduce the chance of rupture.

Option 2: Leave the material thickness to what is dictated by the construction codes. Instead, invest in additional mitigating devices such as danger situation alarms, emergency fluid diversion schemes, emergency fluid containment schemes, training in response systems, etc.

According to Harry Markowitz's theory the second option presents the more prudent course of action.

This should shed some light on why we need containment dikes around reservoir tanks, rather than stronger tanks.

By the first half of twentieth century, the theory of probability was applied very effectively in almost everything done on a large scale such as insurance business, astronomy, behavior of subatomic particles, etc. Indeed it made life easy. Every thing revolved around the basic proposition that the *expected value of an event can be calculated by multiplying each possible value by the number of ways it can occur, and then dividing the aggregate of these products by the total number of ways.* This works out rather nicely long as we are dealing with large numbers and events, which are insulated from external intrusive agents, especially if the action of such agents is dependent upon nature of the earlier outcomes. Games of chance, as conducted in Las Vegas, are an ideal example, where no matter how much you have won or lost, you cannot influence the next outcome.

The above observation is what caused me to think that the theory of probability, in its pure form, cannot be applied to safety enhancement programs for the general smokestack industry. As a matter of fact, Daniel Bernoulli made a similar observation in the 1730s, although his was interested in different applications. He found the hypothesis stated above to be flawed in certain circumstances. His opinion was that such statements couldn't be applied to events on which humans have some degree of direct control. Risk, he maintained, was in the mind of the beholder. An identical set of events can have a different sensation of risk, depending upon the particular circumstances of an individual.

This notion made him the father of the fundamental concept of the *utility theory*: **The utility of a small amount of prospective gain is inversely proportionate to what you already possess.** At the time of conception, it was a revolutionary idea, and since then it has had a profound effect on many facets of life. One of which was the individual income tax structure. The greater your income the higher your rate of income tax, presumably because the more you have the less you feel when you part with some of your money. I personally think that this particular instance represents a gross misapplication of this wonderful concept – but that is a different story.

Thus, Bernoulli gave a human face and soul to the abstract mathematical concepts by combining esoteric numerical systems with human frailties – most important of which is our dubious claim to be rational beings under all circumstances. Rationality is a very elusive animal, as we'll shortly see.

The process of rational decision making involves the maximization of expected utility (which can be loosely translated as usefulness). Even under the best of circumstances when every one has exactly the same information, different people reach different conclusions. Common jury verdicts are a good example of this phenomenon. In an industrial setting the situation is much worse because personal experience, which varies widely from person to person, is used to make most of the decisions. This should explain why most of the new initiatives have a great difficulty in being accepted on the shop floor.

As a matter of fact, it is an irrational expectation to think that you will get a rational situation evaluation and decisions, from your shop floor personnel, especially if you went about it in an uncoordinated manner, and if you included only a few people in the process. You should look at it in a good news/bad news manner. The bad news is that if you rely on a few shop floor people to, say, assign equipment criticality, etc. you are setting yourself up for continuous surprises in the future. The good news is that in this book I suggest a methodology whereby you can convert the opinions of your best people into the "most informed" decisions, by letting them base their assessments on comprehensive, consistent and the best available information.

RATIONALITY, ANYONE?

Let's explore why it is difficult to make rational assessments under ordinary circumstances. This phenomenon has been studied exhaustively by two Israeli psychologists, Daniel Kahneman and Amos Tversky. They call this phenomenon the Prospect Theory. This theory says, in principle, that most of our decision-making processes are not rational due to some common human failings (cognitive difficulties):

- We let our feelings and emotions color our judgment
- Sometimes, without realizing, we do not fully comprehend what we are dealing with
- We tend to invoke the laws of large numbers even when the sample population is limited – which leads to erroneous results

- We have a great difficulty in keeping the big picture in focus. We tend to be influenced by the high profile components of a bigger issue and tend to ignore the low-keyed components which sometimes may be more relevant
- We treat a problem according to how it is presented or manifests itself, rather than its impact on our well being. In other words, as far as our approach to solve our problems is concerned, we are inherently inconsistent.

All of the above were demonstrated to be true by Kahneman and Tversky in a series of experiments which were later recounted by Peter Bernstein in his best selling book.

Consider the following case where a person is presented to choose between the following two choices:

Option A: An opportunity to gain $50,000 with a 100% certainty.
Or
Option B: An opportunity to gain $100,000 with a 50% probability.

We realize that for both of the options the expected value of the gain is exactly $50,000, but most people will select the first option. This shows that we do not like to take risks, and are risk-averse, especially if we are personally impacted by the outcomes.

Now let's look at our inherent behavior in more detail.

Option A: A 70% probability to gain $5000, and a 30% probability to gain nothing.
Or
Option B: A 100% probability to gain $3000.

What will you choose? In this case the expected value of Option A is $3500, but most people will choose Option B, in which they gain only $3000. This shows that even when we stand to gain more in a risky operation, we tend to stick to the slightly less paying but certain options. This is an interesting situation. Present these options to the people you know. You'll be amazed at the results. You'll see that people who are not much up on mathematics will easily select the second option. And surprisingly, people who clearly understand the concept of "expected values" will hem and haw, but eventually settle on the second, less attractive, option. Why? The only reason I can think of is that in spite of the rational contemplative skills of our mind, when push comes to shove, we go with our instinct. Note this concept carefully; later on I'll ask you why you expect a technician to ignore his instincts and make rational decisions – especially when you give him scanty information to base his decisions on. Now let's make things a little more interesting.

Option A: A 70% probability to lose $5000, and a 30% probability of zero loss.

Or

Option B: A certain loss of $3000.

In this case, the expected value of loss in option A is higher, yet most people would choose option A. This shows us to be seeking risk. We tend to gravitate toward a situation that has some probability of keeping us loss-free. It is an irrational choice, but it reflects our inherent nature, and it colors our judgment.

Suppose that a deadly disease breaks out and is expected to kill 1000 people. The public is given the following two options to handle the situation:

Option A: Employ a disease fighting strategy, let's call it strategy A, and save 300 lives.

Or

Option B: Employ another disease fighting strategy, strategy B, which gives a 70% chance of saving none of the 1000 people, and 30% probability of saving every one.

Note that in both of the options and expected number of people saved is exactly the same, yet most of the people will go for option A, in which we talk about saving lives rather than of massive death scenarios (a subject abhorrent to most of us).

Now let us look at the same problem in a different manner and present it as noted below:

Option A: The employment of strategy A results in sure death of 700 people, the rest will be saved.

Or

Option B: The employment of strategy B will ensure that nobody will die with a probability of 30%, while there is a probability of 70% that 1000 people will die.

In this case, it was shown, most people would opt for option B, because we do not like to talk in terms of sure death of 700 people, so we are ready to gamble.

Most of the psychologists believe that we tend to go for activities which on the surface seem more risk-free. When faced with a loss and gain situation we tend to do the following:

- We tend to magnify the potential losses because we inherently believe the situation usually will turn out to be much worse. One of the production managers I worked for, John Shorter, told me his secrets for good estimating: *Calculate the cost for the worst case, double it and then add one-half as much again.* I know of another cost engineering manager, who applied similar logic, and whose estimates were always on the right side of the actual as-built costs. So much for application of scientific principles. No wonder civil engineers use a factor of safety of three for most large constructions. If they stuck with purely calculated numbers we'd see collapsed bridges and structures all over the place. This applies to industrial workers as well. Since they happen to be in the trenches, therefore a potential hazard is more likely to affect their well being than that of a manager sitting in the administrative building. This should explain, at least to some degree, the presence of the never-ending safety item lists.
- On the other hand we generally tend to discount the potential gains. This applies to management who is charged to deliver a return on investment, including those made on safety items. These two points guide us to the root of one of the most insidious problems. Since there is so much natural divergence in the perceptions, the solutions are usually off-mark, Many unimportant things get attended to, and many important ones are ignored. This book helps to unify these perceptions so that time and money is spent on only those things that make sense to all.
- We also we tend to go for gains which we can put our arms around, rather than much greater ones which cannot be explicitly presented. This aspect of our behavior was found by Edward Miller an economics professor, who determined that the size of the potential gain plays a key role in our decision making. Let's look at two options presented to a thirty year old person.

  Option A: Prospects for a weekly income of $50.00 for a lifetime.
  Or
  Option B: An immediate payment of $10,000.00

While the net present value of option A is far greater than the second option, but most of the people are likely to choose the option B.

Other psychologists have also conducted numerous experiments to determine some other interesting human traits, and one of the most important conclusions was that we tend to shy from ambiguity in favor of certain situations. This should explain why, in most industrial installations, time and energy is squandered away on things, which have an immediate high profile, rather than those, which can add enormously to the bottom line in the long run. Granted that the fire-fighting activities need to be attended to, but a higher emphasis needs to be put on other activities that prevent the fire-fighting activities to occur in the first place.

We tend to gamble with other people's, or free, money much more readily than we do with our own. This should explain why some casinos give some money or tokens to start gambling. The idea is that you will more readily start to gamble if you are playing with free money. Richard Thaler, another prominent economist, devised a series of experiments to prove this point. Consider the following two cases.

Case A

A group of people is told that they have won $50.00 and are given a chance of participating in a coin flipping enterprise. If they chose to flip the coin they will get $10.00 if it's heads, and lose $10.00 if it's tails. They have a choice not to participate at all and keep their $50.00 intact. It is estimated that about 70% of the people will participate in the coin toss exercise. The reason is simple: It is free money and we tend to gamble with it. ***Let's not forget the analogy here, if it's somebody else's equipment, we'll tend to gamble with it! It is irrational to expect us to be rational about it.***

Case B

Another group of similar people is given the following options:

Option A: Flip a coin, heads gives you $20.00 and tails gives you $80.00.

Or

Option B: Do not flip a coin at all and receive a certain payment of $50.00.

Notice that for either of the options the expected value is $50.00, but what happens? Majority of us will choose not to flip at all.

SO WHAT DO WE LEARN FROM THE PSYCHOLOGICAL EXPERIMENTS?

All of us try to be rational, but it is very difficult to be so if you are dealing with large numbers, ambiguous situations, stressful environment, incomplete information or the absence of the big picture. Most of us have certain inherent shortcomings, which have been demonstrated conclusively by psychologists. Our reactions and decision-making processes on the shop floor are sometimes influenced by these characteristics. The challenge is not to equate such characteristics as incompetence; instead, we need to understand them and negate them through application of compensatory management systems. In many places management does not provide adequate systems or procedures and hopes that everything will turn out all right. It won't. In such cases the future is full of surprises. An industrial installation simply cannot function without adequate management systems.

Richard Thaler (as reported by Bernstein) carried out an extraordinary experiment that may help explain the constant tussle between unions and management. In many cases, the unions claim the work environment to be unsafe, and they make their cases by showing leaking steam lines, dripping chemicals, bad lighting etc. On the other hand management claims to be very pro-active as far as worker safety is concerned, and they make their cases by showing their rules, training activities and the money being spent on safety issues. I've been close enough to this issue to state that rarely you find gamesmanship at work here – both parties are sincere and earnest in their assertions. The principle reason relates to the differences in appreciation of safety as it is applied to workers – ***how much safety is enough safety?***

Without implying that the current level of safety in the industrial plants is adequate, I can safely state that if by magic and by spending, say $100 million, a plant removes all of the existing safety complaints. Then, within a month's time you'll have another list of safety items and someone claiming that the plant was unsafe. This does not mean that one should do nothing about the safety items, simply because you cannot get rid of the list anyway, so why bother. In this book I demonstrate how safety items can be addressed in an economical and rational manner, while allowing you to have a communication vehicle which publicizes that you are doing the best possible – thereby narrowing the perception gap.

Before we get to Thaler's experiments, let's briefly review a news item regarding worker safety reported by USA Today on February 19, 1997. This item referred to the famous US Supreme Court "snowmen of Grand Central Terminal" case. Apparently this name came about due to the fact that some of the workers were covered by asbestos every workday for many years (thus creating the snowman effect). The plaintiffs were seeking compensation for future injury and discomfort. At the time of claim submission, all were in perfect health. The lawyer for the workers told the justices, "These men were covered from head to toe with asbestos." To which Justice Stephen Breyer pointed out that one is covered from head to toe with chlorine when one takes a swim. The justice also said, "There's nothing in this room that does not have a known carcinogen in it."

On the same bench, Justice Antonin Scalia stated that an elderly person, sitting next to someone with flu, has some risk of contracting a possibly fatal disease. "There are all sorts of risks you face every day," he said.

This raises the fundamental question: How much are we willing to sacrifice and pay to remove a hazard?

Well, going back to Thaler's experiment, he posed the following question to a group of people (I've re-worded the questions):

> "In every day life, how much would you be willing to pay to eliminate a one-in-a-thousand chance of immediate death?" The answer was surprisingly close to $200.00, presumably because there are a lot of one-in-a-thousand hazards.

To another group he posed the following question:

> "If I increased the risk of fatality in your jobs to one-in-a-thousand, how much additional compensation would you require, to be compensated for the additional risk?"

The answer this time was even more surprising: Even $50,000 was not enough compensation.

The value or price of risk varies according to which end of the stick you are at. So not only we are not rational, our station in the scheme of things also colors our judgment.

Reality Check

It is a common complaint in many large industrial organizations that the best talent is kept busy handling day-to-day fire-fighting activities. On numerous occasions, I have studied such emergency work. In all of the cases I found that over 90% of such work was self-created and could have been prevented through application of better management systems. ***In most of such cases the root cause could be traced back to some "rational" act of omission or commission.*** So much for our rationality. Some examples will help illustrate this point further.

Example 1

Consider a common situation where management requests a few of the experienced individuals to prioritize the plant equipment. Usually there is very little dialog or discussion before the priority is assigned. In one of the major mills I asked the maintenance supervisors if their equipment had been properly prioritized. The answer was an emphatic yes, and, indeed, they had used their most experienced people to do so. I asked one supervisor how the priority system worked. He couldn't explain it to me, which was OK, every one is not expected to know every thing all the time, I thought. As an afterthought I requested to meet the technicians who had worked on the prioritization project. I am glad I did that, the technicians told me the following:

> "We just took some wild guesses, some of the equipment we had never even seen or knew much about. We told them we couldn't do it, but our maintenance manager told us that he understood our difficulty but asked to guess anyhow. He said the Champs system wouldn't work without the priority numbers".

The above is a classic example of garbage in, garbage out. As it turned out, each one of the participants assigned higher priority to items he knew about or was somehow fascinated with.

This is an example where the big picture is ignored in favor of something one is familiar with. A smaller certain gain looks more attractive than trying to understand the big picture, which one is not equipped to do in the first place.

Unfortunately, since my first exposure to this type of experience, it has been repeated many times.

Example 2

Let's construct a hypothetical case involving a recovery boiler operator who is facing two problems, either of which could be rectified by the lone instrumentation technician, which the operator has at his disposal.

> **Problem A:** A flashing audio alarm in the control room is indicating that a potable water tank is about to overflow because of an instrumentation problem. In this case, the overflowing of the tank is assumed to be a non-reportable environmental incident. To fix the problem it will take two hours of work of an instrumentation technician.
>
> **Problem B:** A recovery boiler is being brought on line and needs two hours of work by an instrumentation technician before it can proceed any further. The economics of a recovery boiler operation depend upon economics of power purchase and the black liquor inventory status. For the situation being discussed we assume that there is a 90% probability that the delay of the boiler startup will have no negative consequences, and 10% probability that the loss will be over a $100,000.

Such scenarios are played daily in the industrial world. Generally, operators will choose to respond to the first problem. Why? Because he will get an immediate certain gain. This scenario is also similar to the one of "free money" we talked about earlier. This is a case of free money since the operator will have no personal out of pocket loss. As shown before we tend to gamble with free money.

Example 3

In most industrial plants you'll see excellent training programs for easy to comprehend problems such as forklift operation safety, and none for the complicated multi-stage pumps. Why? It is simply because we get an immediate concrete gain with a 100% probability of success from a forklift training program. The fact that the gain is rather small takes the back seat, but it is something you can put your arms around. You can show your work to people, you easily implement the training, you easily keep records of accomplishments and you can easily demonstrate the improvement in safety as far as forklifts are concerned.

On the other hand a multi-stage pump is a messy business. The development of a training program for such equipment takes a lot of time and effort, and the benefits are not easy to calculate. But you do know that the benefits come in many forms, some of the huge benefits have a low probability of occurrence. But under any circumstance the expected value from a pump-training program far outweighs that from a forklift program. Yet we go after the forklift programs because it gives us a certain immediate gain.

Example 4

I know of dozens of places where the operators and plant supervisors routinely allow bypassing of burner safety devices on furnaces, incinerators and pressure vessels. Usually such actions are preceded by a "rational analysis" colored by personal feelings regarding confidence in the ability to handle mishaps and/or the expediency needs. Usually the gamble pays off and it reinforces our inclination to do it again. On many occasions the gamble does not pay off and an explosion occurs. Sometimes, the restoration of the safety equipment is forgotten which eventually leads to trouble.

About this time some of the readers must be asking, If we are so darned irrational how can we really survive in this complex world? This is a good question. Kahneman and Tversky demonstrated that despite our shortcomings we could survive very well in our social and personal competitive environment. As a matter of fact it may be the key ingredient that makes life interesting. However, it is a different thing when unrestrained human behavior is allowed to play a key role in the design of industrial safety systems where lives and livelihood of others is at stake.

Going back to the issue at hand, in my opinion, for industrial applications you can apply pure statistical methods for risk evaluation only if the laws of large numbers can be applied.

It has always been difficult to quantify risk and to decide on the risk level, which could be taken as an acceptable level. In some circumstances we do so in an indirect way. For example, we clearly know there is a correlation between the maximum allowable freeway speed limit and the number of auto accidents and deaths. We know exactly how many lives will be saved if we reduced the maximum allowable speed to, say 45 mph. Yet society allows a higher limit, clearly deciding that the additional accidents, injuries and deaths are worth the convenience of high speed and reduction of wasted time.

There are many other aspects of modern life where we have mastered the risk/reward ratios; life and health insurance is a good example. It is not so easy in an industrial organization. Indeed, in an industrial organization you cannot even discuss the subject in such stark terms.

Over time, many attempts have been made to numerically quantify risk involved in industrial work. William T. Fine attempted the first meaningful work in risk quantification in his paper Mathematical Evaluations for Controlling Hazards (*Naval Ordnance Laboratory, White Oak, Md., NOL. 1971, NOLTR 71-31, publication UNCLASSFIED*). William Fine was probably the first to suggest a practical application of the notion of expected value for risk/safety situations. This notion, was first explored by a sixteenth century physician, Girolamo Cardano in his great book on mathematics, Ars Magna, which was published in 1545. As mentioned earlier the original concept, over a hundred years later, was seen in a different light by Daniel Bernoulli (The Utility Theory).

At any rate Fine devised the mathematical formula:

Risk Score = Consequences x Exposure x Probability

In his paper, Fine suggests some modifications to the formula, which incorporate cost factors and justification factors. I've never seen this formula being applied on routine industrial work. I find the following problems with this approach:

- It is too cumbersome to be utilized on systems where thousands of pieces need to be analyzed
- Many of the guidelines leave too much to individual interpretation, which is likely to result in people "calculating" the numbers and getting answers they want.

The Center For Chemical Process Safety of AIChE published a risk evaluation methodology in its excellent publication, “Plant Guidelines For Technical Management of Chemical Process Safety”. This method utilizes the fundamentals as proposed by W. Fine. On the surface this method looks close to the method which I am proposing, but they are significantly different animals. In the following paragraphs I’ll briefly comment on their method and what I am proposing in this book. I consider the CCPS method, a natural extension to Fine’s work, as an excellent piece of work in the complex world of risk management. It is hoped that my comments are taken as constructive criticism designed to suggest some possible improvements in the future.

The CCPS method (using Fine's terminology) is based on the following key elements:

- Likelihood of Hazardous Event
- The Exposure Factor

- Possible Consequences
- The Risk Score.

On these elements some comments are noted below.

Likelihood of Hazardous Event: In the CCPS system, no methodology is given to determine this number in a reliable manner. One mention is made regarding the need for the mathematical probability for occurrence. The user is required to choose between 0.1 and 10 to quantify this element of the equation. The absence of a good method makes the starting point extremely subjective – thereby making the rest of the evaluation suspect. In various sections of this book I have explained why it is imprudent to use pure mathematical numbers or simple subjectively generated numbers. In my system, I've proposed the generation of a factor called ZBRF (Zero-Base Rate of Failure), which not only de-couples the expected rate of failure from pure mathematical numbers and questionable historical data, but forces the use of uniform common base data to assess failure rates. The result is the generation of a representative number, which is repeatable and far less subject to individual interpretations.

Exposure Factor: This factor reflects the exposure of personnel to potentially dangerous situations. I had some difficulty understanding how this factor adds value to the analytical process. The use of this factor suggests that if something is potentially hazardous one should stay away from it – thereby rendering it less hazardous. For example, say a control system is used to manage a hazardous substance. The CCPS method suggests that if you design your process so that a person will not need to go near it, it will make the situation less risky. It makes a lot of sense when the 'riskee' (the person at risk) constitutes a variable which is independent of the source of risk. Freeway hazards are a good example of this kind of approach, where the more you stay away from icy conditions the safer you will be. In this case the proximity of the freeway user to the freeway is essentially incidental, since he has the option to take a different route or not use the freeway at all. In other words the condition of freeway has nothing to do with whether people use it or not. The industrial situation, however, is completely opposite, where the proximity of an operator:

- may be causing a hazard due to an inadvertent inappropriate action, or
- may be mitigating a potentially hazardous situation by having it promptly noticed, followed by a corrective action.

It would seem, for industrial applications, the approach should be entirely opposite. Hazard-initiating devices should be under greater scrutiny to catch the incipient problems. Usually, if properly monitored and inspected, most of the major potential hazardous events can be caught before they get out of hand. For general industrial applications, unless you can completely automate a process and remove all personnel from the premises it is far better to closely monitor and inspect hazard-causing devices, instead of isolating them.

Secondly, such an application of exposure factor (as suggested by CCPS) renders the model inoperative for some of the environment-related problems. For example, if you were studying the operation of an electrostatic precipitator used to control the stack gas opacity, the term "exposure" loses most of its import and will become a stumbling block for the remainder of the analytical work. Again, this is so because in this case the undesirable event does not pose a risk to the operator and the closer he is to the action, the more he is able to take the necessary corrective actions.

In my method I focus on industrial applications only – where you assume the human proximity as the default condition. Secondly, to be on the conservative side, instead of exposure factor I use failure modes as a variable – since, again, for industrial applications, dynamics of interdependent failures play a very significant role in the overall scheme of things.

I have similar reservations about the remainder of the CCPS method. Having said that I do take my hat off to most of the work done by CCPS in the field of chemical process safety, which I consider to be invaluable, and which serves as a guiding light for the rest of the world. In later chapters we discuss a current CCPS project to construct a central database for reliability of industrial equipment. This is a much needed and very significant project. More later.

3

Does Safety Pay?

It is undesirable to believe a proposition when there is no ground whatever for supposing it is true.

–BERTRAND RUSSELL, 1872-1970

Chapter Summary

Safety does not always pay. In spite of all the rhetoric, large compliance and safety programs do not seem to have an adequate payback. The main reason: they are implemented wrong. One can, however, manage a large program such as that for PSM/RMP compliance to pay, by using a rational approach. One can also ignore the need to manage a large program and face costly consequences, including a plant shutdown. By managing a program properly, besides amplifying the cost/benefit ratio, one can zero in on the real safety and environmental issues, which is likely to create an enormous amount of goodwill with the regulators.

An investment in plant safety enhancement always has a competitive ROI. If you believe that, then I'll request you to be my guest in White Water, Arkansas, I've got a perfect piece of real estate for you.

Does safety pay? How much safety is enough safety?

These are difficult questions. I know the politically right thing to say is, 'Yes it does – the safer the workplace the greater the productivity and profitability.' But is it true?

Well, the answer is Yes and No. I'm not trying to evade the question and sit on the fence on this issue. To determine if something has a competitive ROI, we need to know its cost as well as the benefits that accrue from it. For safety programs, where a lot of the benefits are intangible, it is difficult to do so. Let's look at some of the major elements of this equation. Here we are talking about incremental costs and benefits.

COST SIDE

The cost side consists of the following major elements:

- Program development cost. This cost depends upon the nature of the safety program
- Cost of training delivery. This includes the costs of people while they are in training classes, and the costs of those who are on overtime to fill in the vacancies. It should also include the pro-rata cost of trainers who conduct the training classes
- Most of the time when you implement a safety program, it necessitates some changes to existing procedures, which sometimes take a longer time. Additional safety and coordination meetings, though undeniably important, also cost money. There is a cost element associated with technicians taking extra time due to the procedural changes
- Usually it is seen that the additional procedures, paperwork and formalities create interference with workflow. A good example is the time taken to get additional permits, making of additional records, involvement of additional people who have to interrupt something to participate in some new safety requirement. All this costs money
- Cost incurred due to dis-empowerment of people which results from enforcement of seemingly mindless tasks. Frequently, in an industrial plant, you come across groups of idle people waiting for something to happen, such as modifications to their work permit, mid-work inspection, and so on
- Cost incurred due to diversion of supervision's focus away from continuous, creative and timely intervention in the production processes. This is the most significant price you pay when you install a new program. It is so important and damaging that I almost included a whole chapter on this subject – but we'll take care of it in another book. Nobody is denying the fact that new (safety related) responsibilities are important, but to carry them at the expense of wealth generation processes, as is evidenced in some place, may not make sense. At any rate, this item should not be ignored but considered as a significant cost item

- Revenue loss due to loss of market share resulting from the higher priced product.

BENEFITS SIDE

The benefits side also has many components:

- Increase in revenue due to increase in productivity (due to better thought out production processes)
- Decrease in losses due to reduction in lost time (due to lower rates of worker injury, etc.)
- Decrease in losses due to fewer catastrophic events such as fires and pressure vessel explosions
- Increase in revenue due to the fact that a safer plant attracts higher quality employees
- Decrease in losses due to drop in employee litigation for safety related issues
- Decrease in losses due to fewer and lower OSHA fines
- Increase in asset value. A well-run company with a good safety and compliance record is considered highly on the stock market.

There you have it. If the benefits side exceeds the cost side, the safety program pays, otherwise, it doesn't. It is as simple as that.

So, once again, does safety pay? The answer, again, is Yes and No – with a whole lot of shades of gray in between.

In real life, all of the items in the equation, as noted above, are not in your control. Most of the cost-related variables, besides having a life of their own, are inter-related and difficult to isolate completely. Almost all of the cost-benefit items are of a subjective nature.

At the lower levels in an organization, the benefits side is inflated, therefore, rarely you come across a program which is not said to be justified. At higher levels of the organization the cost-side is inflated, therefore, rarely you come across a safety program, which is considered cost-effective by upper management and voluntarily installed, with no prodding from anyone. The basic reasons for this phenomenon have been discussed earlier. For these reasons, in a large organization, it is very difficult to develop a consensus on the cost-benefit ratio. That being the case, it is difficult for external agencies to get a good handle on the cost-benefit specifics for a given plant. This should explain to some degree why the regulators tend to stick to the letter of the regulations rather than listen sympathetically to people at the higher levels of an organization.

Having said all of the above, in my experience over 90% of the installed safety programs I've seen, make sense. The ones which don't make sense are generally those which result when the letter of the law is applied to those institutions which already have their house in order. It's similar to the traffic laws which are applied in exactly the same manner to a perfectly trained (having taken many defensive driving courses) driver as to a rough-and-tumble driver having a total disregard for his and others' safety. I have also seen many places, where management ignores the fundamentals and merrily drives the operation into ground – facing an eventual shutdown – all to be blamed on the safety and environmental regulations and *those bureaucrats* in Washington DC.

Let's review some of the important items that are in your control or *can be* in your control, and see what you can do about them.

NATURE OF THE SAFETY PROGRAM

This is, literally, the mother of all cost-related variables. If badly conceived and managed, this is where the following happens:

- Resource-rich companies squander away tens of millions of dollars as one-time costs, and institute long-term resource-drains
- Companies with modest budgets focus on wrong targets and waste scarce resources.

This book addresses the nature of the PSM/RMP programs. In this case, the nature (medium) is the message. There are no magic bullets. Manage the fundamental philosophy of your actions appropriately, and you will reduce your cost to a fraction of what it'd be if you did otherwise.

BENEFITS FROM THE PSM/RMP PROGRAM

A large number of companies do not manage the benefits side of the PSM/RMP program. Most are happy in producing and reporting statistics – basically counting the after-effects.

It need not be so. To some degree you can give the right spin to your statistics and amplify their effects – which is likely to come in handy when you face an investigation in the future. This paragraph does not sound right, I know that. It can be very easily misconstrued, I know that also. The message here is not to suggest creation of a phony or glitzy PR effort. The message is exactly the opposite. You need to have a philosophically sound program, and then you need to implement it. After that, besides producing the necessary statistics, you need to sell your work as a duly diligent effort. Your audience is your staff and the regulators. Once every one buys into your diligent approach, they are far more likely to ignore the imperfections in your program (and there will be many, believe me). It gives you time to fine-tune your act, and the wrath of the legislators will lose its fury.

SITUATIONAL PAYBACK

It cannot be taken for granted that the money spent on safety or PSM/RMP regulations will always have a payback or a positive ROI. This is an irrational expectation and can easily induce junior managers towards creative accounting solutions. There are two key elements to the payback picture:

- ♦ The maturity of an organization, as far as safety and productivity issues are concerned, plays a key role in the payback picture. The maturity is very site-specific. A given amount of money spent at one place may have a huge payback and none at another.
- ♦ Compliance with the regulations is not designed to have a payback under all conditions. It is designed to bring about a greater good to society. As a matter of fact, most of the time regulation designers do carry out the cost benefit analysis for regulation proposals, and they do look at the broad picture. The problem with PSM/RMP regulations, as with all regulations, is that it controls and fixes the irresponsible elements at the expense of responsible citizens. But, it is believed, that the value of the greater good brought about far outweighs the costs incurred (sometimes unnecessarily) due to impositions made on the good guys.

In real life the picture is not as rosy and objective as expressed above. Some of the regulations do not turn out to be objective and need to be evaluated and contested by the business community using the various feedback forums.

4

What Makes OSHA Tick?

A year ago, when we met last, a new Congress was huffing and puffing, and hoping to blow OSHA down. I appealed for your support, knowing the turbulent times that lay ahead. But little did I imagine how turbulent the last half of 1995 and early 1996 would be. I often wondered, as we were gearing up for OSHA's 25th anniversary, if there would be a 26th."

JOSEPH DEAR, ASSISTANT SECRETARY OF LABOR FOR OSHA

IN A SPEECH, ON MAY 22, 1996, TO THE AMERICAN INDUSTRIAL HYGIENE CONFERENCE AND EXPOSITION.

Chapter Summary

The purpose of this chapter is to describe some of forces that shape OSHA and make it tick. In spite of a solid underlying mission, OSHA's actions, over time, bob and weave through the tapestry of the industrial establishment. Still, for the industry, it is prudent to respond to the underlying and fundamental OSHA direction, rather than short term dictates, or lack thereof, as they come about. For the long-term compliance it is better to find rationale-based solutions rather than immediate appeasement of the regulators or the shareholders. If solutions of such permanent nature are implemented, then they'll more likely withstand the test of time and would not need to be found again and again.

It is estimated that the industry spends over $20 billion annually on compliance with OSHA requirements! In spite of its near-death experience with the 104th U.S. Congress, OSHA is a powerful organization and will remain so for many decades to come. There is no question about two things:

- Prior to the advent of OSHA, industry did not care much about worker safety. In 1969 from over 75,000 of the covered work sites only about 3000 were inspected. During this time over 30,000 violations were discovered but under 40 actual complaints were filed. And less than five companies were punished. It clearly shows that industry did have an upper hand with very few external encumbrances.
- OSHA has been very effective in meeting its goals. It is validated by the fact that since 1970 the workplace fatality rate in the U.S. has declined by over 50%. This is a big achievement by any measure.

OSHA's record is a good one: **OSHA saves lives.** No question about it. At the same time in many instances the broad-brush approach is counter-productive and unnecessarily costly.

The purpose of this book is not to laud OSHA's virtues but to bring the big picture into a better perspective, where it is possible for OSHA's intents and the industry's concerns to live side by side in a rational acceptance of the other, if not in harmony.

The U.S. industries that use chemical processes of one kind or another are extremely diverse. The substances used by such establishments vary from the relatively benign to those that create extremely hazardous situations for people and the environment. The very mention of the word "chemicals" conjures up unsettling feelings, and the designers of such processes try to take personnel safety into consideration to some degree. In retrospect, by and large, it seems the overall management of the chemical plants has not been as diligent or consistent as warranted. Investigations of major accidents conclude that the root causes include problems with some or all of the following:

- Management and operational systems
- Application of technology
- Human factors
- External events.

Prior to the current era, the inclination of the industry has been to focus mainly on technological fronts with incidental improvements in the management of human systems.

- For over fifty years, it has been understood the primary responsibility for the safety of workers lies with the employer. In the earlier times, immediately after World War II, this philosophy gradually started to take hold. At that time there was a mixed bag of employers. Also, at that same time some of the employers, usually the larger ones, took worker safety quite seriously. But the majority of the employers placed worker safety in the third priority tier, the first two being production and the minimization of capital outlay.

The first serious attention was paid to worker safety during the era of Lyndon Johnson's Great Society. He proposed a bill empowering the Labor Department to establish and enforce worker safety standards that were not already regulated by other federal agencies. During the same period Richard Nixon, a Republican presidential candidate, made this into a political issue and proposed a number of his own initiatives to attract blue-collar workers away from the Democrats. It worked and he won the election. That's how the era of the modern day OSHA began – initiated by a Republican president. The U.S. Congress passed the Occupational Health and Safety Act (commonly referred to as the OSH Act, not OSHA) on 29 Dec 1970. The original language of this Act was rather vague but the intent was clear. The Act clearly required all employers to provide a safe and healthful environment (whatever that means) for his employees. The most significant and all-encompassing clause in the Act was called the General Duty Clause. This clause contained the following language:

> *Each employer...shall furnish his employees a place of employment which is free from recognized hazards that are causing or likely to cause death or serious physical harm...shall comply with occupational safety and health standards promulgated under this Act...shall comply with orders issued pursuant to this Act which are applicable to his actions and conduct.*

Immediately after the passage of the OSH Act, the Department of Labor formed the Occupational Safety and Health Administration (OSHA). This newly formed department was charged with development of safety regulations, inspection of workplaces and enforcement of the regulatory provisions. To become effective immediately, OSHA quickly adopted some of the tried and true ANSI and NFPA standards. Key provisions of the Walsh-Healy Act of 1936 were also adopted at the same time. After that OSHA grew rapidly. At this time, in 1997, it has over 4,000 regulations on the books and an annual budget of nearly $300 million.

From the very beginning, OSHA has been a political football and has had to endure political pressures all the time from practically all directions (main ones being the republicans, the democrats and the labor unions). The first appointee, chosen by Richard Nixon, to run OSHA was George Gunther, a lightweight businessman. He is mostly remembered for his famous "Gunther Memo", in which he suggested to some industry sectors that he'd slow down the implementation of OSHA regulations, in return for contributions to Nixon's political war chest. At any rate, during this initial period, OSHA issued a set of consensus standards, which were widely believed to be useless at best, and silly at worst. One significant initiative, which Gunther did, was to try to delegate most of the power to the states. Irrespective of the fact whether the states were ready to take on the new responsibilities, he approved the state plans as they were submitted to him. Some aspects of this initiative were challenged successfully in court by the AFL-CIO union.

In January 1973, the leadership of OSHA was passed on to John Stender, a former union representative and republican legislator from Washington. He is most famous for pushing a bill through which defined the permissable level of carcinogens in the workplace to "non-detectable". This was interpreted by OSHA as one part per million of any "cancer-causing agent".

In 1975, Gerald Ford appointed Mortor Corn as the head of OSHA. Corn had impressive credentials in the field of worker safety and occupational health, he taught these subjects at the University of Pittsburgh. This began a period where most of OSHA's public relation problems started. It did not occur to most people in power that the standards being used at this time were "national consensus standards", which, by design, were vague and meant to provide general direction only. The original intent was to use them as a starting point and to fine-tune them before any enforcement began. Most of these regulations contained words such as "should not" and "shall", which to most people is the starting point for any enforcement action. Anyway, all this was ignored by the over-zealous inspectors and a barrage of citations were issued for relatively non-serious issues. (Similar to the examples quoted by the 104th Congress – some of which were probably overblown to create an attractive soundbyte). One of the provisions required OSHA to conduct an investigation in response to any complaint stating "reasonable grounds" to believe a violation had threatened the well-being of an employee and someone was in harm's way or in danger. Now this is a very vague language, and it resulted in a lot of confusion and complaints.

The first semblance of "management" was introduced to OSHA's operations when Jimmy Carter appointed Eula Bingham as the head of the agency. During this period OSHA inspectors were provided with comprehensive training and supervision. On the operational front, better inspection targeting policies were developed. OSHA developed a three-tiered policy to handle complaints. OSHA's response to complaints was tied to the perceived severity of the issue.

Bingham also instructed the OSHA officials to find and target the "high hazard" industries for inspections. The determination of hazard classification depended upon the injury data supplied by Bureau of Labor and Statistics, number of employees in potential harm's way and the nature and quantity of hazardous chemicals.

In 1978 OSHA issued a controversial standard regarding lead contamination, which was immediately challenged in court by several industrial groups. The federal appeals court in Washington upheld the standard but determined OSHA had failed to adequately justify the feasibility standard for certain industries. This was a small victory for industry and reinforced its ability to talk back to OSHA. By 1981, OSHA successfully established the standard was technologically feasible for the most part. The only good thing that came out of this exercise was the presumption of technological feasibility requirement for the OSHA standards.

During this period another key point was decided upon. OSHA is required by law to carry out a cost-benefit study for all new regulations, the object being to protect the industrial establishments from going bankrupt by the compliance cost. The petroleum industry took OSHA to court on this using regulations regarding benzene. The court determined that, indeed, OSHA had failed to carry out the cost-benefit test adequately.

All along, on the sidelines a quite battle was going through its course in the political arenas. OSHA proposed a workplace noise standard in 1974, which never went anywhere due to wrangling of one kind or another. A comprehensive standard on this subject was issued in 1978 and the final standard was issued in 1981. As soon as the Reagan administration took over OSHA, this standard was withdrawn completely.

The Reagan administration brought about significant changes in OSHA's view of the world. Thorne Auchter, a construction executive from Florida, was appointed to lead OSHA. Auchter filled key OSHA positions with known deregulators and started to convert OSHA into a non-intrusive and user-friendly agency. During this period OSHA mainly focused on industries with highest levels of safety and health problems. The agency almost ignored the companies with good records or those having active safety and health programs. The regional directors were given powers to negotiate settlements and avoid costly lawsuits.

During this era of "golden" or "dark ages," depending upon one's point of view, many major philosophical changes were brought about. OSHA was required to justify its rules. All of OSHA's initiatives had to go through an OMB (White House's Office of Management and Budget) Regulatory Impact Analysis (RIA). This exercise was conducted to confirm that all major rules had a positive cost-benefit ratio.

During this period Auchter was not known to issue any new regulations. At one time, the unions determined that they'll not get anywhere against the big business lobby at the federal level, and decided to go around it. They started a campaign to influence the states to implement their own "worker-right-to-know" legislation. In the opinion of big business such state regulations would have had a disastrous effect on the shop floor; every state would give it a different spin and there would be mass confusion. Nobody wanted that, so business relented and let OSHA go ahead with the Hazard Communication regulations. So during this period only two new health standards were issued: Hazard Communication and Ethylene Oxide. The former, however, was one of the most significant pieces of regulation. It created "material safety data sheets" (MSDS) which are so common in the industry these days. This regulation also required the employers to provide training to the employees on how to handle hazardous chemicals.

The deregulators under Auchter phased back on the inspection policies by limiting the programmed inspections to the manufacturing and construction sectors only. It was also believed that OSHA should only use the programmed inspections with the most dangerous establishments in a given industry. The criterion used for the programmed inspections was lost-time due to injury in days per 100 workers. The national average was 4.9 days per 100 workers; therefore only those establishments were inspected where the site-specific rate exceeded the national average.

Under Auchter's regime, employers outside of the manufacturing or construction industries didn't have much to do with OSHA. The agency policies required the inspectors to spend time and effort in their offices going through records rather than inspecting workplaces. It's believed that Auchter instituted guidelines that encouraged OSHA inspectors to settle complaints with the employers expediently – usually in the employer's favor. One of the silly rules at this time discouraged follow-up after inspections. It was suggested that a notification from the employers, saying that the issue had been taken care of, should suffice.

During this period, the number of agency inspections dropped from approximately 12,000 in 1980 to 1,600 in 1983. This corresponds to a drop of over 80%.

Also, the number of "willful" violations cited by OSHA dropped from over 1,200 in 1980 to about 110 in 1982. This corresponds to a drop of about 90%.

The Reagan administration, during its first six years, referred only 10 cases to the Justice Department for criminal prosecution. In comparison, Bingham had referred 24 in about three years. This corresponds to a drop of about 80%.

In 1984, Robert Rowland was nominated to head OSHA. Rowland was widely believed to be strongly pro-business. As a matter of fact, he owned a substantial number of shares in petroleum and chemical companies. This announcement did not sit well with the bureaucrats within OSHA and the labor organizations. He lasted as the head of OSHA for less than a year, and was actually never confirmed by Congress.

ADVENT OF MODERN OSHA

In February 1986, John Pendergrass was confirmed as OSHA head. One of the first major jobs Pendergrass had to take care of was the hazard communication regulation and the controversies surrounding it. Prior to this period OSHA had excluded non-manufacturing industries from the requirements of this regulation. Due to pressures from some of the unions and federal court findings, OSHA decided to make this regulation applicable to all industries.

In 1988 and 1989 OSHA tried to impose a generic rule to strengthen the existing exposure limits for about 200 substances and created new ones for about 160 substances. In spite of brave efforts by OSHA to soften the blow to the effected industries, dozens of lawsuits were filed against this initiative. In 1992 the Eleventh Circuit Court of Appeals vacated the entire standard – finding that OSHA had not done its homework and not enough feasibility studies and risk analyses had been done.

Under Pendergrass's leadership, OSHA's inspection policies were changed to follow more scientific principles. The agency decided to make the employers' history of workplace fatalities the key-determining factor instead of injury rate data. Under the new departmental rules, every tenth programmed inspection was conducted in a comprehensive manner, irrespective of the injury rate statistics. Also heightened attention was paid to the physical condition of the plants. If there was physical evidence (or a complaint) to suggest sloppy custodianship, in-depth inspections were carried out.

At this time period, the agency reinstated the "wall-to-wall" complaint inspection policy. For deliberate mishandling of records an employer could be subjected to mega-fines: $100,000 to $1 million. For the industry, the most intimidating aspects of the new policies were the fines based on instance by instance for willful violations. Fines could also be based on the number of employees exposed to a serious hazard.

THE "NEW" OSHA

In March 1993, within months after Bill Clinton was sworn in as President, the House introduced a new version of the Comprehensive OSH Reform Act. This bill was vastly different than the original version and reflected Clinton's philosophy of "reinventing" the government agencies. The bill was not approved, but the Clinton administration kept on working to find new and innovative solutions.

In 1993 Joseph Dear was appointed to head OSHA and he immediately set out to "reinvent" the agency. Two of the key initiatives were the Voluntary Protection Program (VPP) and the Cooperative Compliance Program (CCP). In May of 1995, a three pronged strategy to reform OSHA was initiated:

- ♦ Give employers a choice between partnership with OSHA or the traditional one-sided enforcement by OSHA. The former will result in partnership between OSHA, workers and the employer, where all will work together to solve the problems. OSHA promised that an atmosphere of partnership would go a long way in reduction of red tape and adversarial relationships.

- Use common sense regulations and enforcement. Eliminate confusing and out-of-date standards. Work with business and labor leaders to develop more effective rules.
- Shift focus on results and not the red tape.

Many companies decided to take up the offer. Dear reported that in three years the injury rates at the VPP companies dropped to 45% below their counterparts who had not joined the program. The California Department of Insurance found that big and small employers can cut their injuries and illnesses by as much as 40% if they establish VPP-like programs. On September 17, 1996, in a speech to the National Voluntary Protection Programs Participants' Association Conference, Joseph Dear explained the information noted above and said: "**An underlying premise is that the agency clearly distinguishes between responsible employers and those who neglect their workers' well being**." This is a telling and insightful comment. It opens doors to rational management systems as proposed in this book. Such systems fit in well with the OSHA intent to look for results instead of red tape. This is exactly what Zero-Base™ Compliance gives you: The biggest bang for the buck in terms of worker safety and productivity.

At the time of writing OSHA was going full steam ahead trying to implement a National Safety and Health Program Standard which will have the following key components:

- Management commitment
- Employee involvement
- Work-site evaluation to identify hazards
- Hazard prevention and control
- Health and safety training
- Periodic evaluation of the program.

Zero-Base™ Compliance strategies address the above issues as has never been done before in an extremely cost-effective manner.

> **Partnership works, but only in tandem with common-sense. Serious violators will face serious consequences. Reinvention does not mean putting on the kid gloves. We've upped the ante for employers who fail to care for their workers' safety and health."**
> Joseph Dear in a speech..

CHEMICAL PROCESS SAFETY MANAGEMENT REGULATION

Other than commercial airline crashes, the chemical industry accidents take on the highest profile in the eyes of public. The government has been under the gun to take on an active role in prevention of such accidents. For many reasons (worthy of a full-fledged book) the government has dragged its feet for years on this front. Eventually a few major disasters made this issue too difficult to keep on the back burner. Some of the accidents which, over time, produced a shift in the priorities were:

- In Mexico City in 1984, almost 650 people died in liquefied petroleum gas explosion
- In Bhopal, India, in 1984, over 2000 people were killed by a major spill of methyl isocynate at a Union Carbide plant
- In 1985, over 135 people were seriously injured by a release of aldicarb oxime and methylene chloride, at a Union Carbide plant in Institute, West Virginia
- In 1985 a Phillips Petroleum refinery had a explosion in Pasadena, Texas, killing 23 workers and injured more than 130 others
- In July 1990, a compressor system exploded in an Arco facility in Channelview, Texas, killing 17 people.

All of these accidents and a series of other relatively smaller industrial accidents in the U.S., caused the public to conclude that it was just a matter of time before major catastrophic events occur in their own backyard.

In 1995, the Council for Excellence in Government had a poll conducted. The poll posed many questions to the general public. When asked whether they agreed or disagreed with the statement "Government has gone too far in regulating business and interfering with the free market system", 73% of the respondents strongly or somewhat agreed. The poll also asked if the respondents agreed or disagreed with this statement, "Workplaces are much safer as a result of government regulation than they would be if business was left to its own devices." Seventy two percent of the respondents agreed with this statement.

The first significant initiative on this front came about when the legislators passed the framework for emergency planning efforts through Title III of the Superfund Amendments and Reauthorization Act (SARA). Immediately thereafter, the U.S. Environmental Protection

Agency (EPA) released its Emergency Preparedness and Community Right-to-Know regulations (EPCRA).

To protect the workers against catastrophic events, OSHA promulgated a standard to regulate process safety management (PSM) of highly hazardous chemicals: 29 CFR 1910.119. Prior to this standard, OSHA relied on Section 5(a)(1) of the general duty clause to address hazards other than releases. For citation purposes, national consensus or industry standards were relied upon. As a matter of fact, under OSHA's Hazard Communication Standard (HCS), 29 CFR 1910.1200, facilities are required to develop and maintain written hazard communication programs to train workers about possible risks associated with hazardous substances. But the HCS standard does not address in-plant process hazards.

The purpose of the PSM standard is to protect employees from hazards associated with toxicity, fire or explosion involving highly hazardous chemicals. This application of the act should eliminate or at least mitigate the consequences of major industrial accidents. This regulation is designed to be "performance based", which is a significant departure from previous safety legislation rulings that were of prescriptive nature and identified specific equipment requirements or actions to be taken. This time around, the regulation establishes goals, and delineates the basic elements to be used to fulfill the goals. This is the aspect of the regulation that this book capitalizes on. Such a regulatory approach gives the industrial establishments the flexibility for development of site-specific programs to best meet their needs. This book offers a rational approach which can be used to get the biggest bang for the buck in terms of employee safety and process productivity.

Philosophically the PSM standard is built upon some of the trail-blazing international standards. Most significant among these are:

- ♦ The Sevesco Directive, which was developed by the European Community (EC) in response to some major accidents in seventies. This directive was passed in 1982 and has been revised many times since then.
- ♦ The guidelines developed by the World Bank for identifying, analyzing and controlling major hazards posed by industrial establishments in developing countries.

For application purposes the PSM standard builds upon the existing safety and emergency response regulations:

- ♦ The Occupational Safety and Health Act (OSH Act) of 1970

- The Hazard Communication Standard (HCS) of 1984
- The Emergency Planning and Community Right-to-Know Act of 1986 (EPCRA).

The PSM regulation was created as Section 1910.119 "Process Safety Management of Highly Hazardous Chemicals" in Title 29 of the Code of Federal Regulations. The design of this section was largely based on recommendations from an industry task force, and contains requirements for prevention or minimization of the consequences of catastrophic releases of toxic, flammable or explosive chemicals. The PSM rule consists of thirteen elements:

- Employee participation
- Process safety information
- Process hazard analysis
- Operating procedures
- Training
- Contractors
- Pre-startup safety review
- Mechanical integrity
- Hot work permits
- Management of change
- Incident investigation
- Emergency planning and response
- Compliance safety audits.

The regulators have tried to delineate requirements for each element in as much a clear-cut manner as possible, but this is a very complex undertaking and there is a considerable amount of inter-dependency between the elements. At the time of writing, industry was facing a great difficulty in management of mechanical integrity, which was something new – the other elements being already in existence in one form or another. This element is also one of the most cost-intensive. At the time when the rule was issued there was (and still continuing to do so) much confusion and speculation as to how to implement this element and what OSHA will consider acceptable. This book deals with this element specifically, which obviously has impact on others.

EPA's RISK MANAGEMENT PROGRAM (RMP)

In response to a mandate in the Clean Air Act (CAA) Amendments of 1990, the Environmental Protection Agency (EPA) promulgated the Risk Management Program (RMP) rule. This rule added a new subsection [r] to Section 112 of CAA. This rule is designed to prevent accidental releases of regulated substances and other extremely hazardous substances to the air. Another objective of this legislation is to reduce the consequences of the accidental releases by focusing on preventive measures. Section 112 [r][7] of the Act requires EPA to promulgate "reasonable regulations and appropriate guidance" to cause the prevention and detection of accidental releases and the generation of requisite responses. To implement this requirement, EPA published a final rule on June 20, 1996 (61 FR 31668), entitled "Accidental Release Prevention Requirements, Risk Management Programs Under the Clean Air Act, Section 112[r][7]. This rule is commonly referred to as the RMP rule.

Another key item worth noting is the influence of the regulators is not limited what is specifically spelled out in the RMP rule. Section 112[r] also contains language for a general duty clause, which requires the industrial establishments to operate safely and to prevent accidental releases of extremely hazardous substances, irrespective of the fact whether the substances are formally regulated or not. Philosophically, this rule is similar to the PSM rule in that it is also performance based.

EPA, in promulgating the RMP rule, added new part 68 to Title 40 of the *Code of Federal Regulations*. The new part is further broken down into eight subparts, A through H:

RMP Rule	Title
A	General (includes management)
B	Hazard Assessment
C	Program 2 Prevention Program
D	Program 3 Prevention Program
E	Emergency Response
F	Regulated Substances for Accidental Release Prevention
G	Risk Management Plan
H	Other Requirements (Recordkeeping, Audits)

Here it serves no purpose to go into the details of the RMP rule. Therefore we'll limit ourselves to salient points.

In general the rule requires the following:

- Development and implementation of a comprehensive risk management program
- Submission of the risk management plan that consists of salient documentation and summary of all key information.

A comprehensive (full) risk management program consists of:

- Thorough hazard assessment
- A management system
- A prevention program
- An emergency response program.

In this rule, EPA has adopted a tiered approach to manage and control stationary sources, which are subject to the rule. All of the affected industrial processes are divided into three tiers depending upon the severity of potential hazards. The processes, which present a higher risk to the surrounding general population and environment (outside the plant boundaries), are subjected to more stringent requirements.

Each process is required to be analyzed for determination of the applicable program level (Program 1, 2 or 3). Such a determination is based on items such as accident history of the process, estimation of impact distance of a worst-case release from the process, etc.

For the higher two levels (Program 2 and 3), the employers are required to manage maintenance and the mechanical integrity of equipment. At the time of writing this book, the industry was facing a great difficulty in management of mechanical integrity, which is also, one of the most cost-intensive elements. At the time when the rule was issued there was (and still continuing to do so) much confusion and speculation how to implement this element and what EPA will consider acceptable. **This book deals with this element specifically, which obviously has some impact on others.**

5

Of Visions, Mission Statements, Wishful Thinking And Other Similar Things

Man seeketh in society comfort, use, and protection.

–FRANCIS BACON, 1561-1626

Chapter Summary

The "vision thing" as George Bush used to say, is one of the most misused concepts in the industrial world. This chapter provides a discussion on how effective corporate visions and mission statements can be constructed. Furthermore, a case is made to utilize the corporate vision as a very powerful production enhancement tool–at virtually no incremental cost to the corporation.

*C*orporate vision is the primary driving force for everything we do in the industrial world (probably elsewhere too). A relevant and farsighted "vision" will take you places, and an irrelevant vision will eventually open doors to chapter 11. Funny things, these visions, a good one will make you move mountains, but a bad one doesn't really have any negative impact; it simply leaves you alone and lets you slowly wither away on the vine. All of us know that if we believe in something hard enough and long enough, it'll happen. And, if we don't, not much will happen. You see, this is the root cause for compliance, maintenance, or technician training programs that don't work. People have scant vision about them and don't believe in them long enough and hard enough. It is important to discuss some of these nebulous concepts that relate to vision and how they can be applied at different levels of an organization.

One company that handles the "vision thing" very well is Microsoft (most of the time, anyway). Bill Gates' vision is: ***"A Computer On Every Desk And In Every Home"***. This is a rather simple, but meaningless, statement as we'll shortly see. Fortunately, the shortcomings of this vision are compensated by other business tools employed by Microsoft. One of which is the philosophy to hire nothing but the best talent. Which helps, because a talented person can detect the presence of a tacit vision and translate a simple statement into powerful personal messages.

"All vision statements must address a human problem. All missions must do something for humanity", explained Jawad Khaki, a senior NT Development Manager at Microsoft. I was interviewing him about the impact of vision statements.

"What does your chairman's mission statement mean to you?", I asked him.

He answered: "It shows me true North on a perpetual basis. Many years ago when I was a fairly new manager at Microsoft, a major software developer wanting to do something jointly for IBM mainframes approached me. I immediately knew this idea was outside our corporate vision and therefore rejected it. Did we lose an opportunity? I don't think so. Pursuing something outside our vision for the future would have de-focused us. By concentrating on the vision, we created great opportunities for the corporation."

I asked, "How do you use the corporate vision in your day to day affairs? Do your people know the chairman's vision as well as you do?"

He answered: "Certainly. Everyone is aware of the corporate vision. How do I use it? I've made my own departmental vision based on the corporate vision. It has four components regarding creation of applications which don't exist today:

- Create a distributed LAN and WAN infrastructure for Windows and Windows NT
- Create a premier access server and router for Internet and telco dialup, as well as customer premises
- Create an infrastructure for multimedia network applications
- Create a platform for third parties to make a lot of money.

Microsoft is one of the few cases where the corporate vision (albeit incomprehensible to the non-initiated) actively operates as a management tool. Very cleverly, Khaki had crossed the communication gap. You see, the vision enunciated by Bill Gates means very little to software engineers. Somebody has to translate that into a workable statement. This is where line management comes in: to lead by using a multitude of tools in producing the most good for the corporation.

> **Management must manage.**
> Peter Drucker in *Management*.

Line management must translate the corporate vision into a workable statement. Each department has to have its own sub-vision. Simply chanting the corporate vision serves no purpose other than giving the CEOs a warm and fuzzy feeling. The corporate vision is a tool and must be used as such. From the master vision you need to develop derivative visions, and use them as tools to keep you on the straight path and keep your creative juices flowing; exactly like Jawad Khaki did. The goals he set for his department are tangible ideas that can be used very effectively to unleash the creative minds of software engineers.

Another big tactical advantage you gain, by doing so, is the enormous amount of maneuverability such subsets of visions give you. You can re-focus the whole department in days if you have to.

During my interview with Khaki we reviewed many projects which Microsoft had started with its usual zeal and enthusiasm. Dozens of people poured their hearts and souls into them. Some of the projects were axed with little advance notice, and people were re-deployed very effectively at a very short notice. Its mind boggling to see how teams of highly focused (some working 16-hour days) people can be re-channeled into something completely new and different. This is what a subset of vision does for you. People do not resent a change of course as long as it conforms to the fundamental vision, and has the same leadership to go with it. What people resent is the rudderless knee-jerk exhortations sans the requisite vision and sub-vision, as practiced in many multi-billion dollar enterprises.

How Microsoft made a major strategic turnaround regarding the Internet has got to be one of the most profound examples of vision-at-work. This is based on Bill Gates' writings, information generally available in

Redmond environs and an excellent article *Inside Microsoft* (Business Week, July 15, 1996). This discussion is being presented to highlight how a vision works, whether clearly stated or tacit and whether it is coherent or not.

> ***Oh, our eyes have seen the glory of the coming of the Net,***
> ***We are ramping up our market share, objectives will be met.***
> ***Soon our browser will be everywhere, you ain't seen nothin' yet,***
> ***We embrace and we extend!***
>
> *Battle Hymn of the Reorg*
> Anonymous Microsoft employee
> *MicroNews,* the in-house newsletter.

By 1993, the whole world, with the exception of Microsoft, was getting keenly interested in the World Wide Web. This new communications platform lets you display complex graphics and other material on the Internet, and facilitates rapid jumping around from one Internet computer to another. By the end of 1995, some 20 million people were surfing the net using software that was not made by Microsoft. During late 1994 and through most of 1995, the common rumor was the stature of Microsoft as a giant and a leader will be undone by the Internet, and that the Windows hegemony on the PC was short-lived. It all changed after one full day of meetings on December 7, 1995. On that day Microsoft declared that it was changing its strategy and it would jump into the fray with full force and "Web-ize" all of its products. After that, within a period of six months, Bill Gates did something which has never been done before. He took his $10 billion dollar company and its 20,000 employees and did a momentous about-face in direction and philosophy. In magnitude it'd be similar to what General Motors would have done, had it decided decades ago, that it would re-tool all of its assembly plants for smaller, more reliable fuel-efficient autos to combat competition from the Japanese. And if it did it all in six months. But GM did not do it, nor is it capable of doing it, even if it had the clarity of vision necessary for such an undertaking. Why is that? Perhaps it is a lack of vision permeation. When did you last see a low-level GM manager talking about a single-minded goal to make the GM products the best in the world?

Many others could not do what Microsoft has done. Remember Apple Computer? Its tacit vision for market dominance was all right but it had a defective philosophy to go with it, which did not allow low-cost cloning by others. Neither did Apple go out of its way to attract the best and the brightest prodigies, which presumably could force the founders to stay on the right track. The same thing happened to IBM, but it was sharp enough and did manage to mend its ways before the consumers could shut it down.

Bill Gates did not want to have much to do with Internet since he thought it was free and there was little money to be made there. His lack of interest was noticed by many, and independent Internet startups started mushrooming all over the place, led by Netscape, which had spectacular growth in a very short time. By the end of 1995, Netscape had gone public and launched the internet era which picked up momentum at an astonishing rate. Netscape's Web browser had a stranglehold on the market and Microsoft was nowhere to be seen.

Well, it's all history now. Microsoft realized, just in time, that the world will no longer play according to Microsoft's rules, hence, if it still wants to play the game it must accept the Internet standards – and then dominate the market once it is accepted as a player. At the time of writing, Microsoft had gained most of the lost ground and had found its true North, once again.

> The unofficial and guiding vision is very clear and robust at Microsoft, however, I'm a little confused about the official vision of this organization. Some of the Microsoft people say that since 1991, their vision has been gradually amended to ***Information At Fingertips***, while as late as 1995, it was reported as ***A Computer On Every Desk And Every Home*** as the official vision by Jeffrey Abrahams in his book The Mission Statement Book (Ten Speed Press, 1995).

Taken at the face value, Microsoft's published vision is **A Computer On Every Desk And Every Home.** I've always had trouble with some vision statements; this is one of them. What does it mean? It's a statement, which a futuristic guru such as Faith Popcorn or a techno-politician such as Al Gore would make. Well, let's test it. Assume that Microsoft had missed the boat on the Internet, and Netscape had led the innovation charge for the next twenty years, at which time you'd have seen a computer on every desk and every home, providing a level of service unimaginable today, but sans Microsoft software. Well that would have fulfilled the Microsoft vision, and therefore the situation should be totally acceptable to them. So why did Microsoft have to jump in and interfere with a flawless plan for fulfillment of its vision? Because, mercifully, the publicly stated vision is really not its real vision. And luckily (for Microsoft), senior managers at Microsoft do not pay much attention to this vision statement. Instead they focus on the real vision, an inkling of which is provided by Patricia Stonesifer, a senior vice-president when she says that one of the driving forces is number of dollars per PC (Business Week, July 15, 1996). Aha! So the real vision has nothing to do with proliferation of PCs but to maximize Microsoft's share of the software being used on each PC (and, of course, the more the PC's the better it would be.) Incidentally, Microsoft has little direct control over the number of PC's on tables, at homes or elsewhere, notwithstanding the indirect effect on PC sales by the availability of useful and user-friendly software. If I had to guess Microsoft's vision, my first guess would be **A World Where Productivity and Wealth Creativity Doubles Every Ten Years Using Microsoft Products**. This vision not only implies information at the fingertips, but also suggests a partnership in the process of wealth building and a positive impact on the human condition.

To clarify let me use an example. When John Kennedy, in 1961, decided that it was in the interests of the United States to acquire dominance in space, he did not state his vision in terms of some silly exhortation such as **A Satellite On Every Planet And A Spacecraft In Every Orbit**. It would've sounded nice but it would've been meaningless; though it would probably look nice on tee shirts. Instead he said that his vision was to see a U.S. manned spacecraft to land on the moon "before this decade is out". You see this embodies the best of what a vision statement can do. It's specific, it visualizes some noble aspirations, and, **most importantly, it is measurable**. It did not really care what the rest of mankind (read USSR) does in the field, it talks to what the U.S. must do in this field. You see he was interested in the market share for the USA, and he was very clear about it. After a decade one could easily compare the results with the original vision and take corrective actions, if necessary. On the other hand, a silly statement, other than sounding nice, does not let you do anything of the sort.

A business entity reflects a vision; actually it is created to realize a vision. Therefore the vision cannot really be changed radically, since it is its *raison-de-etre,* any major tampering with it de-facto terminates it (and the enterprise), however, something completely new and different can begin. Therefore the vision can be used as a rudder, set to point in different directions at different times. However, if you changed it too often you may end up zig-zagging or going in circles. It is the most powerful tool which can be used to steer an enterprise, which (the enterprise) is nothing but a dynamic capital and talent mass, used as a wealth generation organism. B.F. Goodrich is a good example of such an organism (Forbes, April 7, 1997).

What comes to mind when you hear of B.F. Goodrich? Tires, that's what comes to mind. Let's take a guess at what would've been its vision, say 25 years ago: **B.F. Goodrich, A Leader Among Suppliers Of Reliable Automobile Tires Having A World Wide Market Share Of No Less Than 35%.** I don't know what its actual vision was, but if this was not its vision it certainly should've been. Here someone is likely to ask: If the company itself has a difficulty enunciating its vision (which is the starting point, after all, and begins with a twinkle in the eyes of the founders), how the heck can you make a guess at it? The answer is simple, you observe the struggles, travails and triumphs of an organization and back-engineer to figure out what it is trying to do. Sometimes you can figure it out and sometimes you can't, especially if it shuts down before others can decipher what it was trying to achieve.

Well, let's get back to B.F. Goodrich. Do you know that it has not made a single tire in almost a decade. It sold its tire business a long time ago and is currently producing aircraft parts and specialty chemicals - two enterprises of completely different nature. Had it used the vision I suggested, it wouldn't do much good today, would it? There is nothing fundamentally wrong with this picture, you can certainly close your books on one enterprise and start another, with a new vision, with your bags of gold and hordes of talent. But as long as you are engaged in an enterprise, it is foolish not to have a clear vision, because it can be used as a very powerful productivity tool.

In this chapter we'll briefly see how a corporate vision can be used as a business tool, and how it can have tremendous impact on safety and reliability of equipment.

I was discussing a training project with an operations manager heading a large industrial complex. I asked him to describe his vision, stating what he sees his operators doing for him. He thought for a few moments and then said: "We want to be the best in the industry, we want to have this operation known as the best of its kind." Well, well, well. He is not the only one. Why do people say that, I've often wondered. I know of one president who was a voracious reader of business and "I'm OK, you're OK" type books. Every week his vision would change and reflect the latest book he'd read.

The operational manager I mentioned earlier is an earnest and hardworking fellow. It was rumored that his plant was being sold, or at least it was on the auction block. To help the sale move along, all the senior managers were publishing all kinds of visions and long range plans. I'm sure this fellow was sincere, but he'd caught the lofty vision bug. I suggested a few ideas to him. I said: "This is a laudable vision, but does it reflect reality? You lay a heavy burden on the members of your staff if you publicize this vision. For the most part you are likely to confuse them. You've told me yourself that you're not getting enough money to carry out some necessary maintenance. The first time an operator looks at your vision statement and then at a hazardous steam leak or a mess created by a pump, which has leaked for months, he is likely to be confused. He will subconsciously weigh the two contrasting pictures, one showing a run-down and neglected operation and the other as claimed in the departmental vision. He has to reject one picture. Guess what he'll reject? After that moment your vision statement will cease to have any meaning for him."

About ten years ago, I had an interesting encounter with a vice-president who was on the verge of getting it right. But the inertia and bureaucracy brought him down. Ironically, he'd created most of the bureaucracy during his earlier managerial assignments. I worked for him as an operational manager with a $30 million departmental budget.

As always, in July, we started preparing our annual budgets and goals for the next year – much like we'd always done. At the front of my budget manual I had neatly added the corporate vision and values. In my budget I'd shown a saving of 3M$, and in the goals I'd shown a drop of 10% in reportable safety incidents. He liked my budget and then asked me a simple question: " Why and how?"

I showed him the details of my budget, he looked at them and asked me the same question again.

Nobody had asked me this question before, and I'd always delivered on my budgets, goals, and commitments. He did not want to embarrass me any further so he gave me a few days to think about it. A few days later I went back to him and made my case explaining that the reason for my actions were the corporate values that, among other things, stated worker safety had the highest priority in the scheme of things. My proposed cost reduction initiatives reflected a corporation-wide goal to reduce costs by 10% (which had also been reinforced by senior managers many times). Anyway, he did not like my answers and spent a lot of time on the nitty-gritty of my tactical plans. At that time a thought came to my mind like a flash bulb. I realized what he was trying to say and why it was so important. I understood the root cause of our difficulty. You see, we were trying to tie the actions at the floor level of the organization to the corporate vision and were constantly stumbling. As he asked me questions, I thought about various situations and described what I'd really be doing. He liked the answers but those were not the things stated in my budget that I needed approval for. For example I had shown a 10% drop in training expenditure across the board. In reality I was planning a huge amount of training activities for one section (where I needed to improve on the reliability), and in others I was planning to defer some similar efforts, which in my opinion could be safely postponed for a while. The new idea was: *Why don't I create mission statements for various sections in my department and make implementation plans to deliver on my mission statements*? *Why not put the corporate vision and the specific departmental mission statements side by side, but put more emphasis on the localized mission statements?* Therefore for the first case a component of the mission statement could be: ***Identify the needs and train technicians to improve the equipment reliability from 88% to 95%.*** The cost estimate for this work was 300% higher than the previous year's expenditure for the section. On the other hand, the mission statement for the other section could be: ***Identify the training needs necessary to avoid serious safety problems and train people accordingly, and postpone all other training efforts for a year.***

So you see, by doing that you energize people with specific mission statements which are relevant to them.

Well, I got his nod for my budget and he took it to the Management Committee where he was told to "give back" another five percent. By this time it was almost the end of the year and he randomly made the necessary cuts, while letting me know that I was still responsible for delivery on the goals. So much for strategic planning.

There are some companies who are the best (as indicated by benchmarking processes), and they became the best through application of appropriate visions. It is hard work; some do it and reap the benefits. Some organizations that are way down on the totem pole need to start a positive journey toward major improvement before they can aspire to be the best. For them an appropriate vision should quantify a substantial improvement, say, over a period of five years. Once they have achieved that, they should re-group and decide if being the best makes economical sense for them, and if it does, they should go for it. This is a very hard process, because there are many reasons (corporate culture) which determine the company's position on the totem pole. To start the process, one needs to do the following:

- An honest evaluation of where you are
- An honest evaluation of strengths and weaknesses
- A hard-nosed plan to get rid of the weaknesses.

All of the above is easier said than done. Honest self-criticism is the hardest thing to do. Whenever I hear of a plant shutting down, I say to myself: There goes a bunch of people who could not face the truth about themselves. On the other hand I've seen numerous success stories, where people are brutally honest with themselves and as result get rid of their weaknesses or convert them into strengths.

Another way is to do what the zulu do. As the story goes, in total awe they were circling a huge elephant they'd killed. Someone asked them how they'll go about eating it. "One bite at a time," they said.

Stating your goal as to be the best, doesn't say much, and can be regressive as far as the morale of the troops goes. If you really want to be the best, pick your battles wisely and a few at a time. You need not be the best at everything, you could be the best at any one of the following:

- Best safety record
- Best productivity of operators
- Best productivity of maintainers
- Best employee grievance handling record
- Best at being pro-active environmentally
- Best at community relations
- Best at employee training
- Best at conservation of capital
- Best at innovation (R&D)

- Best employee retention record
- Best employee compensation record
- Best at new technology absorption
- Best at customer service
- Best ROI to shareholders
- Best at listening and acting on employee concerns
- Best at acting on employee suggestions
- Best at producing more for less (lowest cost per unit)
- Best equipment uptime
- Best at adherence to plans
- Best operational and maintenance practices
- Best product quality
- Best at inventory control
- Best at energy conservation.

I'm sure if you think about it, you'll come up with many more. All of the above are desirable. There is no company in the world, which is best at all of these. At the time of creation, a vision statement (in spite of being specific) belongs in the realm of wishful thinking. The next challenge is to convert it into a working tool.

THE NITTY GRITTY OF CONCEPTUAL STATEMENTS

The statements that encapsulate visualization of a concept come in many flavors. To prepare for this section I reviewed vision statements issued by almost five hundred organizations. I found the following categories heralding similar concepts:

- Basic Game Plan
- Business Creed
- Code of Business Conduct
- Commitment
- Core Values and Beliefs
- Corporate Philosophy
- Directional Statements
- Ethics Statements
- Fundamental Principle
- Goals
- Guiding Principles

- Management Principles
- Mission
- Mission and Aspirations
- Mission, Philosophy and Standards of Performance
- Objectives
- Operating Cultures
- Operating Philosophies
- Operating Principles
- Our Creed
- Philosophy
- Philosophy of Operation
- Pledge to Shareholders
- Product Mission/Social Mission/Economic Mission
- Purpose
- Statement
- Strategic Plan
- Strategies For Success
- Strategy
- The Vision We Share
- Values
- Vision
- Vision for the Future.

All of these terms (individually and in various combinations) are used interchangeably. No wonder people are confused. Ask ten different people the meaning of the term 'corporate vision' and you get ten different answers. Unfortunately, a majority of the people really don't pay attention to them. My opinion is based on the following:

- In many plants, I've asked the lower level employees if they knew what their corporation's mission statement was. Usually I get blank looks, even when I remind them that I'm talking about the statement emblazoned on the building next to the main gate.
- During work on this book, I looked up websites of many corporations. Usually the website had all information under the sun except the corporate mission statement.

This situation poses a few questions:

- What is the purpose of the mission statement (or vision or whatever, since we haven't differentiated between them) if no one pays attention to it anyway?

- If the mission statement is supposed to serve a purpose, then obviously that purpose is not being served. How come no one has noticed the discrepancy and done something about it? Show me one example where someone said, "Hey, no-one is really paying much attention to the corporate vision, let's find out why and do something about it."

Now let's look at this issue more globally, and try to see if we can differentiate between noble statements and useful statements. A serious question: Since no one pays attention to these statements anyway, why do we need to go through the painful exercise of creating a vision statement, why don't we simply adopt some portions of the latest presidential state of the union message as the corporate vision? The state of the union message contains items like:

- We shall increase productivity
- We shall increase the level of worker safety
- We shall make the organization small, cost-effective and more responsive to customers
- We shall be the world leaders in innovation, etc.

There you have it! These goals sound pretty good, why not adopt them and be done with it. Then you wouldn't need to spend time and money. (I know of one company, which spent over 2000 man-hours to prepare one mission statement).

No. You can't do that, because these statements are too global for your purposes. I'm sure that most people will agree that such statements are "too generic", they may be very good for the president of a country, but for an industrial corporation they are pretty useless.

Now the big question. If you think the state of the union message is useless for your needs, why do you think your corporate or divisional mission statement is of any use to your operators? Therein lies the answer to the fact that 95% of the line people do not pay any attention to your vision. It is pretty useless to them.

- Most of your wealth is created by line people. If they cannot participate actively in your vision, then the wealth creation process operates below its potential because all of the spark plugs connected to the vision statement do not fire. (Actually, under the worst circumstances, these spark plugs may fire in a counter-productive manner)

- A vision statement is a step in the right direction. It just needs to be made functional.

In rest of this chapter we'll see how to charge your employees with the corporate vision statement. Let's go back to square one, the absolute basics. What is the first thing that takes place during the genesis of a corporation?

THE GENESIS OF A VISION

In the beginning, there is someone who has some money and resources. This is the absolute first thing. The second thing is the desire to make more money, or to at least not lose what one has, due to inflation. This is the second thing, which germinates the underlying **fundamental goal:** ***To make more money with some available money.*** At this stage of the game, this is a one and only goal. (Here we are not talking about government or non-profit institutions, which have entirely different philosophies).

Next comes a search for ideas on how to make additional money with the available money. (I'm deliberately avoiding terms such as capital and the necessary rate of return.) The quest is to identify an enterprise, which will make the most money with the available seed money. Let's say the analyses show the best idea is to build a pulp mill. Now comes the quest for ideas to make sure the underlying fundamental goal (as noted above) is adhered to in perpetuity. This gives rise to **visions**. One visualizes the state of affairs at some time in the future when perfection (or an intermediate desired state) would prevail, which is consistent with the underlying fundamental goal. This is what visions are all about. Since this need is very specific, hence visions need to meet some very tight and specific criteria.

> **A vision describes the desired future state of an organization. To be valid, a vision statement must endure and not change with every business cycle.**
> Jack Creighton, President, Weyerhaeuser

A valid vision statement meets the following criteria:

- It must describe the general state of the organization at some point in the future. (A specific date would be a powerful element, but most people avoid it since it creates intense accountability. Remember, Kennedy's use of a specific time and what it did to the space program).
- The description must be good enough to be considered as a measurable parameter.
- It must reflect the long-term view; and should not be prone to minor glitches encountered along the way.

Why does it have to meet the criteria listed above? Very simple. This criteria differentiates between corporate vision statements and noble sounding phrases. You see, a noble phrase, while having many uses, cannot be converted into a management tool. Using these criteria, you'll find it an interesting exercise to review the vision statements of some of the major corporations. You'll be amused, I'm sure.

A vision statement serves the following purposes:

- It tells the shareholders that corporate management is on the ball and the **fundamental underlying goal** (this animal has already been described and it never varies) is being adhered to
- It tells the general public what a corporation is all about
- It gives marching orders to the direct reports (no one else will really understand it).

Let's take an example. This example is constructed with bits and pieces from real life phrases from many corporations.

For a corporation, let's assume the corporate vision statement to be: ***Our vision for Delta Oil is to have at least 30% of the market share by 1999, while maintaining the ROI in the top quartile of similar organizations.***

This vision statement says it all. The message is to expand without sacrificing the return on investment. Let's assume that for this hypothetical organization the ROI was poor at the time when this corporate statement was being put together. In this case it could have been constructed as ***Our vision for Delta Oil is to maintain the present market share, while increasing the ROI to the top quartile for similar organizations.***

The corporate vision statement should be followed by the corporate values, some examples:

- Employee and public safety is one of our primary concerns
- We treat all individuals with respect, irrespective of ethnic background
- We believe in environmental conservation. Our operations shall not cause irreversible damage to the environment.

These may sound like motherhood statements, but they are not. Once you start using them, they have profound impact on every day work. For example, I know of one refinery which has chosen to budget for fines imposed by the regulators, instead of fixing its problems. So, obviously one of its values is to find solutions with minimal cost, irrespective of what happens to the environment.

THE MISSION STATEMENTS

To explore this, we'll consider the first vision statement. Let's focus on one of many divisions of Delta Oil. Let's say that you are the division president and you face many problems in your part of the organization. As a part of the larger organization, you have a mission. Your mission is to contribute to the realization of the corporate vision. This is how **mission statements** are generated.

You have reasons to believe the ROI for your operation is in the lowest quartile among similar industries. Major contributors to this situation are:

- Your capital requirements are too high due to frequent replacement of badly operated equipment
- Inconsistent product quality
- Excessive lost time due to injuries arising from unsafe management of the processes.

In real life, as a division president, you'll certainly have many other strategic issues you'd like to take care of. For the sake of simplicity and to illustrate the process, let's limit our discussion to these issues. Looking at the corporate vision statement and your operation, you should immediately realize that you should not do much about acquisitions or penetration of new markets, in spite of the fact that the corporate vision statement calls for it. You need to bring your ROI up. Another division may do something completely different.

Your mission could be something like:

- We shall actively strive to increase the productivity of our existing assets, and by the end of the next five years we shall be in the top quartile of our industry group
- We shall create a safe work place for our employees
- We shall find innovative ways to fully comply the PSM/RMP regulations by 199x
- We shall increase the proficiency of our workers and minimize the needs for new sustaining capital.

Notice that the compliance with PSM/RMP regulations belongs in your lap and has nothing to do with the corporate vision. This is mainly because the regulation is designed to focus on workplaces rather than corporate structures. Having said that, you'll notice these mission statements exhibit a broad-brush direction, which reflects your thinking and may make a lot of sense to the Board of Directors.

No matter how much you publicize this mission, it has no meaning to your production floor staff. In your "communication" meetings all of them will give you a polite hearing. In reality, they are more interested in the doughnuts and coffee. Actually there is a big hint here. I've noticed in most of these high-level communication meetings there is an abundance of doughnuts and muffins. Question: If the mission statements are so on-message, why do you need doughnuts? I've nothing against doughnuts, in some meetings they're the best part.

There is an acid test for mission statements. The mission statements must be meaningful. Ask yourself the question: Do I have the resources and wherewithal to deliver on these commitments? If the answer is yes, the mission statements are relevant. Otherwise they are just nice statements, which if printed properly look impressive.

Wishful thinking is a mission without a plan. A mission is followed by a plan, never the other way around.

The most important job you have as a division president is to sell your mission statements to your key managers, and the development of execution strategies/plans. Smart presidents involve the key managers in the development of the mission statements to avoid an uphill battle later on. Other important jobs include items such as finding sources for capital, etc.

Before your line managers run off and start making plans, ask them to conceptualize solutions and state their solutions in terms of ***their*** mission statements. Their mission statements could be something like:

Within the next five years we shall achieve the following:

- Increase our equipment uptime to 96%
- Reduce work-related employee lost-time to 2%
- Reduce sub-standard product to less than 2%
- Make and implement a three-year plan to fully comply with the PSM/RMP legislation.
- We shall do so by empowering and training our technicians adequately, and removal of the hardware-related productivity bottlenecks.

Now we're getting somewhere. However, it's still not good enough because all of the above still belongs in the realm of wishful thinking. You need a plan of action. The work plan for a production manager may include some of the following items:

- Sell his mission statement to the technicians. Remember he has to sell his mission statement to his troops. This is where most of the failures occur. Some production managers are so in awe of the corporate vision statements that they spend most of the time going through them and ignore the real stuff – **their mission statements.** The appropriate course of action is to quickly go through the corporate and division statements but zero in on statements where you are asking the troops to participate and do something tangible
- Educate the troops regarding PSM/RMP regulations and actively seek their input in all compliance efforts
- Prioritize equipment that contributes the most to the overall downtime statistics
- Identify the equipment that needs to be modernized or replaced. Develop conceptual options addressing when and how an engineered solution can be applied. Select only those options where the ROI makes sense
- Determine how, specifically, the technicians can be trained to improve the equipment uptime. Make and implement 5-year training plans
- Determine how, specifically, the technicians can be trained to improve the injury statistics. Make and implement training and motivational sessions.

Now the acid test. Ask yourself: Can a production manager deliver on his mission statements and commitments laid out as above? Absolutely! Does his mission statement charge him? Yes. None of this could happen if you simply use corporate visions or mission statements.

Now onward to the last stage of this argument. Does the production manager's mission statements have much meaning for your technicians. Not much, but they are certainly more relevant than the divisional or corporate mission statements.

The operators and first line supervision need to develop a mission statement of their own. After they go through a dog and pony show with the production manager they should be asked to develop their own mission statements. This activity will probably need some facilitation. Their mission statement could be something like:

Recognizing that in our place of work:

- Equipment downtime is abnormally high
- Work related injuries are abnormally high
- Sub-standard work percentage is abnormally high
- The company is required to adhere to PSM/RMP regulations.

We shall:

- Help determine and adopt, safe, and productive work practices
- Identify where we need additional training, and participate in the training activities
- Actively seek and identify continuous improvement opportunities
- Find out how the PSM/RMP regulations affect me and what I can do to help.

The foregoing actions achieve the following:

- Your mission statements, rather than being static, become a dynamic credo which permeates through the organization
- All key people author their own mission, hence there is a high degree of ownership
- Everyone has a big picture perspective which is relevant only to himself
- Your PSM/RMP compliance programs have new partners. I know the legislation is too complex for tradesmen, but remember it is

designed primarily for their safety so they have a vested interest in its success. It is far better than occasionally listening to the PSM Coordinator. **Remember:** ***If we want something long enough and hard enough, it'll happen.***

As one goes through the lower strata of the organization, the vision will include some stratum-specific ideas. For example, operators may include items such as improvements in the start-up procedures or confined space entry procedures. Once you unleash your people and treat them like adults, they will act like adults and move mountains for you.

A line manager can reinforce all of the above on a continuous basis. For example, one could have quarterly meeting with each of the operators and ask them questions like:

> "Well, Joe, let's talk about the last quarter, what ideas did you bring up to improve process safety and productivity?". Guess what response you'll get from Joe? A blank look, that's what you'll get. Because Joe is not used to being listened to. Probably the same thing will happen the next time around. I guarantee that on the third occasion Joe will have some nuggets of wisdom for you. To do your part you need to give him a sincere hearing. Some of Joe's ideas, for one reason or another will not be practical. You need to take time and explain to him why. Some of Joe's ideas will be so simple and far reaching that you'll be amazed. Also, only he can unearth some of those ideas, no manager, supervisor or engineer can.

This will not only improve your process safety and productivity. It'll help you get some brownie points from the regulators who want the employees to participate in such activities. You see the appropriate application of vision and mission statements converts them into powerful management tools.

> **When I was in Ford's Engine Plant #2 in Cleveland, one of the hourly workers leading the tour told me about how he had worked with industrial hygienists and plant manufacturing engineers to design the ventilation system for the machine tools he used. As we entered his work area, he asked me to take off my shoes, so I wouldn't get anything dirty. His pride in his work was enormous.**
> Joseph Dear of OSHA in a speech on May 22, 1996.

6

Maintainers Move In Mysterious Ways

Today's performance measures for maintenance truly focus only on reducing the effects of non-performance rather than systematically improving performance. A cause for this is rooted in the fact that maintenance has traditionally been considered by senior management as reactive and "beyond optimization".

DAVID G. PETERSEN

THE BUSINESS OF PLANT MAINTENANCE

CHAPTER SUMMARY

The maintenance departments of many large industrial organizations are over-worked and under-utilized. These departments are kept busy doing things which do not make sense, while many of the important functions stay undone. This is most important of the fundamental reasons which impede improvements in equipment reliability and safety. Huge gains can be made if the maintenance departments can be re-oriented to focus only on those functions which make business sense.
Pitfalls associated with programs like Reliability Centered Maintenance are also discussed, leading to how such problems may be avoided.

I wanted to name this chapter: Do You Know That You Pay Your Maintenance Technicians $100.00/Hr For All The Meaningful Work Done?

How can one find out what the maintainers really accomplish? One way is by asking people who are closest to the action: the operators and maintenance supervisors.

The operators will tell you something like the following:

"God knows what they do. Whatever I ask them to do is never done."

"Destroy our equipment. You know, most of our breakdowns occur right after they finish the preventive maintenance work."

"Whatever they please."

"Don't know."

Other than the above you'll also hear: "We have a bunch of good maintenance people, they keep things running." You'll get comments of this kind perhaps about 25% of the time. Rest of the time you'll hear something like the comments noted above.

Well, you go to your next source: maintenance supervisors, and ask them the same question. The responses will be something like:

"We do whatever we can do. We are severely short-handed, so we cannot do everything."

"Well, you see the place running. We keep it running."

"Everything anyone asks us to do."

"Don't ask me, ask the technicians. I don't have time to go check anyone's work. As long as operations and my boss are happy, I'm happy."

"I'm too busy going to meetings to know what the hell is going on. I just authorize the overtime."

"Emergencies. I have just enough people to handle the emergencies and the mandatory meetings."

"The place is running, isn't it? You've no idea what it takes to keep it running. Every day is full of new challenges – I can't really tell you what we do. We do what it takes."

The above really doesn't tell you much. However, most of us can easily agree on the following without too much controversy:

- Most of the time, the plant equipment does keep on running. So somebody is doing something right
- Most of the time, the users of the equipment do not know what their maintenance counterparts do. On the plant floor their paths do cross, like ocean liners crossing each other in the dark on the high seas
- Frequently the work done by maintenance is driven by forces outside the direct control of maintenance management.

There are numerous systems that track maintenance man-hours and allocate costs to different cost-centers. These are all enumerative exercises rather than evaluative systems. Generally there is no quantification of maintenance accomplishments. An "accomplishment", in a business setting, has only one meaning: a quantification of what is added to the shareholders' bottom line.

To top it all, frequently management fads are inflicted on the maintenance group (among others). One of the favorite objectives of the fads is to "work smarter, not harder." It is easier said than done, obviously the intent is to improve productivity – which, too, is easier said than done. A lot of the plants take a leap of faith and jump into the latest fad with their eyes closed (especially now, since they've found out that such fads are benign and should be taken simply as expensive and time-consuming distractions.) And some don't – they like to find out the starting point before they look for improvements. To find the status of their *existing* productivity they hire consultants and ask them to determine the baseline productivity of the operation. A team of watchers (usually junior engineers, right out of school) descends on the plant and starts to monitor the activities of the technicians. In one plant where I worked the data for maintenance technicians was similar to what is shown below.

On average a maintenance technician spends his time as following:

- Coffee/smoke break: 10%
- Waiting for permits: 9%
- Waiting for or obtaining parts: 18%
- In-plant travel: 11%
- Idle: 18%
- Working: 34%.

To say the least, management was uncomfortable with the data, until the consultant assured it that these were pretty representative numbers. The usual range, for a large industry was 25-40%. He was very careful not to endorse the numbers as normal or the best achievable. He also pointed out that all of the "non-working" time is not necessarily non-productive. In spite of the assurances, all of us involved in this exercise were sure that there was something wrong with this picture. That was in the early eighties. Since then I became very interested in this subject and found that it was very difficult to find objective numbers which can be used for management intervention.

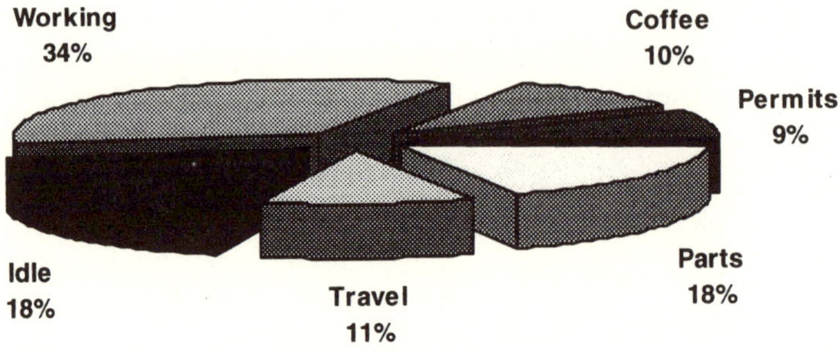

FIGURE 1	This figure shows maintenance activities in general unenlightened plants.

When I started studying this aspect of the business, I found the information and data laid out in layers an onion – each layer is followed by another layer. You could go to any layer, depending upon how deep you wanted to dig.

In many plants I conducted informal exercises and interviews to determine the real productivity issues. In the following section I'll describe my findings as I removed successive layers.

THE FIRST LAYER: THE INITIAL EMANCIPATION

This layer emerges when a maintenance department is subjected to the first set of improvements.

Even today, in about 30% of the large industries, the maintainers are treated as second class citizens. They are regarded as a necessary evil, the less you know about them the better. They are rarely given a pat on the back. At the first sign of financial trouble, the maintenance budget is cut. (Actually this is an exaggeration, the training department is the first to lose money and resources – but the training budget doesn't amount to much so it's practically insignificant to the big picture – at least on the cost side).

This layer emerges when management realizes the maintenance group does play a key role in the big scheme of things, and deserves a spot in the sun. Immediately thereafter, the department is put under a manager who reports directly to someone with real power. The manager is made responsible for cost control and the general management of the department. Generally the criteria for his performance are:

- Expenditure of dollars below a certain number
- Head count not to exceed a certain number
- Overtime hours not to exceed a certain number
- Safety numbers not to exceed a certain target.

In another book (**Zero-Based™ Industrial Maintainer Training - Unleashing of the Maintainer Power**) I explain why these performance indices are inadequate – as a matter of fact, they are counter productive. In this book we'll limit ourselves to issues that are germane to the subject at hand.

Having been burdened with the accountability, maintenance managers try to rise to the challenge. They immediately realize that there is more to maintenance than technology and hard work – namely ***politics***. It quickly dawns on them that there is no way they could take care of everything that is in their plate. To succeed, somehow they need to develop a work plan, which makes sense to them and others. This hurdle is crossed in many ways, but usually it is handled in one of two ways, depending upon the characteristics of the individual maintenance managers. The most effective ones are somewhere between these two extremes, mercifully there are few of those as well.

Departments Headed By Maintenance Managers Who Are Sensitive To Plant Politics

A maintenance manager who has been through enough of team building courses is sensitive to the fact he is not going to amount to much unless he has a constituency, which considers him a team player. For a maintenance manager, it is very easy to function as a team player. All he has to do is to let others (operations, engineering project managers, etc.) play a key role in making of the work-orders and schedule. Industrial plants with leadership of this type show the following characteristics:

- High emergency vs. scheduled work ratio
- Frequent equipment break down
- High maintenance overtime
- High number of maintenance people equipped with beepers and radios
- Unpredictable maintenance costs

- Lack of acrimony between the maintainer and other groups
- Frequent moving of maintenance managers to bigger and better things.

Most of maintenance work in organizations headed by diplomatic managers is prioritized according to whoever happens to be in a position of influence. The rest, precious little, is left to the judgment of maintenance supervisors.

Departments Headed By Management-Systems Oriented Maintenance Managers

These types of managers believe in disciplined applications of technology. Their ideology can be summarized as:

- ♦ In-plant politics is not worth wasting time on. Operations and other users of maintenance resources have to make a case for their requirements. Reluctantly, for good causes, resources are provided to needs determined by others.
- ♦ They view an industrial plant as a conglomeration of large pieces of equipment, which must run in a reliable manner. They tend to ignore low profile items such as soot blowers, analyzers, chemical pumps, alarm panels, etc. To such people production seems to be a hurdle in the way of technology application.
- ♦ They believe that computerized maintenance management programs are the way to go. The bigger the program the better. Experienced and knowledgeable people are seen more as a hindrance rather than as assets. In one plant I noticed a maintenance manager of this type characterize the opinions of an experienced person as having an "adverse effect" on the signal-to-noise ratio – whatever that meant.
- ♦ They believe in strong project management disciplines. Everything in the world somehow revolves around Gantt charts and critical paths.

I know of one such person who insisted on using a maintenance management package to control a large (over $50 million) short-term maintenance project. This computer program was new to the plant and nobody really knew how it worked. The vendors of the program demonstrated flawless algorithms and a myriad of interfaces that seemed to operate like a Swiss watch. Well, the reality was completely different. On the second day of the project huge printouts were handed out to the maintenance and construction crews. There were about 1000 people on the job. The reports looked very impressive and workflow paths, resource allocation and logistics tables were awe-inspiring in detail. Super quality boardroom material! The only difficulty was that many in the field could not relate to the new work packages. Overnight Murphy did his trick and on Day 1 about 5% of the activities had to be done differently, using modified materials, skills and time allocations. For Day 2, even such a small amount of changes messed up work allocations for about 30% of the work force. The project manager was referred to as Mr. Cool in the company newsletters due to his unflappability in times of stress. (Nobody wondered why he got himself in the stressful situations in the first place). Well, anyway, through the sheer strength of his personality he retrofitted the inputs to get some meaningful outputs and people went to work after wasting about half of Day 2. It seemed that Murphy had been specially invited. The next day about 10% of the work went haywire. Again, Mr. Cool prevailed and the people went to work after losing most of the day in waiting for the new marching orders. After that it was total chaos. The division president made Mr. Cool an offer he could not refuse, and on the fifth day all systems were turned over to manual planning. The company lost millions in lost production and idle time for the short-term contract labor.

The characteristics of plants run by such managers are:

- A lot of acrimony between the maintenance group and other groups
- Good adherence to allocated budgets
- Frequent production losses due to seemingly minor issues
- Infrequent large equipment failure
- High reliability of equipment but low production numbers – a classic case of successful operation and the death of the patient.

Well, irrespective of the nature of maintenance management, it is easy to bring about improvements to the first layer. Generally the following elements are tweaked to increase the productivity.

Coffee/smoke break

Everyone is reminded about the company policy and most people respond positively and the time taken for such breaks is reduced to what is allowed.

Waiting for permits

This is a very contentious issue. All of us say that safety is Job 1, but no one wants to take time to make sure that the safety of workers is guaranteed. Dennis Mackenzie, one of the maintenance managers I worked with, used to say: "Everyone wants to go to heaven but no one wants to die." Usually, contrary to common beliefs, in large industrial organizations, management is far more safety-oriented than the technicians. To ensure worker safety, management creates numerous rules and regulations. One of which is the safe work permit system. As generally applied, such systems increase safety, but they act as great de-motivators. The designers of such systems usually ignore the human element. Workers are humans and humans are easily motivated to not work. Take a typical maintenance worker who starts work at 7 AM:

06:45
He comes to the plant, all gung-ho to work.

06:45-07:05
He banters about this and that while he changes in the locker room. He is in a good spirit. A coffee to start the day.

07:05-07:20
Group exercise to loosen up. General foreman gives a short update on some accident, which occurred the previous week.

07:20-07:35
His foreman assigns him and his buddy to a welding and pipefitting job. It is supposed to be a two-hour job, and the foreman has other jobs lined up for this pair for rest of the day. The foreman gives him some safety pointers as well. All done by the book.

07:35-07:40
He walks over to the control room to get his permit to work. There are many other workers waiting to get permits as well.

07:40-07:45
The following dialog takes place.
Maintainer: "Permit for 13T-A pump?"
Operator: "What? Don't tell me you're doing 13T today?"
Maintainer: "Sure, that's what the boss man says." The operator looks at the message board and in his log.

Operator: "Yeah. You're right. I don't know if the graveyard shift got it ready or not. They have taken a gas test though. Let me check."

07:45-08:15
The operator ignores the maintainer for about half an hour while he takes care of his other operational responsibilities and other maintainers who are also waiting to get their permits. To the maintainer we are tracking, it looks like as if the operator really doesn't care and that he is being ignored. The operator's coffee cup really bothers him. Finally the operator speaks into his radio and gives instructions to somebody at the other end. "Bill is going to check it out," he informs the maintainer, who by this time is feeling a little bit frustrated. "Well, its part of the job," he says to himself and moves back into a corner.

08:15-08:30
Nothing happens and the maintainer starts to lose interest in the job.

08:30
The operator informs the maintainer that indeed the night shift had prepared the equipment for maintenance, but he has to take another sniff test since the earlier one is no longer valid.

08:30-08:45
The maintainer is issued a work permit. By this time he has lost a great deal of interest in work.

08:45-09:15
The maintainer walks over to the job and finds, as he has done many times before, that there is a lot of similar equipment, redundant piping, and bad lighting. And most of the identification tags are missing. He has a good idea but he is not certain about the equipment he is supposed to be working on. Should he take a chance? His chances of being right are over 90%. What if he is not right? He decides not to take a chance. He decides to call the control room.

09:15-09:45
He asks, "Say, you've got two pumps down, which one is 13T-A?" "The north one, actually more like the northeast one, don't do anything, I'll radio Bill to go over", the operator in the control

room instructs. Bill comes over and identifies the equipment to be worked on. By this time our maintainer is not a happy camper at all.

09:45-10:00
While Bill puts on his **DO NOT OPERATE** tags; the maintainer puts on his safety tags and sets up his equipment. Then he realizes that it is time for a coffee break.

Usually, in-house safety committees design the safe work permit systems. Members of such committees are charged to make the plant working conditions safe. Unfortunately, the design of such far-reaching and multi-tentacled systems is done without the benefit of "management" disciplines or an in-depth cost-benefit analysis. It usually happens because the overworked supervision and management personnel do not take time to go away and work in think tank-like situations. As a result, the system design is left to people who can most easily be roped in, technicians and safety specialists. These people do bring valuable knowledge to the table and do the best they can. They tend to look at issues in a one-dimensional manner – from a pure technical point of view.

A given level of safety can be attained by many different ways. On this subject I'll limit myself to only a few comments since it does not belong in this book

Consider an example where the safety committee makes the following statement: *"Since the operators have the best knowledge about plant operational status, henceforth all maintenance work must be preceded by a safe work permit. Also, the operators are responsible for ensuring a safe work environment for the maintainers."*

Superficially, the above statement makes a lot of sense and you'll find few that will disagree with it. Now review some real life examples.

Example 1
Consider the case where an electrician has to change a light bulb, a mere ten-minute job. By the time he gets his permit for such a low priority job, half a day is gone. Some additional problems are also created:

a. Since it is such a hassle to change a light bulb, most don't get changed. This should explain some of the dark areas in the operating plants that have not been seen by a human eye for decades.

b. A ten-minute job, such as tightening of a pump packing, takes hours to complete. In other words it costs close to $100.00 to do a ten-minute job!

A Possible Solution: Train the maintainers in the fundamentals of plant operation. This type of training, including site visits should not take more than two days for each operating unit. After that empower them to carry out non-critical tasks in an unhindered manner. In one plant, the maintainers needed a permit to pick up garbage! Even for production equipment, once it is shut down and safed, I don't see any harm in handing it over to the maintenance technicians and letting them do their thing. This will save a lot of time without jeopardizing safety.

Example 2

Now consider a hot work example. Before the work permit can be issued, a sniff test is required. What happens if, three hours later, there is a hydrocarbon leak? How can operators be responsible for keeping the work environment safe? As a matter of fact, under such conditions, the operators will probably be busy responding to the situation causing the emergency – they may not even know that a combustible gas has leaked out.

A Possible Solution: Train the maintainers and equip them with continuous inexpensive combustible detectors. This will not only save time, but will increase worker safety.

Tampering with safe work permit systems is a dicey business. The only point being made here is that safety committees should not be charged with making the work environment safe but to create management systems for safety issues. A little bit of innovation can make almost any safety program pay. But this can only happen if management does not shirk its responsibilities and manages the work design. Conversely, any safety system can become a liability if a broad point of view is not taken. The system designers must consider the following:

1. The do-ability of a solution in a practical sense

Consider the usual case where the operators are responsible for depressurization of lines and vessels prior to any maintenance work. Numerous maintainers are injured and killed in accidents resulting from cutting into a pressurized system. A simple time-and-motion study will indicate that it'll cost less if operators and maintainers jointly depressurize tricky systems. In such a system the primary responsibility of making the work environment safe should still stay with the operators. But the person in charge should decide how to go about it. Our plants are getting old; many drains don't drain and many isolating valves don't isolate. It's dangerous to put one group totally in charge of something for which they have fewer skills than someone else.

Another example is racking in and out of the low voltage electric breakers. In many places the operators are not allowed to touch the breakers. It creates many problems that senior management does not know about. On numerous occasions the electricians open or close the wrong breaker, and by the time the situation is analyzed and rectified, considerable damage is done. Electricians spend a considerable amount of time doing this silly work – sometimes on overtime. In most locations when a person is called out on overtime he is paid for at least 4 hours, while the breaker operation does not take more than twenty minutes.

The breaker operation assignments are randomly assigned among electricians. Sometime the assigned electrician is not knowledgeable in the specific process, which the breaker controls. This increases the probability of an error, and decreases the probability of coming out of the upset unscathed, should one take place.

Possible Solution: Train and empower the operators. Any operator can be trained to operate a low voltage breaker safely with only a few hours of training. It'll not only add to the safety, it'll save money. This is what I meant when I stated that a little innovation can make any safety program pay.

2. Effect on worker morale.

3. Cost in terms of lost operator and maintainer time, effects of de-motivation, etc.

Remember that when a person does useless work, sometimes most of your loss does not occur in the form of lost time, rather in shape of important work, which does not get done.

4. Training and empowerment of the person who has the most control over the situation.

Unfortunately, the above comments can be easily misconstrued to indicate that cost control is more important than safety. Not at all! The point being made is that you can attain the same or increased safety levels with properly designed systems that cost much less. Just because one believes in safety does not give one a license to tie up the whole operation in knots.

Waiting for parts

Waiting for right parts chews up a lot of time on the plant floor. Let's follow our maintainer a little more.

10:20
He and his buddy are back on the job site.

10:20-10:40
The maintainer realizes that the gaskets he has been given by the planners are the wrong size. He calls up the planner, who tells him that what he did was right according to the latest set of P&IDs and specs he has. Nevertheless, the planner instructs the maintainer to take measurements of all the piping he intends to work on so that the correct gaskets may be obtained.

10:40-11:30
The maintainer takes the required measurements and walks over to the planner's office, only to find he is in a meeting. He waits. When the planner emerges from his meeting and they have a discussion. The planner orders the right parts and informs the maintainer that it is not likely that the warehouse will deliver the parts before 1 PM, so the maintainer should go and do something else.

11:30-01:00
The maintainer has his lunch break, and waits until the warehouse delivery truck shows up. He could probably go and pick up the parts himself, but then he reminds himself that a lot of the warehouse staff has been laid off and its going to be a long line up there, anyway.

Under the circumstances and conditions similar to the above, sometimes the maintainers, in their effort to save time and do some useful work, decide to use scavenged or incorrect parts – for which a big price is paid later on when the equipment fails.

The challenges such as these (which do not involve system design philosophy, but are more focused on logistics) are usually addressed by time and motion studies, and application of common sense. Most companies hire consultants to do so. Actually this type of problem is best solved by in-plant people. They hate to use incorrect parts and waiting for spares. Given half a chance they will come up with great ideas. Of course, most of their ideas will not work out at first, but since they are the inventors, they will keep on tinkering with the systems until they get it right.

When all is said and done, the improved condition looks like:

- Coffee/smoke break: 7%
- Waiting for permits: 9%
- Waiting for or obtaining parts: 10%
- In-plant travel: 7%
- Idle: 18%
- Working: 49%.

This result looks great until you peel off the second layer.

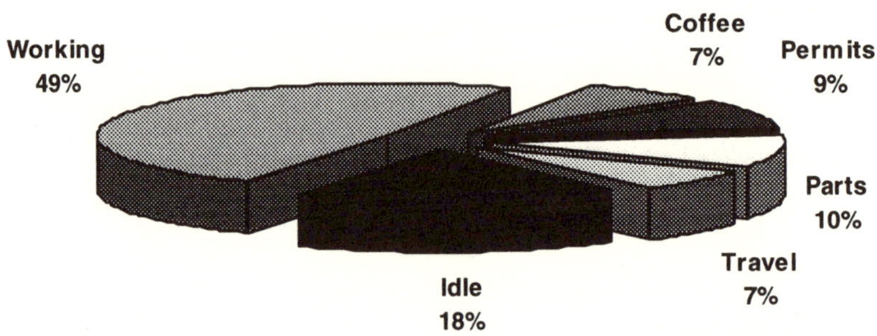

FIGURE 2	**This figure shows maintenance activities at the first layer of maintenance management onion.**

THE SECOND LAYER: THE FAD FODDER

I call this section the Fad Fodder because external consultants love to get involved in such issues. And they keep at it for years since it doesn't quite work out.

This layer is invoked by maintenance management due to its dissatisfaction with the results as outlined previously. In this layer maintenance management looks outside to find technologies on how to manage and execute maintenance functions. The key element, *what should be managed,* is ignored – more on that later.

These are difficult times. The era of captive markets is gone. Now it seems anyone can make anything and sell it anywhere, and it will sell as long as it is cheaper or better. Twenty years ago, if you walked into a large department store, you'd find that almost 80% of the goods were of U.S. origin. Today this number has dropped down to a low twenty percentile. At one time almost all of the video recorders were made here, now none are made in this country. There are many such examples.

The offshore competitive forces are usually blessed with cheaper raw material and labor, which creates enormous challenges to U.S. industry. To stay competitive, one must produce a quality product at a low cost. Since the margins have shrunk, one needs to produce more to stay financially viable. The production equipment must work as long and as hard as it can. The highly profitable plants are operated at or near design capacity. Available capacity is inversely proportional to the equipment down time (irrespective of the fact whether the down time is caused by planned or unplanned events). It is the function of maintenance to deliver highly available capacity numbers for the key production equipment.

A few years ago "quality" was the buzzword in the industrial world. Somehow the quality revolution did not touch the practice of industrial maintenance in any meaningful manner. In most of the industries, the maintenance component is not perceived as a business function. Therefore it is easy to ignore the quality component. From the operations and corporate point of view, the performance of maintenance is measured in equipment up time terms. Maintainers, on the other hand, complain that they have little control over the up time since it depends upon the down time, which is generally caused by equipment abuse by operation, more so than improper maintenance procedures.

In my opinion, both parties are wrong. First of all, the maintainers do not have their house in order – their business lacks fundamental philosophies. There is a universal law at play here: ***Your rights to uncalled for criticism quickly vaporize if you do not bother to put your house in order in the first place***. In this book and a companion book on maintenance training, I've suggested solutions for maintainers to get out of this conundrum. After maintenance management put its house in order, it can start influencing what operators do – you'll be surprised at how much influence a well-run maintenance organization has on overall operation. In some places maintenance people have so much credibility that almost nothing happens unless the maintainers buy-in or lead the charge.

Usually the performance of maintenance is measured in the speed by which they return the equipment to service after a catastrophic failure. Their credibility depends upon how they handled the last emergency, and it changes weekly if not sooner.

The current buzzwords are Reliability Centered Maintenance (RCM), Reliability Based Maintenance (RBM) and Total Predictive Maintenance (TPM). These concepts generate systems that are far better than the earlier ad hoc programs. Yet they have some weaknesses, which I'll point out in the following discussion.

The TPM provides a big picture strategy to control the maintenance process. The fundamental premises being that an empowered employee will do wonders for you.

The RCM (which is also called *joint loss time analysis)*, on the other hand deals mainly with the technical aspects of maintenance management. The RCM is based on the fundamental assumption that performance of all of the equipment can be improved and should be improved.

What's wrong with this picture?

These strategies are politically correct. They sound nice and take care of the technical nuts and bolts, but ignore the business aspect. The selection of equipment for performance improvement is done rather shabbily – and it drives the cost up for these systems. Many maintenance managers shy away from these systems because they intuitively know the payback is questionable. It takes deep pockets to finance expensive fads. You'll find most of these fads only in large plants that are estimated to be about 20% of the U.S. manufacturing facilities.

The RCM concepts were pioneered by the U.S. airline industry. Historically the airline maintainers have used inspection-based or time-in-service parameters for component replacement. Over time, as the number of components grew exponentially, they found both of these methods to be unsuitable. The inspections required too much down time (an aircraft only makes money when it is in the air). And since the quality (material and manufacturing tolerances) of components kept on improving, it made no sense to throw away components with significant residual life.

One has to be very careful with the RCM strategies because its fundamental premise (*performance of all of the equipment can be improved and should be improved*) is not fundamentally sound under general circumstances. It is easy to latch on to this principle and randomly start improving the equipment. It can yield very expensive and useless results. Come to think of it, the easiest thing in the world to do is to improve something, all you need is better material, frequent inspections, etc. The difficult thing is to find what needs to be improved and then improve it according to service requirements. This should explain why, in some cases, battalions of maintainers are constantly busy, yet the plant loses money due to low up time.

I know of one expert on RCM strategies who went about explaining some of the elements of the RCM implementation procedures as discussed below. My comments are noted in italics.

A. Make a physical inventory of the equipment. If nothing else you will have a good list for your work order system.

I find such statements bothersome, where valuable man-hours are talked about in such a flippant manner.

B. RCM should not be applied to all of the equipment to eliminate what should not be included in the RCM process.

How do you know what to eliminate? This is a crucial weakness.

C. Determine the criticality of the equipment to the process.

How? The proposed methodology by the RCM experts is very arbitrary and shallow.

D. Find out what the equipment is doing at the present time. Say you are considering a pump bearing. Let's say at present the bearing fails once every two years. Decide on what you want to get as future performance. For example, you want the bearing to run for two years before failure.

How do you do that without considering the cost impact? Why not four years? I find these targets are set rather arbitrarily.

E. Use a cross-functional team to find a solution. The team members should include operators, maintainers, vendors and engineers.
Another reason why the maintainers are always busy.
F. Implement the solution.
What? What solution?

The proponents of the RCM strategies see an eventual cultural change and it becomes a continuous improvement effort. Which is true and an excellent goal, but only if the fundamental philosophy is clearly enunciated and contained within well thought out boundaries.

This is what this book is designed to show: Concepts like RCM, RBM and TPM cannot be applied cost-effectively in a strategic sense. However, if Zero-Base™ concepts are applied as the strategy, then these concepts are likely to yield tremendous results at low cost.

THE THIRD LAYER: THE NOT SO OBSERVABLE REALITY

All through the preceding sections, one thing is very obvious while another is glaringly missing.

It seems obvious that most of maintenance managers look at themselves as custodians of equipment with the primary responsibility of making sure that their equipment keeps on operating. It is not so at all. **The primary goal of maintenance management is to make as much money for the shareholders as possible in safe and environmentally sound manner.** In this book I show that most maintenance people work under two major misconceptions:

They equate high maintenance productivity with high profitability, which is rarely true. While this is a sound proposition, the difficulty lies in the fact that most people associate a technician's productivity with his actual time on the job, which is not appropriate at all. In the auto industry they use man-hours per car produced as a criterion for productivity, which is very appropriate. In the smokestack industry no such criterion exists. The relevancy of what a person does is far more important than most of the other things we do in our maintenance management functions.

Secondly, it is widely believed, due to self-inflicted reasons, plant maintenance is a cost-center and cannot be considered as a profit-center. By thinking like this, the maintainers shoot themselves in the foot. If you think you are cost center, the less you do, the less the expenditure – hence, it follows, reduction of your budget results in direct savings. It is possible, as I show in this book, to formulate easy-to-monitor performance criteria. And, yes, it is possible to make money while increasing your compliance with regulations

The conversion of plant maintenance from a cost-center to a profit-center requires three steps:

Step 1: Acquire an understanding of what maintenance really does at the present time

Step 2: Determine what is appropriate for the maintenance department to do

Step 3: Do what is relevant to the big picture in a competent manner.

The first step is really not necessary. However, by doing that you will be able to paint a good ***before*** and ***after*** picture, which does wonders to the share price on the stock exchange floor.

The third step is also not really earth shaking. Since all of us have years of experience at doing something. As long as someone puts something in front of us, most of the time we do it well. The cure for not doing something well is not a subject for this book. It is covered adequately by a myriad of books on worker motivation and empowerment.

The crucial step is the second one, which makes or breaks us. Business journals are full of stories about plants shutting down. Most of the time we tend to blame unfair competition from overseas. Not really – we do it to ourselves – we cannot differentiate between the important and the frivolous, and make wrong choices.

In this chapter we will only discuss the first step. The second step is discussed at length elsewhere in the book. The third step involves work planning and execution, which is outside the scope of this book.

What Do Maintenance People Really Do?

In this section I give you some unvarnished truth which is revealed after you peel off the third layer of the maintenance management onion.

Over the last ten years, I've observed and conducted numerous informal surveys and developed some general ideas.

In general, especially in older plants, the maintainers are poorly trained. In my opinion the main reasons for the poor quality of technical training are:

> **Management Is Not Interested In Training Of Its Work Force**
> This reason is true for about 40% of the industrial plants. In such plants, management's position is that when they hire a journeyman he should know how to handle most of the things related to his discipline, the rest he should be able to pick up quickly. In such plants the technicians behave in a strange manner. For some reason they do not say something like: "Hey, I do not understand the workings of this piece of equipment. I realize that you have given all of the vendor brochures to me, but they don't make sense to me. Whenever I look at a generic vendor drawing it seems that our equipment is slightly different. I realize that the vendor rep also gave us a one-day training session. But he did not go into enough details, besides he did not have any lesson plans or testing documents. Please train me." Out of pride or fear they simply do not say that. ***Or probably they think it is normal for them to maintain a certain degree of incompetence and muddle through their job.*** This is an interesting situation. On the one hand management takes the tradesmen to be competent in their function, and on the other hand the tradesmen keep their problems to themselves, and nothing happens (other than the eventual shut down of the plant). There is no mechanism to determine and flush out the competency problems. Irrespective of what tradesmen think or do, it is a management problem (Remember: Management Must Manage–Peter Drucker). Management must devise means to identify and take care of these issues. There are many indicators that can be used to gauge the knowledge and skill level of the tradesmen, some are listed in the following sections.

Determine how often a job needs to be redone.
This is one of the best indicators about technical competence. Surprisingly this indicator is rarely used. If you are not sure whether such an indicator is valid in your plant, ask the users (operators). Ask them point blank about this issue. You are likely to get an exaggerated answer but it will put you on the right track.

Determine how readily people accept assignments.
In most of the plants, for some pieces of piece of equipment, only one or two of the maintainers have the required expertise (or at least that is how it is perceived) – all others shy away from assignments involving this equipment. This is also a very interesting situation. I've found that the so-called experts have attained this status out of default. Nobody really trained them, they fumbled their way through some of the initial problems and everybody sort of enshrined them as gurus. In many cases such gurus told me that they probably know about 30% of what they should really know. But the good thing is that they have a blank check and are allowed to fumble their way through any problem. Their trial and error methodology (especially when they are called out at midnight) is considered by all as diligent and hard work. One of such gurus told me that for every two-day training session with proper training material, he'd save the company at least 100 hours of unnecessary work, mostly at overtime rates. ***Without exception all gurus told me similar stories.***

Determine how often the maintainers huddle during an assignment.
This is usually a good sign that the maintainers lack training. Most of the time maintenance huddles are assumed to be generating new and innovative ideas due to cross-pollination of experience. In some cases it is true. Usually the poor tradesmen are trying to figure out the basic stuff and how to take a stab at the problem without making it a bigger.

In this book I describe how maintainer training can be highly focused so that it can be done at low cost to compare to the usual broad-brush approaches.

Perhaps it would be appropriate to talk about a universal law at play here. **Maintainer training is like the force of gravity*: It will flow to the maintainers whether you like or not, it is like an unstoppable force of nature.*** It is similar to that famous ad for an auto filter: You can pay me now or you can pay me later. The only difference is that if you organize training you achieve competence at a very low cost. Otherwise the technical training process will take its own natural course:

- The process of trial and error, which the maintainers need to go through, will be enormously expensive
- The process of trial and error never quite ends. During different phases of useful life, a piece of equipment shows different problems. Also many will repeat the same mistakes in their personal learning efforts
- Only a handful of the employees will subject themselves to the rigors of such a voluntary tortuous learning process. The rest will ignore the problems and try to gloss over them somehow (Band-Aids) – to the detriment of the operation
- During this period of trial and error you may go out of business.

Management Does Not Know How To Train Its Work Force

This type of problem is perhaps the most common. In most cases, management, while thinking that it is doing a great job of maintainer training, it is simply not doing so. It does not know how to go about training its people. It is, however, diligent about allocating funds and resources. Management feels that just because it is liberal about letting people go on courses and conferences, besides having a fully funded training department, it has done its job. Not so! The function of technical training is to enable people do a better job. If that does not happen, the training effort has failed.

The training department organizes courses and delivers them, sometimes it does post-course evaluation and testing as well. But it does not deliver the goods. It is very easy to verify my contention. Walk into any large plant and ask this question: *Did your management give you technical training so that you can do your job in a safe and efficient manner?* The answers you will get will floor you. Notice that I did not formulate the question as:

Are you satisfied with your technical training? This is a useless question, and you can never get an objective answer to subjective questions such as these. When I was a maintenance manager I used to take a hard line approach to these types of issues. I would not let anyone touch a piece of equipment unless he was properly trained to do so. I used ask people about their training needs and prune it down to what was strictly related to the job (about 30% of the wish list). The result was an unprecedented level of reliability at an unprecedented low cost.

In organizations where technical competence can be improved, usually the efficiency of training is measured in terms of:

- Number of courses developed
- Number of courses delivered
- Number of attendees
- Cost of course development
- Cost of delivery
- Degree of participation by the in-plant people
- Comments on smile sheets.

Many of the courses are soft courses about team building, communication skills, etc. Which is well and good, as long as we also address the really hard-core issue about how to troubleshoot and fix a piece of complex machinery.

In the above you will not notice any parameter which measures the actual effect on the bottom line of the operation. I fully realize that it is not easy to measure the effect of training on the bottom line (I've addressed this issue in a different book). For the time being forget about the hard numbers, I'd consider a training department to be at least 70% successful if, after the training sessions, you get positive response to questions like:

- Do you feel that the technical training provided to you was adequate to enable you do your job in a satisfactory manner?
- Did the technical training, provided to you, help make you competent maintainer?
- Did the technical training give you everything you expected from it to do your job in a competent manner?

Well, now we can get back to issue at hand: ***What do maintainers really do?***

There is a general spectrum of activities, which a tradesman goes through. The nature of the spectrum, however, varies according to discipline and trade. To simplify the message I've combined the trades into two major disciplines: E/I Trades and Mechanical Trades. For the purposes of this discussion, I've discarded items such as coffee breaks because there are much bigger issues to deal with. The study of coffee breaks is a favorite with some consultants where they want to demonstrate that the main reasons for low productivity lie with the technicians. It is not so at all. The main reason is management that refuses to manage (or does not have time to do, since there are so many other demands on their time). Let's look at the findings.

Mechanical Maintainers

- Research/study for the job: 2%
- Waiting for permits: 9%
- Waiting for or obtaining parts: 10%
- In-plant travel: 7%
- Idle: 18%
- Re-doing earlier work: 14%
- Working: 40%.

Electrical/Instrument Maintainers

- Research/study for the job: 20%
- Waiting for permits: 4%
- Waiting for or obtaining parts: 15%
- In-plant travel: 9%
- Idle: 10%
- Re-doing earlier work: 12%
- Working: 30%.

I hope the above numbers do not create any irrational exuberance, because some really bad news follows in the next section.

Well, this is it. This is real life. The preceding numbers reflect an average from about ten large industrial plants. I doubt if we'll ever get reliable a database involving a larger number of participants. Most people shy away from subjects such as "idle time" and "re-work percentages."

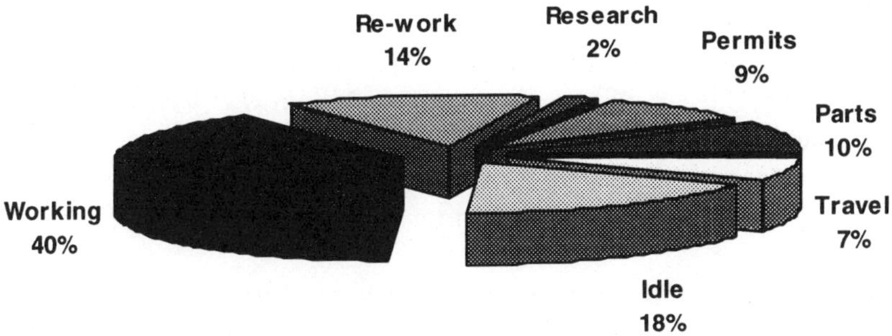

FIGURE 3	**This figure shows the mechanical maintainer activities under the third layer of maintenance management onion.**

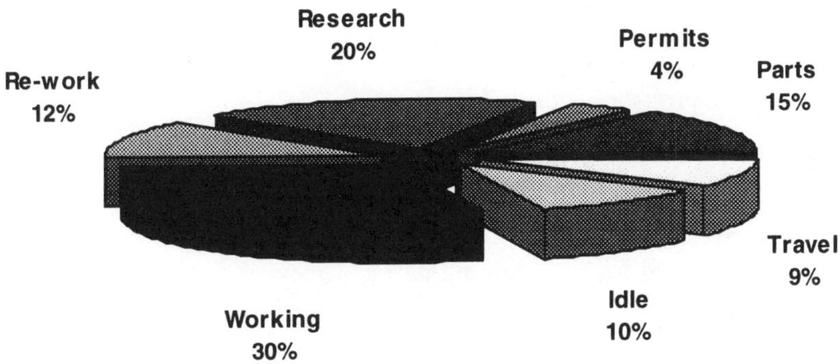

FIGURE 4	**This figure shows the electrical maintainer activities under the third layer of maintenance management onion.**

THE FOURTH LAYER: A CLOSER LOOK AT REALITY

In the preceding, we discussed how the maintainers went about their jobs, but we did not discuss the ***nature of the tasks performed***. In the later chapters we will learn how maintainers spend a large amount of their time doing inappropriate tasks. Through no fault of their own, tradesmen rarely know the importance of the equipment they are working on.

In my estimation, and you will agree with me after you've finished this book, a certain amount of work done is not relevant to the big picture of the operation and does not add to the bottom line. The following tables show the delineation between the useful work and the inappropriate work.

Mechanical Maintainers

- Research/study for the job: 2%
- Waiting for permits: 9%
- Waiting for or obtaining parts: 10%
- In-plant travel: 7%
- Idle: 18%
- Re-doing earlier work: 14%
- Inappropriate work: 15%
- Appropriate work: 25%.

Electrical/Instrument Maintainers

- Research/study for the job: 20%
- Waiting for permits: 4%
- Waiting for or obtaining parts: 15%
- In-plant travel: 9%
- Idle: 10%
- Re-doing earlier work: 12%
- Inappropriate work: 12%
- Appropriate work: 18%.

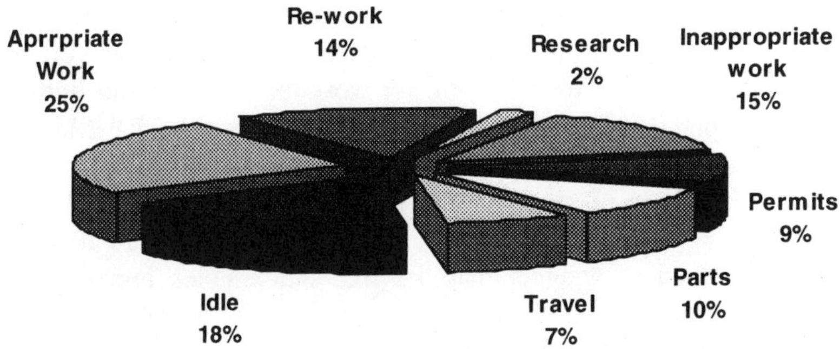

FIGURE 5	**This figure shows the mechanical maintainer activities under the fourth layer of maintenance management onion.**

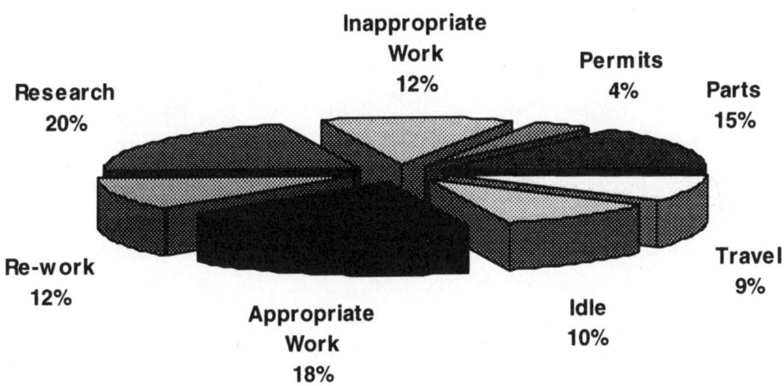

FIGURE 6	**This figure shows the electrical maintainer activities under the fourth layer of maintenance management onion.**

Let me hasten to add that inappropriate work cannot be called useless work; any work done by a technician in good faith usually has some use.

Irrespective of how we cut it, generally speaking, really productive work accounts for about 25% of what a maintainer does during a week. This is what my contention is based on when I say that you may be paying a maintainer over $100/hr for work that adds to your bottom line. With proper training and the application of Zero-Base™ Maintenance concepts, this number can be increased by at least 100%.

If you increased your manpower by 20%, the situation will remain exactly the same. Since the industrial revolution we are dealing with huge mechanical gadgets that act like black holes and can suck in anything you throw at them. Believe me, there are no Maytag Men in the smokestack industries.

I participated in two labor strike/lockout events and became aware of some interesting phenomena. In each case management and non-unionized staff took over the operation. After the first ten days, I noticed the following:

- The housekeeping improved markedly
- Safety incidents dropped to almost zero
- Production levels went up and became steady
- Worker morale was very high, everyone enjoyed doing a hard day's work.

After the strike was over, everything went back to what it was before, within about ten days.

I am also aware that the above phenomena are not universally common, but it is prevalent enough to draw some interesting conclusions from. I have validated these findings by interviewing many people from many plants.

One senior manager, Steve Newcomer, related the following to me. At one of the plants where he worked, the hourly people went on strike and management and the non-unionized staff manned the production processes. His experience was very similar to mine. After the strike, Steve noticed that one of his planners was planning a lubrication job to be done by two people for two hours, and to be done every week.

He was puzzled, and said: "Doug, don't you remember, during the strike, we used to do this job in one hour. We never did it automatically, we kept an eye on the oil condition and replaced it every two weeks or so. And it only took one man!"

There are thousands of such incidents. The only conclusion I can draw is: "In large industrial undertakings people, when given an opportunity, people can only prioritize what they can do with their own hands; they have a great difficulty prioritizing work for others." This principle applies to all levels of organization. Hourly staff and technicians, especially when left on their own (as in socio-tech environments), do as well as anyone else.

There is no organization of any reasonable size where work is not prioritized. But what is prioritized is pretty simple stuff, which anyone can do either intuitively or through application of simple weighing factors. It is nowhere near what is required for PSM/RMP activities. It is extremely rare to see it done properly.

To do it right, you need to:

- Rationalize the work. Find out what is important and what is not so important
- Prioritize the rationalized work.

A lot of times we confuse prioritization with rationalization. The act of rationalization involves looking at a piece of work to determine if it should done in the first place, if so, with what degree of rigor. Rationalization is driven by the nature of the production processes and can be used to categorize equipment in a number of different ways depending upon the criticality of the equipment.

On the other hand, the act of prioritization involves allocation of resources to work, which has already been put in a pecking order according to its usefulness to the overall process. Prioritization is driven by the availability of resources. Depending upon the operational conditions, the rationalized work belonging to the same category may be scheduled in different execution priority.

A rational process to do all of this will involve the following steps:

- Identification of all the equipment
- Categorization of the equipment in an hierarchy depending on its value to the process as far as its impact on safety, environment and production is concerned
- Identification of requisite maintenance actions for each class of equipment
- Application of maintenance resources to equipment in accordance with the above-mentioned analysis. This is where the process of prioritization comes in – after all the rationalization is completed.

As we will see in the later chapters, the second step is the most crucial of all. It involves application of sound business management principles. Traditionally, this step has been missing in all maintenance activities. In most of the industrial plants today maintenance management ignores this step and jumps right into work, based on some hit and miss prioritization system. Business management in this manner is almost sinful, and results in:

- Enormous amount of maintenance resources being squandered away on inappropriate tasks
- Compliance with PSM/RMP standards is impossible. Not only that, it usually puts management in indefensible positions, if litigation were to follow safety system audits
- In the case of worker injury, management can quickly find itself in an indefensible position, especially if faced with criminal negligence charges
- During periods of economic downturns, there is no way maintenance can be scaled back in a logical manner. Since there is no rational basis for maintenance activities, it is likely that some of the cutbacks will be inappropriate and will result in unbearable loss of revenue
- There are no meaningful maintenance management performance indices. Therefore, irrespective of how well or poorly they perform, their work job remains a high pressure, thankless job.

In this book I have tried to solve these problems. You will be amazed at what can be done to a department once you structure its function on sound management principles. The results of using such an approach are:

- You can accomplish a lot by spending a little
- You have a rational approach to addressing PSM/RMP related issues (limited to mechanical integrity aspects)
- You have a defensible position against worker litigation. If your actions are based on sound principles it is very difficult for someone to charge you with criminal negligence. In the eyes of law there is a big difference between an injury resulting from a known and consciously accepted risk, and an identical injury resulting from an ignored situation which was never really examined.

7

Fundamentals Of Zero-Base™ Methodology

When nature's way was lost, honesty was invented.
When honesty was lost, laws were invented.

–LAO-TSE, TAO TE CHING

Chapter Summary

The driving philosophy behind the Zero-Base™ concept is very simple: **Situational Effort**. Our present day maintenance effort is like a carnival, there are many experts being driven by themselves or others to continuously perform feats of endurance and daring to the indulgent and sometimes indifferent masses. If we can harness all that talent and apply it where it really counts, we can get miraculous and unprecedented results. That is what Zero-Base™ methodology does for you. It is designed to harness the available talent and apply it like a precise surgical tool to the situations that warrant it.

This chapter presents the fundamentals of the Zero-Base™ Compliance concept. This chapter also deals with the basics of some hazard analysis techniques insofar as their relation where the ZBC concepts are concerned.

"*W*hat about Hazops? Don't hazops do pretty much the same thing?" I'm frequently asked this question. In this chapter we'll answer this question as well as go over the fundamentals of Zero-Base™ Compliance philosophy.

FUNDAMENTAL ZERO-BASE™ PHILOSOPHY

For the last twenty years or so American industry has constantly been under the gun to improve productivity and quality. At the beginning of this period some thought industry was lagging so far behind that it would never catch up and gradually wither away. As a matter of fact, as late as the early nineties, most of the think-tanks were saying that for the next few decades, industrial leadership will pass on to the pacific rim countries and then to the European Common Market. Well, that did not happen, nor is it likely to happen for the next decade anyway.

Nevertheless, a lot can be improved on the American industrial scene. There are many factors that are holding the U.S. industry from optimization of worker safety, productivity and environmental impact. The quality and viability of industrial performance is adversely effected by:

- many questionable notions enshrined as gospel
- self-imposed constraints
- elements of unrealized potential.

All of the above translate into a host of needs that can be fulfilled (mousetraps waiting to be made). This fact gives rise to industrial management fads which come and go. It is interesting to note how a fad comes about. Somebody, somewhere becomes aware of a problem belonging to any one of the above-mentioned categories. He uses an innovative way to solve that particular problem. *Voila!* A fad is born! When he takes his idea to the public, very few can disagree with him since his idea does respond to a real need. Not many can argue with his solution either, since he did employ a clever method to solve a problem. The more people listen to the new concept, the more want to get on the bandwagon. Thus, the life cycle for a fad begins.

Well, then how does a fad die? You see the fad sponsor and the temporary fad users make a few mistakes. They ignore the overall relevance of the fad to the operation. An industrial operation is like a living organism, it has a huge momentum and slowly labors along in a certain direction, which may not represent true north for that time and place. Nevertheless, in spite of being erroneous, the natural movement of such an organism is controlled by its inherent philosophies and sustaining paradigms, which give it life and nourishment. If a fad is not consistent with the organism's natural dynamics, it dies. This is why fads die: they are irrelevant to the fundamental dynamics of the operation. How many times we have we heard people say:

- Nothing changes here
- The more things change the more they stay the same
- You simply cannot change anything around here
- It's very difficult to bring about a change here!

Well, now you have the answer to comments such as: *It is very hard to go against the inertia and momentum of an organization, irrespective how good a new idea is.*

In my observations, as noted above, I did not mean to imply the natural behavior or direction of an industrial organism is necessarily appropriate for its long-term well being. I simply acknowledged its existence and noted the enormity of its momentum.

To change the direction of an operation to follow a more profitable path requires visionary corporate management. It is a hard and momentous task and requires implementation of innovative visions. Such changes require paradigm shifts that must address the corporation in a holistic manner. Many leaders are successful in doing this, and the corporate boards recognize it and reward senior management accordingly.

The Zero-Base™ methodology proposes such paradigm shifts. It is not limited to a one-notion fad but addresses many issues and the rewards come about in many forms (see the chapter titled **The Bottom Line**). In the discussion that follows, we gradually develop the main elements of Zero-Base™ methodology.

Intuitively, in an industrial setting, we know that we have the wherewithal to produce our product profitably in a manner, which is socially acceptable. Our beliefs are based on hundreds of years of precedents and many analytical exercises. We should not be in business if we did not believe that. This is a very important basic notion, which I intend to use as a launching platform for my argument. Let me re-emphasize, in an industrial setting we believe that we have the resources to produce our product without jeopardizing the safety of our employees or the environment.

Having said so, let's take a reality check. In real life, some elements of the society (OSHA, public et al) sometimes think we are putting employee safety and the environment at an unacceptably high level of risk. There is nothing wrong with that – the owners (the public) of society have a right to think in any manner they want. After having presented our point of view as an input to the opinion formation processes, it serves no purpose to ignore or be discontent with the prevailing notions. We, however, should strive to present our case in the best light.

Our challenge takes a new two-headed form:

- If we think that our operational systems do need improvements regarding worker safety or the environment, how do we go about solving the problems without going bankrupt?
- Or, on the other hand, if we think we are really doing OK, how do we mount a credible information campaign?

Let's consider one item at a time.

CASE I: IMPROVE WORKER SAFETY AND ENVIRONMENTAL IMPACT WITHOUT GOING BROKE

As we said in the beginning, we happen to believe that we do have the resources to conduct our business in a profitable and safe manner. Note that we did not say we have unlimited resources (very few organizations do). We only said that we believe to have adequate resources to manage our business. I realize that I'm belaboring the point, and I'm deliberately doing so since the limitations on resources is a fact of life and the new initiatives should not lose sight of this fact. You can solve any problem with unlimited resources. If that is your situation then you are wasting your time reading this book, because this book is designed to bring about the most good with limited resources.

Having established the above notions, let's review the salient components of our station in life:

- As business managers, we are reasonably certain that we spend an adequate amount of money in our business. For the purposes of this discussion, let's assume that we do not want to exceed our current expenditure unless someone shows us a bulletproof ROI
- We, and others, also think we could use some improvements in our safety and environmental impact programs.

Well, doesn't it follow that we must be doing something wrong if the above statements are taken at face value? We are spending adequate money, yet desirable results are not there. Where is the money going? Is it possible that we are doing some things that need not be done, and we are not doing other things that should be done?

This leads us nicely into the first element of the basic philosophy of the Zero-Base™ Compliance Strategy:

Element 1: To get rid of preconceived notions and to identify the desirable work elements, we must study a business from the ground up.

We need to look at the fundamental nature of how we do business (here we are limiting ourselves to the maintenance functions only). We should **"zero"** out everything we currently do pending a process of rationalization.

Having zeroed everything out, we need to find out what work our maintainers should be doing. The maintainers do everything that is put on their plate. From our experiences, and those of others, we know that we can quickly load up our maintenance forces in no time flat. Give me a thousand maintainers and I'll get them busy by coffee time; by early afternoon at least 20% will be back making a solid case for overtime work. And I challenge anyone to find an iota of useless work in all that is being done – all work looks and feels like useful work. This is so that all work is useful to someone somewhere. ***There is no dearth of work, and therein lies our problem***.

So, what do we ask our maintainers to do? A quick answer is that they should be doing what is important rather than something that is not so important. How do we determine what is important? Prioritization, of course. Well, how do you prioritize work? This question will yield many answers. In other chapters I demonstrate that all of them would be wrong. But here, for the sake of argument, let's go ahead using the conventional wisdom. The conventional wisdom says that we should use a group of knowledgeable people and let them assign priorities to work. (For now we'll ignore that the fact that a similar approach got us in trouble in the first place). But to make things more interesting let's do a test, which I've done many times. Why don't we assign this task with identical parameters to a few independent groups, and see what happens? You'll get a multitude of conflicting answers. How can all be right? In other chapters I have demonstrated that such an approach does not work in large installations, simply because the number of variables at play is simply too large. So, what do we do? We go back to square one and try to find the maintenance issues that are most important and try to handle them first. It is not easy to do so. If it were, you wouldn't have too many reliability problems.

The importance (or criticality, for want of a better term) of a task depends upon the function of the associated piece of equipment in your process, and its reliability. Notice that there are at least two variables in this equation: function and reliability.

To take my argument forward, I beg your indulgence to let me assign a certain meaning to the word "critical". This word is the most abused word in the industrial world and practically means nothing (it probably has more emotional connotations than tangible substance). For now, only for this chapter, let's define it to indicate the "relative importance" for a piece of equipment, to the output of your process. Note that the output of your process is defined in terms of the widgets you produce for the market, safety of your personnel and the environmental impact of your production processes.

> **For example:**
> A piece of equipment, failure of which is likely to cause a serious injury, is very critical; and, on the other hand another piece of equipment, failure of which causes a ten-minute shutdown of the process (with no production loss) is not so critical.

Using this definition we can describe our problem a little better. For each of the following scenarios, the warranted level of the maintenance effort is different:

- Highly critical equipment which is very unreliable
- Highly critical equipment which is very reliable and simply does not fail for years on end
- A piece of equipment of low criticality which is very unreliable
- A piece of equipment of low criticality which is very reliable.

The above represents just a broad spectrum of the possibilities, there are literally hundreds of thousands of possible combinations, each one of which warrants a distinct level of maintainer attention.

You waste money if you pay a lot of attention to a very reliable piece of equipment of low criticality. On the other hand, you set yourself up for trouble if you do not pay adequate attention to a highly critical piece of equipment with questionable reliability.

From the above discussion it is clear that if we want to get anywhere we need to understand and evaluate the following:

- Reliability of each and every piece of equipment employed in the production process
- Its criticality to the process in terms of the impact of its failure on employee safety, the environment and production throughput.

Once we have determined the above two variables, we can start evaluating the "risk" (or threat) a piece of equipment poses. The risk posed by a piece of equipment is a function of its reliability and its criticality.

If we know the risk posed by each and every piece of equipment, then we can list them in a descending order and start taking care of issues that pose the highest risk. This is what Zero-Base™ methodology does for you. Now let me capture all of the above in the form of salient elements of the Zero-Base™ methodology:

Element 2: Reliability of equipment

The Zero-Base™ methodology provides a means to determine the equipment reliability which reflects **the real life as much as possible**. This method does not use unrepresentative published reliability numbers or random guesswork by the shop floor people. It is based on a very regimented assessment carried out by experienced people, based on about a dozen variables and miscellaneous pieces of other information. Since the reliability of a piece of equipment is dependent on its rate of failure, an innovative approach is proposed to determine the failure rate: **The Zero-Base™ Failure Rate**.

Element 3: Configuration of equipment

The Zero-Base™ analysis considers how a piece of equipment is integrated in the overall scheme of things. Such a consideration enables one to study the impact of failure, mitigating circumstances, and interdependency of failures.

Element 4: Impact of failure

The Zero-Base™ system considers the failure impact in terms of worker safety, the environment and the production throughput.

Element 5: Determination of threats (risk) posed by equipment

The Zero-Base™ technique evaluates the threat posed by each piece of equipment to the process. To present the quantification in relative terms, threat indices corresponding to the three areas of interest (safety, environment and production) are developed. A composite index (for each piece of equipment) is also developed which uses the three areas of interest in a weighted or raw form.

Element 6: Development and implementation of threat (risk) reduction strategies

The analysis, as noted above, leads into easy development and implementation of risk reduction strategies.

Since the Zero-Base™ methodology yields results in a numerical form, you can dial it up or down. As a matter of fact, you can dial up or down any of the individual components: safety, environmental or production. Such decisions can easily reflect the corporate vision, mission statements or fiscal year targets.

Also, we should not lose sight of the fact that by going through this exercise we do determine what is important and what is not, therefore we save an enormous amount of money compared to broad brush approaches that, besides being expensive, may or may not yield the desired results. Remember, in an unanalyzed situation you cannot be sure if you are focusing on critical items – even if you decide to ignore the money being wasted on things that may not be appropriate.

In my estimation, the Zero-Base™ system leads you to make a case that if you take proper care of 15% of the equipment, you automatically achieve over 95% of the compliance needs.

Now let's consider the second case.

CASE 2: IF WE THINK WE ARE DOING OK, HOW DO WE MOUNT AN INFORMATION CAMPAIGN?

If you do not a employ system such as the Zero-Base™ methodology, there is no way you can mount a credible campaign. Without a strategy all you have is the data about how much money you are spending on the safety programs and your safety statistics. This data is probably adequate for an audience of engineers and economists, but when you are dealing with the public, it's a different ball game. Especially if there is an accident, then this type of data goes out of the window really fast.

On the other hand if you follow a strategy such as the Zero-Base™ methodology, you can make your case by explaining the following:

- How you determined the risks to the operation
- How you determined the impact
- How diligently you went after everything which posed a significant risk
- How you developed an overall strategy to address the risky issues.

Most people will accept the above as evidence of responsible and diligent effort.

HOW DOES THE ZERO-BASE™ METHOD DIFFER FROM HAZARD ANALYSIS METHODS SUCH AS HAZOP?

I'm frequently asked this question. These two are completely different animals and are used for different purposes. One cannot replace the other. A hazop study identifies the design problems and suggests mitigating actions. On the other hand a Zero-Base™ analysis takes the design at the face value and studies the real life risks to the operation by evaluating the equipment reliability, real life operational issues, and the consequences of equipment failure.

A good quality hazop will get you a robust design, and a good quality Zero-Base™ analysis will give high levels of mechanical equipment integrity, especially for those pieces of equipment which pose the most significant threats to the operation.

There are many methods that can be used for Process Hazard Analysis (PHA); Hazop is one of them. For the purposes of this discussion let's use Hazop (Hazard and Operability Study) techniques as an example.

Purpose and Application of Hazop Studies

Hazop studies are a very important component of safe plant operation and regulatory compliance. The hazop methodology was created in 1963 by the British chemical giant ICI. The original purpose was to use this system to build safer plants. As a matter of fact, even today this company uses hazops during all key phases of a new plant construction:

- **Exploratory phase:** Determination of suitability of potential sites
- **Flowsheet design phase:** Determination of hazards associated with design of major process flow streams
- **Detailed design phase:** Determination of hazards associated with bells and whistles of the detailed design
- **Construction phase:** Verification and confirmation of viability of earlier determinations
- **Commissioning phase:** Determination of hazards associated with commissioning
- **Post-commissioning phase:** Determination of hazards potentially created by modifications, etc.

If hazops were conducted in the above manner, then the PHA's as envisaged now by OSHA would be unnecessary. Unfortunately, most of the plants built in the U.S. do not go through this degree of rigor and need to be retrofitted with hazard mitigation systems. Nevertheless, the original purpose and the fundamental strength of a hazop study lies in its ability to determine design weaknesses and mistakes.

I've lead and participated in dozens of hazop studies and I've come to the same conclusion: It's an excellent method to ferret out the design problems.

A properly carried out hazop study will answer many questions including:

- What type sealing mechanism is used on the pumps? Could mechanical seals do better job?
- Is the gasket material consistent with the fluid being handled?
- Does the location of key isolation valves make sense? Accessibility problems?
- Are there enough isolation valves and/or spectacle blinds?
- Are there enough pressure relief devices?
- Does the process warrant double-block-and -bleed mechanisms, if so, have enough been provided?

Problems with hazop studies

Despite the wondrous results obtained by a properly conducted hazop, it does have a few inherent weaknesses. A few of them are noted below.

1. A hazop study assumes the plant will be operated by competent technicians and management, a rather idealistic situation. Trevor Kletz, perhaps the most knowledgeable person in the world regarding hazops, comments on the foregoing assumption in *Hazop and Hazan* as: ***"If these assumptions are not true then hazop and hazan are a waste of time. It is no use identifying hazards or estimating their probability if no one wants to do anything with them; it is no use installing trips and alarms if no one is going to use or maintain them."*** The Zero-Base™ analysis does not use ideal situations. The risks are evaluated while accepting the plant operation and culture as it exists.
2. The results of a hazop study are usually tabulated under the headings: Guide Word, Deviation, Possible Causes, Consequences, and Action Required. All deviations can cause one kind of problem or another; hence one is obliged to note all of the possible consequences as well as the corresponding mitigating actions. Many times, piles of recommendations are made for rather inconsequential issues. Each of the recommendations is also graded as high, medium and low according to the desirability and severity of consequences. It is a highly unscientific way of handling rather serious issues, which causes management, on many occasions, to ignore many of them. As a matter of fact the sheer volume of recommendations is causing many larger facilities to use other hazard identification techniques (usually What-If/Checklist) rather than hazop studies.
3. In the standard application of a hazop study, it looks at the process changes via system lines (pipes). It ignores the hardware such as controllers, pumps, etc. Although some researchers have recommended modifications to the basic system to include such hardware.
4. The standard application is designed for continuous process operations. It is difficult to apply it to batch operations. We should not lose sight of the fact that in most plants there are many auxiliary batch systems. In a batch operation, many of the

variances (NONE, MORE OF, etc.) on which the hazop study is based are normal, which makes it difficult to find abnormal conditions.

5. A hazop study is oriented toward systems using physical fluids and cannot be easily applied to electrical power systems or digital control systems.

> **The traditional method of identifying hazards was to build the plant and see what happens–"every dog is allowed one bite". Until it bites someone, we can say that we did not know it would. This is not a bad method when the size of an incident is limited but is no longer satisfactory now that we keep dogs that may be as big as Bhopal.**
>
> Trevor Kletz in *Hazop and Hazan.*

In conclusion I want to emphasize that the Zero-Base™ analysis is not designed to replace hazops. As matter of fact, a Zero-Base™ analysis will be highly unsuitable for a PHA project. However, after doing your PHAs when you apply a Zero-Base™ study to improve the plant mechanical integrity, it will not only guide you toward highly efficient and cost-effective solutions, but it will also take care of many of the weaknesses left behind by the hazop studies.

In the next few chapters we'll develop the main elements of the Zero-Base™ technique, followed by a chapter in which we pull all the elements together.

8

The Zero-Base™ Failure Rate (ZBFR)

Custom, then, is the great guide of human life.
–DAVID HUME, 1711-1776

Chapter Summary

In this chapter you will find:

- A discussion on why it is difficult to determine the expected rate of failure for industrial equipment using conventional or ad-hoc methods
- A discussion on why it is important to determine a representative rate of failure in a realistic manner
- A method for determination of a representative rate of failure (Zero-Base™ Rate of Failure – ZBFR) in a reasonably rational manner. The presented method surpasses all other alternatives in cost, accuracy and practicability.

*M*ost managers of industrial processes are interested in determination of the likelihood of failure of equipment. After years of experience they find that it is very difficult to do so, especially if one is interested in a representative number which gives the expected rate of failure ***for the future***. It is rather easy to find some sort of failure rate data which is usually unlikely to represent any given specific field conditions and cannot be used for general industrial applications. The conventional terms such as **reliability** and **failure rate** carry some undesirable baggage:

- Firstly, they are heavily weighted by the historical data, which usually renders them useless, unless the nature of industrial processes, the service conditions and the manufacturing materials do not change over time

- Secondly, they usually ignore the soft field information, which is difficult to get and is generally of a qualitative rather than quantitative nature.

One way to build a useful database is to start from scratch and remove (zero out) all the contaminating bells and whistles. After that add only what is relevant to your plant, and application, and assess the likelihood of future failures for your specific application . We refer to such data as the Zero-Base™ Failure Rate or ZBFR.

This piece of information is critical to your maintenance, compliance, productivity and asset management programs.

The very cornerstone of the foundation of your programs is the realization that your equipment does, and will fail. If you had a piece of equipment which was failure proof, you'll not need any care-taking programs and you will have very few compliance problems. You really do not need any maintenance programs for pieces of equipment which are guaranteed and accepted as failure proof. But, unfortunately, there is no such thing. Given time, all equipment fails.

At this time no one can adequately provide you with a numerical number for Zero-Base™ Failure Rate for general industrial equipment. There are, however, some exceptions to this, two of which are:

- Electric power distribution industry equipment (excluding all generation aspects)
- Aerospace industry equipment.

In the future there may be additional exceptions, especially those arising out of initiatives in hand with the Center For Chemical Process Safety (CCPS) – more on this later.

The reasons which drive these exceptions are rather meaningful and can be replicated anywhere.

- For these two industries, in a comparative sense, the diversity of service conditions is rather limited and well defined
- Availability of an enormous amount of data which does represent the field conditions to a much higher degree
- These industries have rigid and well thought out certification programs for technicians (better training).

Despite varied ambient conditions, electric power distribution equipment lends itself far more readily to analytical study, than say slurry handling equipment used in a mining operation.

Second, traditionally, the electric power industry is classified as a public utility (though the current de-regulation climate is rapidly eroding away at this status). Which means, among other things, a good rate of return is guaranteed on the capital invested. The more money the investors are allowed to invest, the more money they make in the form of fairly secure dividends. For this reason, for decades, it has been rather easy to find money to study and optimize equipment operation. Easy availability of money combined with fairly predictable operating conditions, has resulted in a wealth of knowledge about equipment failure.

The aircraft industry is a high exposure industry. For some reason, the public is very interested in following and knowing the nitty gritty about commercial aircraft failures. If an aircraft crashes and kills 50 people, it is big news for months. The investigators spend tens of millions of dollars trying to get to the bottom of the cause (remember TWA flight 800). The investigations are usually followed up by recommendations for new rules and improvements. These recommendations are usually implemented in a diligent manner, and flying becomes safer yet. The additional cost is passed on to the consumer, and is accepted very readily as the price of safety.

> **On an average day in our country, 17 workers are killed in workplace accidents, and an estimated 137 more die from occupational disease. Just imagine if one plane crashed every day, killing 150 people. The public would be outraged and demand action. But since these deaths normally occur one or two at a time, at different worksites around the country, most people just don't notice the problem.**
>
> Joseph Dear, Assistant Secretary of Labor, addressing the U.S. House of Representatives, July 26, 1995.

There is a curious phenomenon here. The conventional wisdom states that free market forces automatically find the equilibrium between quality and price. It doesn't seem to be the case for the aircraft industry. In many other parts of the world, where free market forces have much more sway, commercial flying is far more hazardous than in the U.S.. The only difference is that in the U.S., the quality of commercial aviation safety is driven by government regulation rather than voluntary initiatives by the industry. So OSHA may have a point, after all.

The net result is that the aviation industry responds in a very conscientious manner and delivers the goods. In the airline operation, design and reliability managers handle this aspect of their business in two major ways:

- They build redundant systems. In the U.S., it is almost impossible for an aircraft to fail due to one or two equipment-based initiating causes. Generally many systems need to fail within a short period (flight duration) to cause an aircraft failure.
- They study (under real or mathematically simulated conditions) component performance, and determine the flying hours needed for a failure to occur under usual service conditions, including material fatigue. Having determined that, it is rather easy to make sure that no component stays in service for a dangerous length of time.

Given the resources, in spite of the large variety of service conditions which an aircraft may have to endure, it is possible to create meaningful failure data.

On the other hand, consider a case where 50 people die in an industrial explosion. It is news for a few days, after that the public interest is nowhere near what it would be for an airliner crash.

To be fair to the ground-borne industry, there is one difference between the aviation industry and, say, an oil refinery. When one (i.e. the public) buys a quart of oil, one really does not care if the operator got killed or injured in the process of making the product, as long as one gets a quart of oil in a nice clean container. On the other hand when one buys an airline ticket, one really has two objectives:

- To be delivered from point A to point B
- It is also desired that the operator (the pilot) reaches there in one piece as well; because if he doesn't, no one else does.

It is a crude example, maybe an exaggeration as well, but therein lies the difference. The public identifies an aircraft disaster as something which is far more likely to have an impact on their well-being than a fire in an oil refinery.

Some key points need to be made here:

1. In our general smokestack industry, the number of variables and the variety of service conditions which industrial equipment faces, is far more extensive in diversity than that for electrical

power distribution equipment and the aircraft industry. Given the diversity, it is practically impossible to simulate representative service conditions and generate generic failure rate data.

2. Even if it were possible to find some means to simulate representative service conditions, there is no source of funds or a venue to do so.
3. The above discussion may lead one to believe the general smokestack industry is inherently less reliable than the aircraft industry. I do not think that is necessarily the case. In my opinion there is a lot of ground to be gained by better management practices before such sweeping statements can be made. As a matter of fact, I happen to think that U.S. industry can be made as reliable in a cost-effective manner as the aerospace industry. Probably, we have no choice but to do so – if we want to survive in the new open world. To stay competitive, this may turn out to be the only edge we could turn to. But we have a long way to go – once we have optimized management practices, only then we will know if there is any inherent performance differential between these industrial sectors.

SOME KEY CONCEPTS REGARDING EQUIPMENT FAILURE

The failure of a piece of equipment is a stochastic phenomenon. That means that even under the most controlled laboratory conditions, there are enough random variables to yield inconsistent results. Let me make this point by giving three examples dealing with equipment failure:

- Insulation failure
- Bearing failure
- Computer disk drive failure.

Insulation Failure

Most of the failures concerning electrical equipment occur due to insulation failure. A variety of reasons cause electric insulation to fail:

- Substandard insulation material
- Age of insulation
- Inadvertent mechanical damage to the insulation
- Atmospheric dust and humidity

- Ingress of water or some other undesirable fluid
- Presence of corrosive gases in the atmosphere
- Presence of erosive material in the environment
- Lightning or switching surges
- Inappropriate application.

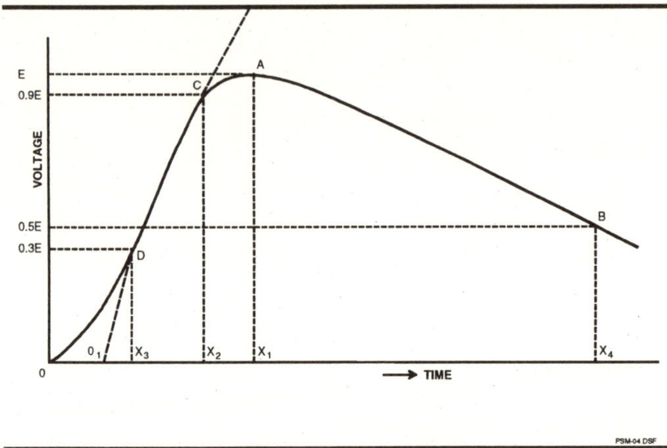

FIGURE 1	This figure shows the key parameters of high voltage test curve.

Let's see how high voltage insulation is designed. Field testing forms an important part of insulation development. Many tests are conducted to confirm the insulation characteristics, the most important of which is the ***withstand voltage*** test. It is accepted, in the long run, the most stressful voltage will be the service voltage applied under normal service conditions. However, tests are conducted to determine the highest voltage which the insulation will stand without failing. The insulation failure depends not only on the highest voltage value, but the rate of rise of voltage as well. It is very difficult to design tests which represent real-life conditions. The alternating voltage, which we commonly use, has a cyclical form – it varies between a positive and a negative value – as it does so, it passes through the zero line. As it passes through the zero point it endures a very high rate of voltage change, which is highly stressful for the associated insulation. So the test voltage has to have at least two representative characteristics, the highest value and its rate of rise. Voltage spikes caused by lightning and switching surges generate very high rates of voltage rise. Since in real life no two voltage spikes have the same characteristics, how do you design a test spike? Along with the nature of the test spike, there are many other variables, as listed above, which can cause insulation to fail. Therefore it is very difficult to state a unique specification which ***will*** cause it to fail. To overcome this problem, the designers create artificial voltage waves (spikes) which can cause an insulation to fail under lab conditions. An example of such a wave is given in figure provided here.

From the figure, notice that the voltage wave rises sharply, and then gradually deteriorates. This wave-form is chosen since it is easy to create and it does reflect high voltage spikes in a general manner. A wave of such nature is applied to the insulation being tested. The shape of the curve plays a key role in this application:

1. The steeper the front end of the curve causes the insulation to fail more readily. In other words, a rapid rise of voltage at the front end, even if the magnitude is not very high, makes insulation more prone to failure
2. Insulation failure also depends upon duration of the high voltage stress applied to it.

Some Definitions

The Critical or Minimum Flashover Voltage is given by the crest voltage of the wave that will cause a flashover at the tail-end of the wave 50% of the time.

The Critical Withstand Voltage is given by the crest voltage of the wave which is just below where the disruptive discharges begin to occur (there may still be some flashovers)

The Rated Withstand Voltage is given by the crest voltage of the wave which does not cause any flashovers.

Now remember all of these values will change as soon as we change the shape of the curve or the ambient conditions. Therefore it is difficult to predict the performance or life of insulation in real life applications. This fact can be easily checked out if you visit the electrical shop in any major industrial plant. You will see piles of motors with burnt out insulation–and, for a majority of the cases there will be no explanation for the failure. Having said that, the number of industrial motor insulation failures can be greatly reduced by better management of the local power distribution system and the maintenance and operational practices.

Irrespective of the uncertainties, we need to establish some measure to define the insulation characteristics. We do this by standardizing the wave shape. This creates a common basis for different types of material being tested. Generally, the designation for a wave shape is given by the time in microseconds for the impulse to reach the crest, followed by the time in microseconds for the wave to reach half the magnitude. Thus a 1x40 microsecond wave takes 1 microsecond to reach the crest of the wave, and 40 microseconds to reach half the magnitude on the downhill side.

Having defined the designation criteria, we face a few other practical problems. Under most conditions, it is very difficult to accurately ascertain the zero (O) point and the crest (E) location for an impulse wave. To avoid confusion and to establish a common base, the test engineers establish a virtual zero time point at O1, which is determined by a line drawn through 0.3E and 0.9E points on the wave front. For example, a 1x40 microsecond wave will have an O_1X_1 value of 1 microsecond and O_1X_4 value of 40 microseconds.

The standard wave which is generally accepted for such testing is designated as 1½ x 40 microsecond wave. As mentioned earlier, this wave is useful for standardization purposes only–and is likely to have no resemblance to real life conditions – especially when we introduce a large number of other significant variables into the picture.

I realize the previous comments do not do much for our quest for certainty in the field of equipment failure, but there are ways to manage all this, as we will see later in this chapter.

Source for the preceding information: Westinghouse Electrical Transmission and Distribution Reference Book, published by Westinghouse Electric Corporation.

Bearing Failure

Bearing manufacturers keep on improving their product. They are constantly testing and developing better raw materials. To improve the reliability of their product they use highly precise manufacturing and inspection methods. As a part of the quality control system, they randomly sample their product and operate them to failure.

One would assume the bearings constructed with identical material and manufactured in an identical manner, would fail in a reasonably identical manner.

Not so. The figure given here shows the result of a representative sample of 30 bearings. There is an amazing degree of variability as far as the expected life of the bearing is concerned.

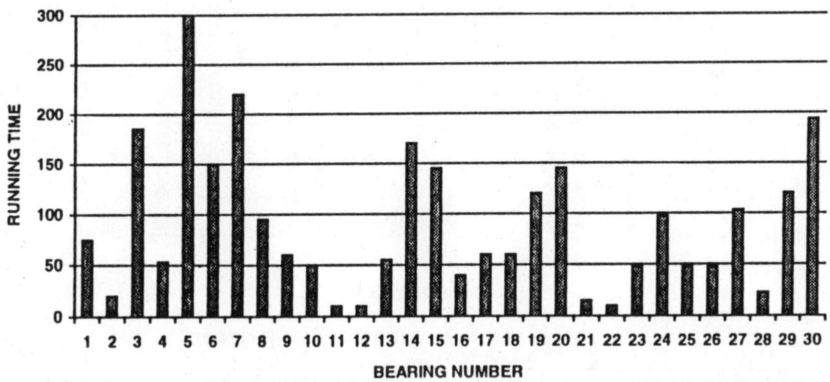

FIGURE 2	**This figure random failure of bearings under controlled conditions.**

Again, don't forget that these results are obtained under ideal laboratory conditions. Just imagine what will happen to the uncertainties if we apply the real life conditions where numerous other factors play a role in the expected life span for a piece of equipment.

Source for the preceding information: The case against preventive maintenance, Ron Moore, Reliability Magazine, March/April 1994.

Computer Hard Disk Drive Failure

Over the last few years the reliability of hard disk drives has gone up considerably. You do not hear of hard drive failures as you used to five years ago. There are two reasons for this. First, most people do not get an opportunity to operate a hard drive to failure. The expected life span of a hard drive is about five years. Five years is a long time in the world of computer technology, most people do not use a hard drive for such a long time. Generally one replaces a hard drive within three years with something faster and having a larger capacity. Second, the industry is using better materials and more precise manufacturing processes.

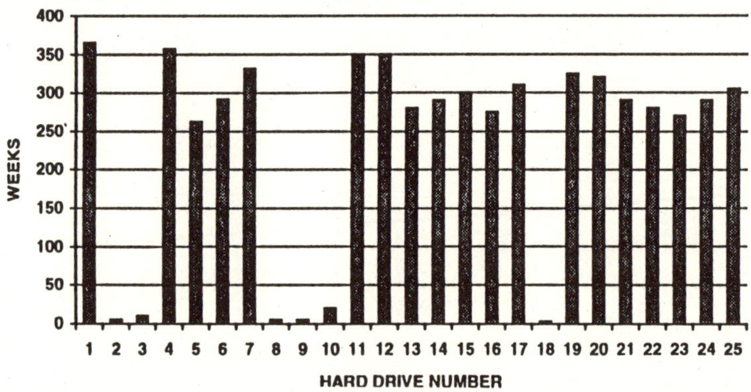

FIGURE 3	**This figure random failure of computer hard disk drives.**

This figure shows the result from a typical hard drive test bench. You will notice a few interesting things in this figure.

If a hard drive survives the first few weeks, it's likely to run OK for a long time, usually five to seven years.

Most of the hard disk manufacturers provide a mean time between failure (MTBF) rating of 300,000 hours or longer for their products. What does it mean? Does it mean that a disk drive is likely to operate trouble free for 300,000 hours (that is over thirty years)? No. You will notice that the vendors also state a "design lifetime" for the hard drives – which is usually about five years. These ratings mean that if you were to run one drive at a time, replacing it with an identical unit as it reached its design lifespan, you would experience one unexpected failure during 300,000 hours of operation.

Most manufacturers offer two to five year warranties for their hard disk drives. It pays off for them, because most failures occur within the first month. So if a drive can outlast the first few weeks, it is almost as likely to last three years as five years. Second, the suppliers realize you are not likely to keep your hard drive for that long a period anyway.

Failure mechanisms for other types of equipment have their own peculiarities. But in general most failures of general industrial equipment have some commonalties:

- Even under the ideal and controlled conditions, the failure mechanism has poor repeatability
- For real life operational conditions, which vary greatly from place to place, it is almost impossible to develop generic data which will lend itself to general applications.

So where does that leave us? Especially when we realize that the expected failure rate is the cornerstone of all analytical work as far as management of operational reliability is concerned.

From the previous discussions it is easy to conclude that it is impossible to obtain perfectly reliable data regarding the expected rate of failure for industrial equipment. It is not true. Useful generic data can be developed if done in a regimented and scientific manner as demonstrated by OREDA for offshore petrochemical equipment.

But what do you do if you do not have good quality data available at this time. To overcome this hurdle we have devised a system which is likely to yield the best possible information and data. Please note that no claim is being made to generate 100% reliable data. The Zero-Base™ technique does not yield perfect answers, but in the absence of OREDA-like data, that being the best of all options, it is likely to generate data of highest possible quality. There is no such thing as perfection, it is simply a state of least imperfections.

The concepts for generation of Zero-Base™ Failure Rate data for general industrial equipment, are based on the following principles:

- All external factors as well as the plant-specific variables must be considered
- Plant-specific field experience and expertise must be considered
- Published statistical data must be considered when available

- Other than the above, the common operational conditions, which reflect real life unique to each plant, must also be given due consideration.

A careful examination of the above principles will convince you that, if you use these factors meaningfully, you cannot help but get failure rate information of the best possible quality.

DETERMINATION OF ZERO-BASE™ FAILURE RATE

The method used to determine Zero-Base™ Failure Rate (ZBFR) is based on the assessment of a set of comprehensive collection of information. The new idea being presented here is the ***assessments are forward-looking and use all of the plant specific factors.***

To make an assessment for the ZBFR we use the following steps:

- Gather technical and all other relevant information
- Make and record the ZBFR assessment.

An illustrative example is provided in Appendix B, however the general ideas on how to handle this exercise are provided in the following steps.

Step 1: Define The Process Area You Want To Study

Carefully analyze your process and determine the boundaries for the components which are covered by PSM/RMP regulations. Usually it is very easy to do so; OSHA and EPA guidelines are reasonably explicit. In some cases you may need to ask OSHA/EPA for a ruling or interpretation. If you happen to be doing this exercise purely for production related issues, then you don't need to worry about the regulatory guidelines.

Step 2: Determine And Show Energy Levels

Obtain a set of Process and Instrumentation Drawings (P&IDs), and inscribe the significant energy (pressure, temperature, voltage, elevation, etc.) data at the appropriate locations. The operative word here is ***significant***, do not chase demons that don't exist or don't matter.

FAILURE-IMPACT-THREAT FORM **Form ID Number:** **Date:** **FORM 1**

Main System: **Subsystem:** **Ref:**

Component	ID No.	ZBFR	Failure Mode	Safety Impact						Environmental Impact						Revenue Impact						OTI
				None	Injury	Dis-ability	Fatal-ity	TI	STI	None	Non-Report-able	Report-able	Catas-trophic	TI	ETI	10K<	11-50K	51-100K	>100K	TI	RTI	

WITO-Form 1 Rev G. 04/97

Step 3: Prepare An Equipment List

Using the Process and Instrumentation Drawings (P&IDs), make a list of "equipment" as defined in CFR 1910.119 (j) Mechanical Integrity. At the time of writing it covered the following equipment:

i. Pressure vessels and storage tanks;

ii. Piping systems (including piping components such as valves;

iii. Relief and vent systems and devices;

iv. Emergency shutdown systems;

v. Controls (including monitoring devices and sensors, alarms, and interlocks) and,

vi. Pumps.

Looking carefully at this list you will notice that you will be hard pressed to find an item on a P&ID which is not included. To make the list we use Form 1: **Failure-Impact-Threat Form**. At this time we will only use the first few columns of this form. A form like this is used for each subsystem.

A convenient way to make a list is to take one process stream at a time and follow it through. As you add an item to your list, mark it off on the P&ID with a yellow hi-lighter. Do not forget to include the piping runs between flanges. It seems to make sense to consider a welded joint as an integral part of the pipe (unless it has additional elements such as bellows type expansion constructs). However, a bolted flange (which can leak) or a pipe run (which can also leak) should be considered as discrete pieces of equipment. Larger equipment should be considered in terms of major components. For example a large pump should be considered as having the following components:

- The pump housing and impeller
- The pump sealing system
- The driver (steam turbine, electric motor, etc.)
- The coupling
- The lubrication and cooling system
- The control system.

The delineation of components should represent practical considerations reflecting the likelihood of operator or maintainer intervention.

The system and the subsystem are identified at the top of the Form 1. Usually it is helpful to give these forms some sort of identification numbers for reference purposes – noted on the right top corner. For clarification of other items some examples are given below:

Main System
Alcohol Plant

Subsystem
Column T4 and its heat exchangers.

Reference
Here we usually note the identification of P&IDs and PFDs used in this analysis. Example: 23-H-14 (rev-d), sheets 2-5.

Component
In this column the name of the component is noted. Examples: Pump 23-P-1, Exchanger 23-E-3, Pipe segment D12, etc.

ID Number
In this column you need to note the unique identification number for the component. Usually equipment tag numbers are used for this purpose.

There is a potential problem here. Invariably you will come across some pieces of equipment which do not have unique identification numbers. Sometimes smaller valves, expansion joints, analyzers, etc., do not have unique tag numbers. In such cases, assign a temporary tag number to them. For ease of record keeping and traceability, the temporary numbers are based on the P&ID numbers. Examples:

- P14/1
- P14/3, etc.

In such cases the temporary number is also noted on the P&ID as well. Such marked up P&IDs should be kept in a safe place for future reference.

This concludes the list making part of the work. Now we can begin gathering of data for the listed items.

Zero-Base™ Failure Rate (ZBFR) **Form 2**
Raw Data Collection and Assessment

System: Subsystem:		Form 1 Identification No:	
Component			
Model No.		Years in service:	
	Design maturity: ☐ Mature; ☐ New; ☐ Not sure	Manufacturer's reputation: ☐ Good; ☐ Not good; ☐ Not sure	
Ambient Conditions	☐ Located in open air ☐ Located indoors ☐ Clean, dry ambiance ☐ High humidity ☐ Presence of corrosive gases	☐ Occasional water and pollutant splashes ☐ Controlled temperature ☐ Frequent detrimental high temperatures ☐ Occasional freezing temperatures	
Application Severity	☐ Primary equipment, continuous service ☐ Usually on standby ☐ Steady continuous service ☐ Intermittent service, frequent stop/start	Inspection/Testing Information:	
Operational Conditions	☐ Always warmed up (pre-start) as required ☐ Usually warmed up (pre-start) as required ☐ Never warmed up (pre-start) as required ☐ Frequently overloaded ☐ Never overloaded	☐ Frequent routine observation by technicians ☐ Infrequent routine observation by technicians ☐ No routine observation by technicians ☐ Always kept clean ☐ Sometimes kept clean ☐ Rarely cleaned	
Operator Competence:	Formally trained to operate this component: ☐ Not formally trained to operate this component: ☐		
Maintainer Competence:	Formally trained to maintain this component: ☐ Not formally trained to maintain this component: ☐		
Failure history–last 5 years	Actual Number: _____; ☐ None; ☐ 0-2; ☐ 3-10; ☐ >10		
Has the reason for these failures been positively eliminated	Yes; No; Not sure		
Published rate of failure: Units:		Data Bank:	

Assume that this piece of equipment is made fully operational by using your normal construction, maintenance and operational practices. **In your opinion, how many times is it likely to fail in the next five years, if it is operated without any maintenance activity, under *your* usual operational conditions and using your usual operating procedures?** To answer this question, ignore all maintenance including preventive maintenance–irrespective of who provides it. In making your assessment, consider all of the information provided in this form.

			Guidelines	
	Maint. Tech.			
	Area Operator:		A:	Number of failures around 2
	Field engineer:		B:	Number of failures around 4
	Selected value:		C:	Number of failures around 8
			D:	Number of failures around 10

© WITO Inc. 1994, 95, 96, 97 WITO Form 2 Rev E	Date: Approved:

Step 4: Collect Raw Data For The Listed Equipment.

In this step we collect all sorts of raw data pertaining to each specific piece of equipment. The object is to collect as much data as possible so that an expert may be able to make an assessment regarding the most probable rate of failure *for the future.*

The form (Form 2), illustrated here is used to consolidate the data for each piece of equipment. After some experience, it is easier to do so by using a spreadsheet type design where twenty or thirty pieces of equipment can be processed at the same time.

You will notice from the form that the data gathering exercise is very thorough – it is only limited by the availability of historic and design data. This reflects absolutely the best information you can have. Sometimes, while gathering the data, you will notice significant gaps in your management systems – make a list of your recommendations and pass them on to appropriate people for action. Having done this exercise, and having become sensitive to some of the flaws in your systems, you will see an automatic tendency to seek out improvements. This is so because for senior management to act in a useful manner, it is crucial to have a well identified problem definition. ***Nevertheless, irrespective of the completeness of data, you will be surprised how meaningful and useful the output is.***

I realize that the form looks very cumbersome, it is really not so. It is a tool to facilitate logical thinking. After practicing with the form for a few days you will find that it is not time consuming and one can zip through enormous amounts of data fairly quickly. Many of my clients have used this form or its earlier versions, and all have found it easy and expedient to use. I have yet to hear a complaint about a need of excessive effort or wastage of time. The main reason for this is the fundamental principle we follow: ***On the form, reflect the real life in your plant as much as possible, and do not chase demons which add little value.*** For people who are close to the real action, it is not a big deal at all–in minutes, surprising a amount of information comes pouring out.

Following types of information is noted on the form:

- System identification
- General physical and operational information
- General maintenance related information
- Technical and historic information

- Failure assessment information.

In the following paragraphs, some brief comments are provided on the form content. Later on in this chapter, these items are discussed in fuller detail.

System Identification

This information ties this form to Form 1, and can be provided by any knowledgeable person such as the project coordinator, an operator, a process engineer, etc.

General Physical and Operational Information

This type of information can be readily provided by a knowledgeable operator.

General Maintenance Related Information

A knowledgeable maintainer can provide this information readily.

Technical And Historic Information

This information can be dug up by a field engineer, an operator or a maintainer.

Failure Assessment Information

This information is based on input from an operator, a maintainer and an engineer.

A convenient way to manage this part of the program is to form a small group, consisting of the following key people:

An operator: This should be a person who has field experience with the equipment under question.

A maintainer: This should be a person who has field experience with the equipment under question. You will need help from different trades at different times. Ideally, you should collect all the forms pertaining to a specific discipline and ask an appropriate person to go through it.

A field engineer: This should be a person who is thoroughly familiar with the nuts and bolts of the operation and has worked extensively in the field.

In some cases, especially in small plants, your group may have only one or two members who will be able to provide all of the information. In others you may have four or five members (but no more than three at any one time). The intent is not focus on the number of people, rather involvement of the people who are best qualified to participate.

The first thing you need to do is train the participants in the basic concepts being used here. The key items you need to cover in such a training are:

- The reasons for doing this exercise
- The basic concepts of this analytical system
- The importance of having focused discussions
- The importance of looking for real and significant issues only.

FORM 2 DETAILS

The top part of the form deals with equipment identification, which is self-explanatory. The remaining parts of the form are discussed below.

Design Maturity

It is important to think about the design maturity of the component you are considering. Sometimes newer designs, especially those from lowest bidders from foreign lands, need to go through a teething period before all the bugs are ironed out. On the other hand the design for a piece of equipment which has been through a few revision cycles over a few years may be far more stable. For example, I have noticed, in each plant, there is always a pet list of equipment which suffers from the design maturity issues, one example is the flame scanning equipment. Some of the newer designs either lack the robustness or too readily pick up spurious radiation; however, if a particularly new design has worked well in your plant, then you really do not have much to worry about.

You can walk through any plant and pick up numerous stories about lowest bid design which did not quite work out.

Manufacturer's Reputation

Maintenance people seem to have an opinion about most of the common manufacturers. In some plants there is a constant battle between the purchasing department and the maintenance people about the vendor selection process. Frequently you will find identically rated equipment made by different manufacturers to have different reliability. Once the information is cataloged as suggested here, it may be far easier to convince the non-believers to see the light and deal with as few manufacturers as possible. That, of course, is not the purpose of what we exploring here.

Ambient Conditions

Ambient conditions play an important role in the reliability of equipment. I know of many cases where low levels of corrosive gases (mainly SO_2) create an insulating coating on relay contacts, which causes random relay failures, and the consequent unsafe conditions.

Ambient conditions such as humidity, dust and grime have a distinctly adverse effect on the equipment reliability. Unfortunately, in many places, I have noticed that management prefers to keep on replacing expensive equipment rather than improve the ambient conditions. Perhaps an exercise such as this will unfold the bigger picture a little better and more informed decisions can be made.

The equipment which is installed outside, directly exposed to the elements, is designed accordingly. In spite of this fact you should be careful with the auxiliary equipment which may not be designed with as much care. Steam tracing systems are good example for this. I have frequently seen steam tracing systems and the associated steam traps in poor operating conditions. In such cases, irrespective of how well the main equipment is designed, it is bound to become failure prone if its steam tracing system operates erratically.

Application Severity

Generally, industrial equipment will last a last long time if it is properly loaded and run continuously in a steady manner. Unfortunately, real life is different. In real life, a piece of equipment may be used continuously, intermittently, or occasionally. It may also be frequently underloaded or overloaded. All of these factors have a bearing on the equipment reliability. In some plants management gets so frustrated with non-performance of the standby equipment, that it tends to keep as many pieces of equipment in service as possible, irrespective of the additional energy costs. We know, in many cases, an identical piece of equipment which is run intermittently may have a lower reliability than its twin which is run continuously.

Operational Conditions

The most important aspect of reliability of a piece of equipment is determined by how well it is operated. A piece of equipment will give you decades of reliable service if the following conditions are met:

- It is properly prepared for start up (warm-up, coolant flow, quality of lubricant, etc.)

- It is loaded according to manufacturer's recommendations
- It is frequently observed by operators and minor problems are taken care of in an expedient manner.
- It is kept in a state of good housekeeping.

In your assessment of probable rate of failure, you need to determine and consider how the equipment is operated.

The reliability of a piece of equipment frequently depends much more on how it is used and operated than how well it is designed. Thus two identical pieces of equipment may have widely different ZBFR values. This should underscore my contention that a third party reliability database may not be as relevant as the technical literature leads us to believe. **You really need to look close and hard at your operation if you want to improve it – there are no mail-order magic bullets which are of any value.** High-priced consultants and thick reports may impress some, and possibly keep the regulators and shareholders at bay for the short term, but are not likely to add any value to the bottom line of your operation.

Getting back to the point, situation analyses, as proposed here, are likely to open many eyes and dangle some far reaching inexpensive solutions which are too difficult to resist.

> **Example**: At the end of such a study you may find that a particular pump has a high threat index-TI (we will discuss criticality or threat indices later in the book). A closer look will immediately show you the root cause for the high TI, which could possibly be any one of the following:
>
> a. Operators are not routinely monitoring it. An inexpensive solution: Add the pump to operators routine checklist.
>
> b. The standby pump is kept shut down. An inexpensive solution: Keep the standby pump running.
>
> c. The pump is routinely overloaded. An inexpensive solution: Amend your standard operating procedures, proscribing the overloading of the pump.

Operator Competence

To get the most out of a piece of equipment, you need to have properly trained operators. I have seen numerous cases where management thinks that the operators know how to operate a piece of equipment, but the operators have no clue. Usually a few of the operators do know enough to do a competent job, but the rest have no idea. In such cases the operators who do know their job acquire their knowledge through personal hard work, sometimes in their own time, not because management trained them. Every one knows who these operators are because they are the ones every one turns to during times of trouble. Most plants have a small cadre of such operators. I have noticed a curious phenomenon with these hot-shot operators. They tend to be aloof and do not readily share the tricks of the trade – so it seems. Superficially it seems that they tend to be arrogant and secretive. It is not the case at all. I have talked to dozens of such people and have startling findings to share. The hot-shot operators seem arrogant and secretive because:

- The knowledge they possess is acquired through trial and error, and they are not comfortable in exposing it to scrutiny which may result in embarrassing situations. I have worked with many of these operators, once they know that the process of information sharing is just that – professionals sharing ideas with no finger pointing or mud slinging – they pour their hearts out and freely discuss their doubts, strengths and weaknesses. Sometimes they demonstrate astonishing insights – far beyond the grasp of any one design engineer. At other times they show fundamental shortcomings which they readily rectify once the correct path is shown to them. Astonishingly, over 90% of the super operators possess great strengths as well as mind boggling fundamental weaknesses. Intuitively they are aware that all of their knowledge is not sound, and as a result they are not given to open discussions about what they know or don't know.
- They have seen too many programs come and go and they do not believe that management really wants to improve the plant performance. This makes them wary of new initiatives and they are reluctant to become a boy scout overnight.
- They mistrust management, sometimes with no good reason. It seems to me that trust abhors vacuum – if management does not actively foster a trusting environment, mistrust sets in.

Well, getting back to the point, in many large industrial plants management has ignored operator and maintainer training for decades and, thus, they have large bodies of poorly trained industrial operators. In many such plants management has been paying lip service to technical training (sometimes spending good money in ill-advised ventures) without really getting anyone trained. Unions have played a role in this fiasco as well – but in retrospect, it is the job of management to train the operators in spite of unions or any other hurdles. In some enlightened instances, management did rise to the challenge and motivated the unions to work with it in a productive manner. Lately some of the unions have been at the fore-front to bring about a positive change.

At any rate, in many industrial plants, due to lack of operator knowledge and skills, many disasters are always waiting to happen, and they strike when a wrong mixture of events takes place, usually at a time when the wrong people are on shift. In all such cases, on a day to day basis, the production equipment keeps on chugging along not because it is operated well, rather because it is designed well, and can take a lot of abuse.

So, in assessment of probability-of-failure, it is very important to consider the level of operator training. You may choose to go a step further and review the situation a few years hence, when some of experienced operators may reach the retirement age.

The analysis, which I am proposing here, will take care of most of these problems. At the end of the analysis you will find a list of equipment with high threat indices. From this list, isolate those which are in the list due to poor operator training. Now, for this short list make sure that the operators are properly trained. This can be done rather inexpensively. You would not need to carry out any broad-brush across-the-board training. This would be a giant step forward as far as prevention of disasters is concerned.

I have hundreds of case histories to back up my contentions as noted above. They cover the complete spectrum of poor operation, from day to day mishaps to lost opportunities to major disasters. I tend to believe that the major disasters are preceded by hundreds of minor problems; if a corporate culture is developed to get rid of the minor issues the major ones will take care of themselves. Here I am presenting some of the minor ones which tend to get ignored.

Operator Competence Case History 1

We all know it is critical for large rotating equipment to be properly warmed up before being put in service. Nothing could be more critical for the operation of, say, large steam turbines. In one place I found that the turbines had been in operation for over twenty five years without any consideration for proper warm up. The operators would warm up the turbines from the low pressure end only, and force the machines into service. Everyone thought the senior operators knew what they were doing. Not only did the operators not know how to warm up the turbines, they did not even know the location of casing drains – usage of which is absolutely critical during the warm-up phase. A review of maintenance history showed numerous problems and expensive fixes. During the period in question, the department management group had changed many times. Not one of them had tried to find the root cause of the problem – all were content with expensive rectification efforts supplied by the manufacturers' field engineers. Every five years or so the manufacturers kept up on selling them new and supposedly better control equipment and other gadgets. Talk about geese which lay golden eggs!

> **Practice doesn't make perfect–it only makes it permanent.**
> Warren Buffet (Forbes Jan 13, 1997)

In such a situation, the operators cannot be singly faulted – they were doing the best they could. They learned the tricks of the trade, some good, some bad – and passed them on to the next generation. A curious thing about this type of training, over time the good is gradually attenuated away and the bad takes on deep roots. Anyway, in such cases the operators (especially the experienced ones) do not have the heart or the courage to confront management and demand proper training. The operators think they are inherently expected to know how to operate, and if they don't it's a failure on their part, and the less said about it the better. And management thinks that the operators do know how to operate. So the matter is never discussed seriously. It's a classic as far as things falling through the cracks is concerned, the only difference is that the cracks in this case are huge chasms. Both parties don't realize that it is a critical management function to manage and enhance the potential, capability, and performance of all wealth generation assets. The operators certainly belong in this category.

> **Management must manage.**
> Peter Drucker in *Managemen*t.

Fortunately, most of the time, when these challenges are pointed out to management, they rise to the challenge and pay attention. Unfortunately, hard work always takes a back seat to the management fad of the day and, sometimes, it is very easy to forget about the effort needed to bring about improvements, and everything reverts back to the good old times.

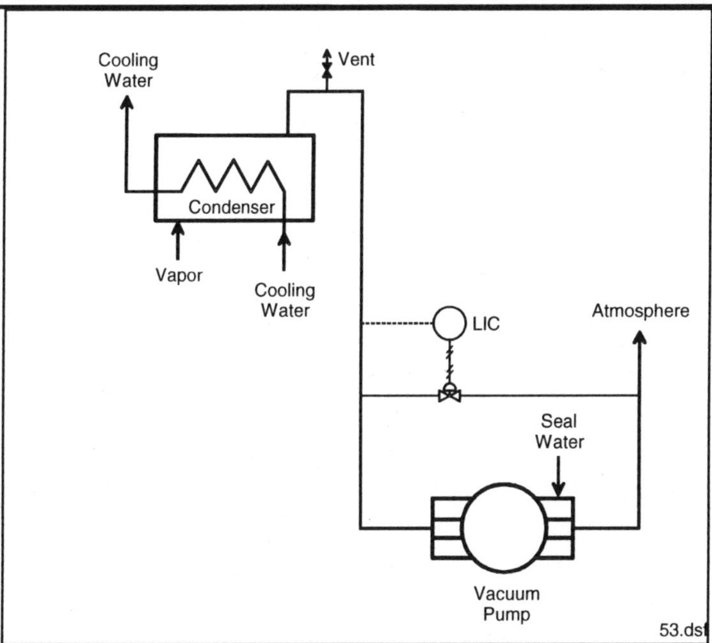

FIGURE 6	**This figure shows a vacuum pump connected toa condenser.**

Operator Competence Case History 2

In a chemical plant I was discussing some what-if scenarios with the operators. I asked them how the vacuum was maintained in a condenser. Nobody seemed to know anything other than knowing that a vacuum pump was always kept running. Then we discussed the control valve shown in the figure, and someone volunteered that it was there to bypass the vacuum pump when the pump was not working! Most of the operators seemed to think that they were supposed to open this valve completely in the event of vacuum pump failure! As it turned out, in their minds, the pressure on the upstream side of the pump was higher than the pressure on the downstream side. A few times they had done it with disastrous results, but no one had bothered to determine the route cause of the problem and train the operators correctly.

Getting back to the "Operator Competence" section of Form 2, it is recommended that you should only check off the top line if all of the operators have been formally trained to operate the piece of equipment in question. You will, obviously, consider only those operators who are or may be called upon to operate the subject equipment.

The near-future retirement of the experienced people should also be considered as a factor. Let's say you have only four people (one on each shift) who are properly qualified to operate some equipment, and half of them happen to be retiring during the next year. If the company has no plans to train the replacements then it should be a factor, since in the real sense you would **not** have any trained people after the next year. You'll be surprised to know how critical the retirement factor is in many of the large industrial plants.

Maintainer Competence

Maintainer competence also plays a key role in the determination of the ZBFR for a piece of equipment.

In many plants a considerable number of failures occur just days after a piece of equipment comes back from a scheduled maintenance activity. In some place I have witnessed members of management wonder why they inflict this unnecessary pain on themselves. "If we are going to have a failure anyway, why not let the pump fail, rather than overhaul it and forcing it to fail?", they ask.

Well trained maintainers add a lot to the reliability of a piece of equipment. Unfortunately, maintainers are far worse off as far as technical training is concerned, compared to the plant operators. The main reasons for this contention are:

- Maintainers are rarely under the gun to perform in a timely fashion. This enables them to ask someone knowledgeable to help out. Thus nobody knows about the presence of poor skill level. In larger plants there are a few go-getter maintainers who keep themselves abreast with the current knowledge–these are the people who are called in at night when no one else can figure out the problem.
- Technology changes too rapidly for an average maintainer to keep pace. This is a marked contrast with the operators, where the nature of plant operation changes at a slow pace.

Numerous accidents occur due to maintenance carelessness, errors, and inadequate training. During the last few years I have seen a marked increase in interest in maintainer training by management. In some places, management has gone to great lengths to determine and fix the shortcomings. They seem to be on the right track.

Maintainer Competence Case History 1

Two men wanted to repair a raw-water pipe. The raw-water in that area contained traces of bitumen. The standard company policy required a sniff test before any hot work. A specific maintenance procedure also called for a sniff test, but nobody had been trained on that procedure for years. The maintenance foreman ignored the policy since they were working, after all, on a water line which was located in an open area. What could be safer? The pipe line was drained and the workers proceeded to cut a section off with a welding torch. That immediately set off an explosion. One fatality. Subsequent investigation showed the high points in the pipe were filled with a hydrocarbon based explosive mixture.

Maintainer Competence Case History 2

A maintenance worker wanted to leak test a set of refrigeration coils. To do that he acquired a nitrogen bottle, but was too lazy to find a pressure regulator. He did not believe in too many fancy controls and yearned for the good old days when he could do anything he wanted. After all what could a small bottle of nitrogen do. As soon as he opened up the bottle to the refrigeration coils, he heard a boom and promptly blacked out. He was hospitalized for a week with serious head and chest injuries.

Maintainer Competence Case History 3

This incident is similar to the one above. Only in this case, maintainers in a pulp mill were trying to purge a natural gas line with nitrogen. They made the same mistake: ignored the need to use a regulator on the nitrogen bottle. A boom was heard and a control valve on the line being purged was found to have exploded. Fortunately, no one was near the valve and no injuries resulted. But the people involved will never forget the experience.

Now back to Form 2, do not check off the first line in the maintenance training section unless all of the maintainers who are expected to work on the subject component have been formally trained. Formal training could be as expedient as an hour long training session with a competent person. Formal training does not mean a week long course in Phoenix, Arizona. Any form of training is acceptable as long as the following criteria are met:

- The session is designated as a training session. It could be as short as an hour or less. Informal discussions during coffee breaks cannot really be qualified as training sessions
- The trainer is qualified in the subject matter and has prepared a lesson plan
- A test is conducted after the session
- A record is kept of the training session and the results.

Again, you should only be concerned with those maintainers who are actually expected to work on the equipment.

As in the case of operators, the near-future retirement of the experienced people should also be considered as a factor.

Failure History

The system being presented here is a forward looking one, yet, it is important to review the equipment history for the past five years to see if some useful information can be gleaned out. In spite of considering as many plant specific factors as feasible, it is possible to overlook some significant variables. Some examples of such oversights are:

- welding procedures and competence of welders
- calibration-shop practices
- competence of contractors
- effects of absenteeism (temporary move-ups).

For these reasons it is important to consider the real life failure history of the plant equipment. Usually such data is available from maintenance records or operational incident reports.

Going through the failure history, you will usually notice patterns of cluster failures for specific pieces of equipment. Sometimes it takes a piece of equipment to fail a few times before the root cause is identified and eliminated.

> **Every dog is allowed one bite.**
> Trevor Kletz in *Hazop and Hazon*

Let's consider a five-year failure history of two pieces of equipment: Let's say the equipment A had 37 failures and the equipment B had 12 failures. Let's further assume that the root cause for failure of equipment A was identified and removed two years ago, and it failed only once during the past year. In the case of equipment B let's assume that it ran fairly good during the first four years but it failed nine times during the last year. If you feed this data into a purely statistics-based system, the system will spit out instructions for you to invest more effort on operating and maintaining of equipment A. In real life, however, it would not make any sense. This is one of the major reasons why major institutionalized failure rate data sources have little relevance in most cases.

Despite the above-mentioned reservations, it is a good idea to gather historic data and review it to see if most of the troublesome issues have been sorted out. The equipment operational history should also serve as an important consideration when you decide to make an assessment regarding the projected rate of failure.

Failure Data From External Sources

In the end you should determine if some failure rate vendor has some information which could be applicable to your situation. If so, write down the published rate of failure and the data source, and give it due consideration in your deliberations. You will rarely find useful published data. However, if you do find some data which reasonably reflects your operating conditions, you should use it as a base number and then massage it to make it more representative. An appendix at the end of this book provides a list of some of the important equipment reliability and failure data sources.

The American Institute of Chemical Engineers'(AIChE) is at the forefront of initiatives to develop data and facilitate risk assessment for the U.S. chemical and hydrocarbon processing industries. No organization has done more work in this field than the Center for Chemical Process Safety (CCPS). This organization has published numerous guides and books to educate the chemical plant designers and operators. Two of the best books on this subject, published by this organization, are noted below:

- Guidelines for Chemical Process Quantitative Risk Analysis
- Guidelines for Process Equipment Reliability Data.

To overcome data quality and standardization problems CCPS started the **CCPS EQUIPMENT RELIABILITY DATABASE** project in June of 1996. This project is headed by Lester Wittenberg and coordinated by Joe Mettalia. During research for this book I interviewed both of these gentlemen, some of their comments are provided in a paraphrased form below:

> "The object of this project is to generate a database for equipment reliability information. There are all kinds of data sources available at this time, the best one is the one created by OREDA for the equipment associated with the North Sea offshore oil facilities. One could use any one of the available databases as long as one understands its limitations and the concepts utilized in its creation. Most of the databases do not use standardized terms or reflect real life conditions. Before being put to use, most of the databases (other than that of OREDA) need to be carefully looked at for the integrity of the following aspects:
>
> - How is the term "failure" defined? The definition of this term determines the failure rate numbers. Depending upon the definition the numbers can vary between many degrees of magnitude
> - The maintenance culture at the data source: Breakdown maintenance, preventive maintenance, predictive maintenance, etc.
> - Data "confidence", which is determined by the number of pieces used to calculate the numbers
> - Data "tolerance", which is determined by the integrity of data as a function of service variability
> - Equipment boundary delineation quality. Does a pump include the coupling, the driver, the start-stop switch, etc.?
> - Competence of the technicians at the data source. The impact of humans is far more relevant to the reliability of a piece of equipment than any of the technical factors."

The CCPS project is based on published OREDA concepts and the evolving ISO database standards. However, taxonomies and equipment boundary conditions will be modified, when necessary, to be relevant and useful to the equipment in use in the chemical and hydrocarbon processing industries. Many large industrial facilities are sponsoring this project by paying a sponsorship fee and participation in data collection activities. It is expected that the database will be in operation in January 1998, and will be available to the sponsors. I think in years to come the products of this project will play a key role in operation and management of large industrial complexes. In my opinion it's a worthwhile investment to join this project. For information call Lester Wittenberg at 212-705-7673.

I am certainly looking forward to seeing how this project fares. In the meantime, what do you do if you do not have "unimpeachable data", to use Joe Mettalia's terminology? This is where the Zero-Base™ Methodology comes in, and massages the real life situations, warts and all, into a fairly useful and consistent operation and maintenance strategies.

Having all of the above information in front of you, neatly captured on Form 2, you should pose the following question to area experts (an operator, a maintainer, and a field engineer):

> "Assume that this piece of equipment is made fully operational by using your normal construction, maintenance and operational practices. ***In your opinion, how many times is it likely to fail in the next five years, if it is operated without any maintenance activity, under your usual operational conditions and using your usual operating procedures?*** To answer this question, ignore all maintenance including preventive maintenance–irrespective of who provides it. In making your assessment, consider all of the information provided in this form."

This question has the following characteristics:

- ♦ It is phrased in terminology with which the field and experienced people can easily relate to.
- ♦ We deliberately do not ask about ask the reliability of equipment as a consequence of the ongoing maintenance effort. If we did that, it would "grandfather" some of the existing maintenance activities which in the final reckoning may turn out to be inappropriate. We want to determine the "zero-base" situation – which is stripped of all voluntary action. We want the reliability data for a piece of equipment corresponding to its inherent characteristics and its operational.
- ♦ Our field testing has shown that operators and maintainers associate reliability in simple numerical terms as explained below. Note that these numbers correspond to the conditions and assumptions as noted in the question being posed. The failure rate under actual plant operating and maintenance conditions is expected to be far less than what is noted here.
  - **Highly reliable, not likely to fail:** Two or less failures every five years are considered to belong to this category.
  - **Acceptable reliability:** 2 to 4 failures for every five years are accepted as reasonably good reliability.

- **Unreliable:** Any piece of equipment which will fail about four to six times every five years is considered to be unreliable.
- **Failure prone:** A piece of equipment which fails more often than once per year is considered to be failure prone.

The failure rate groups, as shown on Form 2, are designed to facilitate a dialogue with the operators, the maintainers and the field engineers. Since each plant has its unique sensitivity to equipment failure, the groups as shown are not designed to propose any standard for the failure rates.

The assessors are not asked to guess the exact number as far as the failure rate is concerned – selection of the appropriate band is good enough – and people can readily do so. In the beginning I'd spend hours discussing probabilities with field people without much progress. Then I realized field people don't think in mathematical terms, they like to think in terms which are readily meaningful.

The question being posed seems difficult. In reality it is not so. I've posed this question thousands of times to the people as noted above. Surprisingly, the operators and maintainers relate to this type of assessment very readily, and there is remarkable consistency between the numbers given by operators and maintainers. As cumbersome as this method may seem, in the field it is handled in a very expedient manner.

Each one of the assessors is asked for his opinion. After that, the project coordinator massages the opinions into one representative number. The selected number or letter is the ZBFR for the subject piece of equipment.

In the end the form is dated, signed and filed away in a suitable manner.

In the later chapters (also in Appendix B) you will see that the ZBFR is used as the starting point for further analysis – which can be done manually or through computers. For manual systems the four distinct ZBFR levels are adequate and yield excellent results.

However, this system is available in a computerized form where large masses of data can be easily handled and additional fine-tuning can be done. Essentially the data input to the computerized method permits some intra-band fine-tuning. For example, while staying within the B band, you may decide to assign two different ZBFR numbers, say 2 and 4, to two different pieces of equipment. This will help differentiate between many pieces of equipment one is fairly familiar with. This too, people find easy and useful to do.

9

Interdependent Failures

For want of a nail, the shoe was lost; for want of a shoe the horse was lost;
For want of a horse, the rider was lost; for want of rider, the battle was lost;
For want of a battle, the kingdom was lost!

–GEORGE HERBERT, 1593-1633

Chapter Summary

The effect of the failure of a piece of equipment is dependent upon the plant operational conditions at the time. In this chapter, definitions for three modes of failure are developed which take the plant conditions into account. In the later chapters these definitions are used in the analytical processes.

A failure of a piece of equipment usually poses a threat of one kind or another to the operation. Not only that it increases the vulnerability of the operation to additional problems, should something else also fail during this period. There are many levels of threat posed by any given piece of equipment. The least amount of threat is posed when a piece of equipment fails while everything else is operating normally. The level of threat is higher if the said piece of equipment fails while the operation is suffering from some other kind of failure related to the system in question. And so on.

This brings us to the nature of the threats we need to consider for an industrial operation. We can take the most benign piece of equipment and argue that it can cause a serious threat. To argue this point you are only limited by your imagination. On this subject in one of my meetings with maintenance planners, an interesting discussion took place. We were exploring the logical limits of this issue. One of the participants wondered about the equipment in Men's Washroom. His argument went something like:

> If the washroom equipment fails, management will be forced to bring in temporary portable facilities (which were usually installed outside the main gate). This will necessitate technicians to take longer breaks, creating longer absences. A long absence of a technician may coincide with a forced shut down of a piece of equipment on which he has the most expertise. This may cause a safety hazard or a production loss. Therefore the equipment installed in the Men's Washroom is of a serious critical nature.

Well, well, well. A fertile imagination can result in getting everything designated as critical. All of us think in patterns unique to our personality, making it very difficult to come up with objective assessments on our own. A group think, while politically correct, is only slightly better. The best approach is to use a group think, facilitated by thinking aids which provide guidelines as well as set boundaries.

We need to consider threats in meaningful terms. We can look at many modes of failures:

- A piece of equipment or a system will pose some threat to the operation if it fails independent of everything else, while everything else is running normally. Such failures are referred to as **single independent failures**. This type of failure is the most likely one. Unfortunately, many people in the industry believe that no mishap is caused by a single failure, a series of things have to go wrong before a catastrophic event occurs. What they are really saying is that prior to the catastrophic event many single-item failures take place which do not catch anyone's attention. ***The trick is to find the minor things which lead to a catastrophic failure and make sure that they stay in order.*** It is fairly easy to do so if you start thinking in terms of threats rather than general maintenance functions.
- A bigger threat will be posed to the operation if a piece of equipment fails while something else, directly associated with the failed equipment, is already in a failed condition. It is called a **double interdependent failure.** The probability of occurrence of such events is far less than the single-item failure. At this

point many will disagree with me, since they see such occurrences all the time. As mentioned earlier, such events take place not because they are very likely, but rather due to the absence of appropriate systems designed to catch and rectify the single-item failures.

- A still bigger threat to the operation is posed if a piece of equipment fails while two other related systems or component failures are already present. It is called a **triple interdependent failure**. Such events are have a very low (almost negligible) probability of occurrence as long as there are systems in place to identify and rectify the single- and double-item failures.

As described below, I take a much broader view of the term "system failure" and include everything which can cause a system to fail.

It is far more meaningful to consider actions designed to ward off meaningful threats, rather than those dictated by some misguided preventive maintenance notions forcing one to jump up and grease the squeaky wheel, and all other wheels in sight.

Any abnormal event which can pose a threat to the operation should be considered a failure. A failure may be in any form, including the following:

- An operator missing his daily inspection rounds
- Forced outage of a piece of equipment
- An explosion
- Flooding of the lower floors by rain water
- An operator carrying out a task he is not trained to do, thereby jeopardizing the whole operation
- A maintainer carrying out a task he is not trained to do
- Flow of a non-standard fluid
- Absence of spares.

Usually in the HAZOP or WHAT-IF/CHECKLIST studies only a double jeopardy (two-item failure) is considered. Also most of the time such studies ignore the human element.

In the application of Zero-Base™ methodology, we consider three modes of failures, and also include the human element.

MODE 1

A system fails, while the rest of the operation is functioning normally, and causes an undesirable event to occur which has a negative impact on the safety, environment or cash flow. Obviously, there can be many possible impacts, but we are only interested in the worst possible outcome for each category.

MODE 2

A system fails while the process is suffering from another related failure, problem or abnormal situation. The nature of the other problem can be in the form of failure of another piece of equipment, a procedural failure, operator negligence, etc.

MODE 3

A system fails while the process is suffering from two other events of the type mentioned in Mode 2.

In the analytical processes which follow, we'll be considering the three modes as described above.

10

Pulling It All Together

Rules and models destroy genius and art.
–WILLIAM HAZLITT, 1778-1830

Chapter Summary

In the earlier chapters many of the fundamental concepts of the Zero Base methodology were discussed. In this chapter all of the concepts created earlier are put together like pieces of a jigsaw puzzle. Definitions of equipment criticality, which are consistent and make sense, are developed. This chapter also provide a framework to create maintenance work strategies which not only make business sense, but are likely to be appreciated by the regulators as well as the shareholders.

THREATS AND OPPORTUNITIES

*A*ll problems are opportunities in disguise. I fully ascribe to this notion. However, in this book I've chosen to use the word "threat" instead of "opportunity", because I think the urgency of the issue at hand warrants it. However, people accustomed to usage of the word "opportunity" can freely do so, with no loss of message.

One of the premises this book is based on is: Search and remove the threats, and your performance will reach the optimum. On the other hand if you do many good things but ignore the threats lurking in the shadows, you're not likely to see optimum operation.

A perfectly well-run plant should operate at the design levels safely, for an indefinite length of time. However, in real life, a plant may not do so due to threats posed by:

- Acts of omission and commission by management
- Acts of omission and commission by the operators and maintainers.
- The inherent design problems

This can be looked at in one of two ways:

- There are many opportunities for better operation
- There are many threats which may stop us from doing what we are supposed to do.

Both interpretations eventually mean the same thing. Once we recognize the problem in either one of its forms, we are on our way to problem resolution. But which interpretation gives us bigger bang for the buck. An "opportunity" is a weak agent of change. You can take it or leave it. It is, however, more user-friendly in the psychological sense. But in some context it becomes rather meaningless. For example, consider a plant which is heading toward shutdown due to bad operation. We can characterize such a situation by saying : “We have a set of opportunities which will help us keep the plant running”. Or we can say: “We have a list of factors which are threatening to shut us down. Let’s take care of these threats and save the plant”.

The usage of the term “threat removal” evokes a sense of personal responsibility and of participation in a good cause. It’s a strong agent of change.

I’ve done some informal field testing on usage of this terminology. Overwhelmingly I get a better reaction and response to “removal of a threat”, than “capturing of an opportunity.” Either one of the approaches will eventually get the job done.

In another chapter we have discussed what a maintainer thinks his job is. One of the frequent answers one gets is: ***To improve the performance of the equipment.*** This seems to be a safe answer, after all who can argue with improvements in the plant performance.

What about the operators? When they are asked what their job is you get two types of answers: the serious type and the frivolous.

“I don’t know. I come here for the money”

“Beats me. Ask my No. 1 Operator”

“Babysit the controllers.”

“To keep the production going. No matter what”

"To keep the equipment operating"
"To keep the tanks full with (product)."

Let's analyze what the real function of a maintenance department is in an industrial organization.

When you buy a piece of equipment, it comes with a certain performance expectation. Whether those expectations are realized or not is dependent upon your state of readiness. But as far as the performance of the equipment is concerned it is fixed, ***it can only go downhill***. Granted, on occasion, plant maintenance modifies or retrofits the equipment with additional gizmos to coax out some additional performance. These are genuine continuous improvement type activities where you identify and capitalize on some potential, which the original manufacturer had failed to see. This is very good and should be encouraged (as long as sound engineering principles are followed). Having said that, one has to realize such activities are not the primary function of the maintenance department.

The primary job of the maintenance department is to ***identify and remove hurdles which will prevent the equipment from performing at the required performance level.*** This is a very meaningful statement. The required level may or may not be the optimum level. We need to be cognizant of the fact that the performance of the equipment has to be considered in short as well as the long term: You require a piece of equipment to operate at a certain level for the short-term as well as the long-term. Sacrifice of the long-term operation for the sake of short term gains, does not meet the requirement. In this context, note that the function of the maintenance department is **NOT** to:

- make sure all of the equipment is available for operation all the time
- make improvements to achieve the optimum design performance for all pieces of equipment.

This is a fundamental paradigm shift which divorces the maintenance department from the technology aspects and aligns it to the needs of business. You see, it's very easy to do things better (by using better material, newer gizmos and expertise – anyone can do that, especially if you are using someone else's checkbook), but it's rather difficult do things which make sense for the business. To summarize, the role of the maintenance department is not to make random or poorly selected things to operate better, but to remove the threats which jeopardizes the operation of carefully selected equipment at the *required level.* To do that, obviously, at first you need to identify the equipment which is threatened, along with the nature of the threat.

The same concepts apply to the operators' primary function. Their job is to identify and remove hurdles which will prevent the equipment from performing at the required performance level in the short and the long term. This statement does not validate the job functions described by the operators as listed earlier on. It speaks to the necessity of careful and mature custodianship of equipment so that it does what it is supposed to do today, next week and ten years hence, in a safe manner.

HOW DO YOU DEFINE "CRITICAL EQUIPMENT"

In my talks on this subject, I ask the members of the audience to write down their definition of the word "critical" on a piece of paper and pass it on to me. I've got hundreds of entries in my collection. In each session, at least fifty percent of the people give differing answers. My collection shows over 25 uniquely different answers, some of the common responses are:

- Equipment which the vendor does not support any more and the warehouse is out of parts
- Equipment which is used to monitor toxic gases
- Beats me. It's different every week
- Anything which can cause an explosion
- Anything which can cause production loss
- Anything which can cause an injury or a fatality.

Amazingly, all of the above, while bearing no resemblance to each other, are correct, in the context of the writer's vision of what really matters.

This tells us that we tend to see and evaluate the world in our terms. From an individual's point of view it's very difficult to define what is critical to the operation, in spite of the fact that he is exposed to exactly the same corporate messages as every one else. The criticality of a piece of equipment should be driven by what the corporation holds dear – its values. Well, how does a run of the mill corporation tells its employees its values? Corporate mission statements? Slogans?

These days you can hardly go anywhere without coming across a slogan or two. Most of the people are inundated by statements like the following:

- Our People Are Our Most Important Asset
- Safety Is The First And The Last Job.
- No Task Is Completed Until The Paperwork Is Done
- Safety Is Everyone's Responsibility
- Our Survival Depends Upon Continuous Cost Reduction
- Only Production Will Bring The Unit Cost Down
- We Are Good Corporate Citizens. We Must Do Our Share Of Environmental Conservation.

All of these statements are supposed to generate a set of values which, in turn, are supposed to define what is important and what is not.

In some plants they put a small team together to create a definition for the word "critical", and make a list of the critical equipment. Usually such activities degenerate into political horse trading, where the favorite equipment of the individual members (which they *really* believe to be critical) eventually makes the list. Since there is no logical or uniform underlying basis, such lists eventually evaporate and the whole thing is repeated every 3-5 years.

The relevance of a piece of equipment cannot be determined by simplistic notions (which, incidentally, work very well as slogans) like "Safety Is The First And The Last Job". Let's see why simplistic slogans lead to confusing solutions. This slogan means that any piece of equipment which jeopardizes personnel safety should be classified as critical. If you really think about it, you'll notice that almost all components in your plant can cause one type of safety problem or another. Consider some examples:

- A pressure vessel may explode and cause injuries and possible fatalities. Does that make a pressure vessel critical to the safety of the people? If so what can a technician do about it? Should he worry more about the pressure vessel or a pinhole leak in some piping elsewhere from which superheated steam at 1000 psig is leaking out.
- A pipe may rupture and spill a toxic substance. Does that make this pipe an important pipe? How about other pipes? As a matter of fact most pipes can theoretically rupture and create hazardous conditions. Does that make all pipes critically hazardous pieces of equipment?

- A controller may malfunction and cause a tank to overflow. As a matter of fact, most malfunctioning controllers can cause a hazard of one type or another. Should all controllers be classified as critical.
- A person may trip over an obsolete pump and seriously hurt himself. What do you think of this situation? Can an in-operational pump installed in an awkward situation be hazardous? Can it be defined as a critical piece of equipment?

Especially if you take two-event scenarios where you consider malfunction of a particular piece of equipment while another undesirable condition exists, you'll be hard pressed to find anything which has no safety hazard potential. This may lead you to consider almost everything as critical to the safety of the personnel. This is the reason why in some plants "emergency work" never ends–people keep on finding "safety items".

Similarly if you analyze production, and to a lesser degree environmental impacts, you will come up with similar answers.

So how do we find out what is critical (read ***really really important*** for now, since we have not developed a definition for this word yet). To demonstrate how the criticality for a piece of equipment is really not fixed and can change, let's consider a boiler-turbogenerator unit, which is fed by a single feedwater pump.

Conventional wisdom will guide you to consider the feed-pump, under such conditions, as a critical piece of equipment to the process. Every one will agree with that, because if the pump goes down the generator, goes down. What about the feedwater control valve for the boiler, surely it is critical to the operation too? Yes it is, but if you really look at it you will notice that it is equipped with a bypass valve and if the main valve goes haywire it can be safely bypassed for a short period of time. The boiler water level can be manually controlled while the main valve is being fixed. So it seems that the feedwater valve is less critical to the operation than the feedwater pump.

Now let's go back to the pump again and see what happens if we install another 100% capacity pump. In this case only one of the pumps needs to be available for full operation, and therefore either of the pumps is not as critical as before. The failure of a single pump does not pose any threat to the operation at all. The feedwater control valve, on the other hand, does expose the operation to some risk – since manual control of feedwater flow is not an easy task and should only be undertaken as a short-term emergency provision. So now we've talked ourselves into considering the feedwater control valve as more critical to the operation than either of the feedwater pumps.

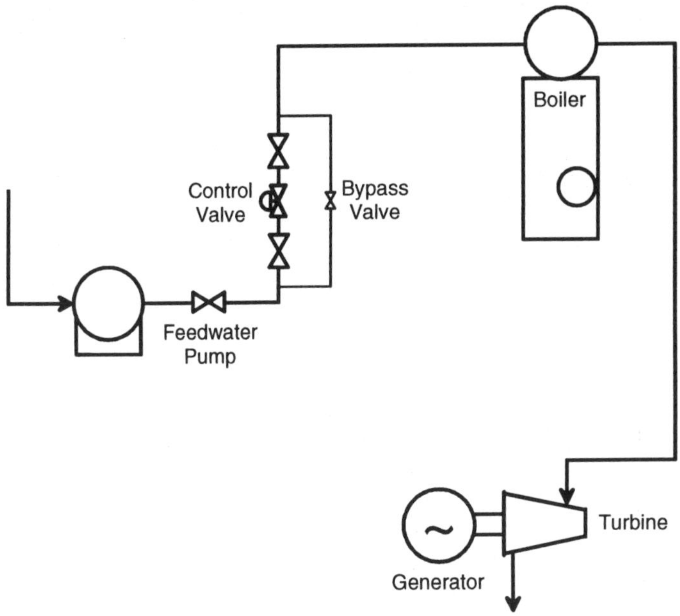

FIGURE 1 | A Unitized Boiler-Generator System.

Why are we bothered about knowing the criticality of a piece of equipment in the first place? A short answer is: **we need to identify threats to the operation so that we can do something about them.** This is a key statement. When all is said and done, we need to do the following:

- Identify the threats to the operation
- Take action to reduce the probability of occurrence for the threat-causing events
- Take actions to minimize the possible impact of the threats.

Now let's wade into slightly deeper waters. We left our example where the feedwater control valve was more critical to the operation than either of the feedwater pumps. What does it really mean? It means that you should be far more interested in taking actions to prevent the failure of the feedwater control valve than that of either of the pumps. Now let me throw another curve ball at you. What if we replaced the feedwater control valve with one made to nuclear specifications with an expected failure rate of once in a thousand years? Under these conditions you'll be more inclined to babysit your pumps rather than the control valve.

You see, the criticality of a piece of equipment is a function of many variables and changes from situation to situation.

From the above example we see that it is a mistake to be hardware and technology oriented. We need to be process and business oriented. We need to find means to identify threats to the operation which have the potential to jeopardize safety, environment and production.

To do just that I've coined the term **Operational Criticality Index – OCI**. For a piece of equipment, the OCI is defined as a standardized measure which quantifies the level of threat posed by the subject equipment to the operation with respect to safety, environment or production. Therefore, a piece of equipment will have four OCI numbers. The first three deal with safety, environment, and production. And the last one will represent a composite number combining the three individual ones.

A standardized OCI does not depend upon hardware and technology only. Its numerical value is dependent on many factors, some of which are listed below:

- Its Zero-Base™ Failure Rate (ZBFR) which in turn is dependent on the following:
    - Design maturity
    - Manufacturer's reputation
    - Service ambient conditions
    - Application severity
    - Operational conditions
    - Operator competence
    - Maintenance competence
    - Five year failure history
    - Externally available statistical information.
- Process configuration
- The impact of failure on safety, environment or production.

The higher the OCI number, the higher the threat. Once you have quantified the OCI numbers you can start looking for the requisite management actions to mitigate the threats as necessary.

The equipment with a higher OCI requires more maintenance and operational attention in comparison to those with lower numbers.

Usually through application of inexpensive and innovative ways, the high-end OCIs can be reduced.

The underlying premise of this definition is that all of the plant equipment, as well as the tasks carried out by the technicians, are important and, for any analytical work, should be considered to appreciate the full spectrum of issues. It will also put everything in an objective perspective. After all, if they were not important why would you have that piece of equipment installed, or have that task done in the first place? The only difference is that some are more important than others.

The primary function of the OCI numbers is to delineate all of your equipment according the relative importance of each piece to the operation. As a matter of fact, it goes further than that. Once the OCI concept is widely accepted, it can be used as a standard benchmark (or as a guideline at the very least) for various bands on the scale. For example, the equipment of highest criticality can be defined as that which has an OCI of 85 or more. This number can be different for different plants, but serves as a unique benchmark for a particular plant. So, if through the application of superior management problem-solving disciplines, you reduce the OCI of all of your equipment to a level below 85, you eliminate the need for many expensive Band-Aid type programs designed to handle emergencies. Let me hasten to add that I am not advocating doing away with the emergency response plans. Not at all. Perhaps an example will help me make my point.

Let's consider the case of a large deaerator using 75 psig steam as a heating and scrubbing medium. The deaerator is installed at 150 ft. elevation to provide adequate suction head to four 800 hp boiler feedwater pumps installed on the main floor. These pumps are of a multi-stage (5 stages) construction, requiring a certain minimum flow to act as a coolant. A low or no flow causes the pump impellers to overheat and seize up, requiring very expensive maintenance attention. Normally such systems are equipped with protection against low-flow conditions. Usually such protection is provided by monitoring the deaerator water level, and the low water level condition causes an immediate automatic tripping of the pumps. One plant I've in mind did not subscribe to this idea – the operators wouldn't allow it – they were afraid of spurious trips caused by instrumentation malfunction. Instead, they have a red strobe light which illuminates on the main floor indicating a low level condition in the deaerator. When the operator sees the light he is supposed to do a few very well defined things, and is forbidden to do some others. All the operators have been clearly told of the process. And to be helpful, there is a laminated sheet with instructions clearly written out installed near the pumps. The instructions are clear and logical, all the exceptions are listed – however they do take up most of the page. Theoretically, everything should work fine. However, real life is always full of surprises:

- On occasion the light does not function (bad light, burnt fuse, breaker off, etc.)
- Sometimes the operator is not close enough to notice the light when it does come on
- Sometimes the operator is in the middle of another emergency when the light comes on. He is forced to choose between the two emergencies. In other words he is forced to analyze quickly to identify the worst of the two evils. Half the time his analysis is faulty
- During such emergencies, in spite of the training, without exception, the operator runs to read the instructions to refresh his memory. On some occasions he finds the sheet to be too grimy to be legible, on others the area is inadequately lit
- During the past five years, one of the operators (one of eight) had a history of perfect responses, and always saved the situation, with no adverse effects. So the system does work, it is the operator who sometimes need to be more careful – or so it is thought
- One of the action items, if not handled expeditiously, causes a surge of water through the deaerator.

The net result is:

- During the past ten years they have seriously damaged the feed pumps numerous times. Every one of such events was accompanied by serious safety hazards – though no injury resulted, yet
- The process surges destroyed the deaerator internals (trays and the like) on three occasions, requiring a major maintenance effort.

For the last few years, the engineers in this plant have been trying to Band-Aid the pumps and the deaerator internal construction to withstand the short-term, though violent, transient conditions. All expensive and time-consuming solutions.

Out of curiosity, I applied the Zero-Base™ methodology to this situation, and quickly found out that the most critical element in the system was not any of the pumps or the deaerator, but the low level alarm system. The OCI of the level alarm drops to a very low level if the alarm system is duplicated and if the pumps are tripped (only if both of the sensing systems show a low level in the deaerator). This solution, however, is against the industrial norm, where generally either one of the signals would be used to trip the pumps. However, the proposed solution does meet the constraints set by the operators: avoid spurious trips at all cost. Thus a few hundred dollar solution works far better than solutions which cost thousands of dollars every year – without really delivering anything.

When the principles expressed here become one's philosophy, three ideas come to mind.

- First, since we have limited resources, let's make sure that we do the most important things diligently.
- Second, let's select a target for the high side of OCI, and modify our systems to make sure all of our equipment is below that number – as long as modifications can be brought about in an inexpensive manner. If not, we need to make sure our mitigation actions and alarm responses are up to snuff.
- Third, let's have another look at items at the lowest end of the criticality list. Baby sitting them may not be necessary at all.

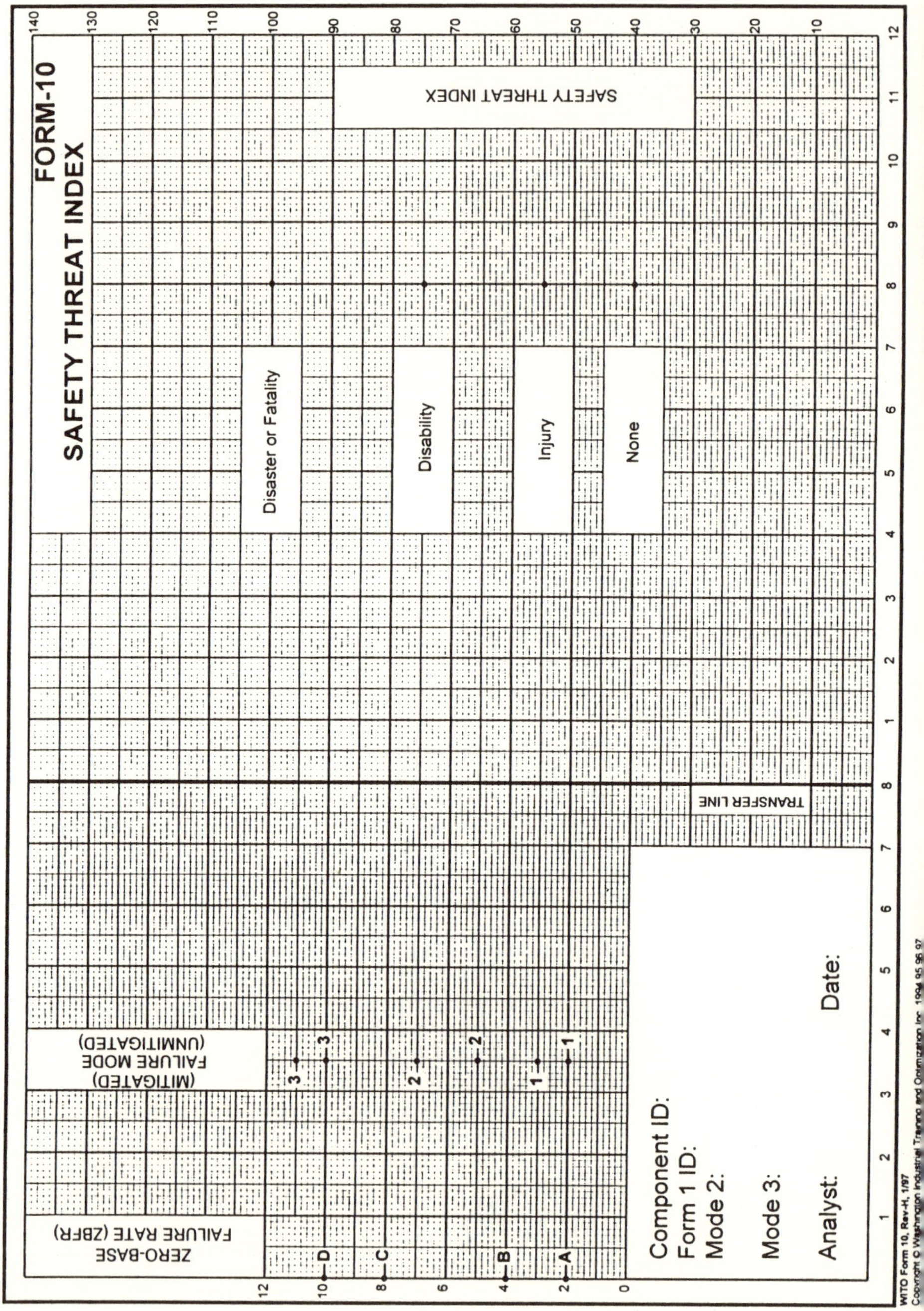
FORM-10
SAFETY THREAT INDEX
SAFETY THREAT INDEX
Disaster or Fatality
Disability
Injury
None
TRANSFER LINE
ZERO-BASE FAILURE RATE (ZBFR)
(MITIGATED) FAILURE MODE (UNMITIGATED)
Component ID:
Form 1 ID:
Mode 2:
Mode 3:
Analyst:
Date:
WITO Form 10, Rev-H, 1/97

HOW TO DETERMINE MEANINGFUL OPERATIONAL CRITICALITY INDICES (OCIs)

We are nearly at the end of the book. Let's review where we are in the process and where we want to go. So far, in the earlier chapters, we have gone over the following:

- For each piece of equipment we know how to determine the Zero-Base™ Failure Rate (ZBFR)
- We've determined that we are interested in examining the impact of three modes of failure (Mode 1, 2 and 3)
- We have also established the concept of threat indices associated with each piece of equipment.

With the above knowledge in hand, we are well equipped to determine the value of threat indices for all the equipment.

Three graphical tools are used for this determination. Of course, a computer program is also available to speed up and automate the graphical maneuvers. Let's examine the tools briefly, a copy of which is included in this chapter.

WITO Form 10: Safety Threat Index

First, one of these tools is WITO Form 10 which deals with various types of safety impacts associated with system failures. The left hand y-axis shows Zero-Base™ Failure Rate (ZBFR) numbers. Recall that we ask the field technicians their assessment in the following broad bands:

A: Likely number of failures to around 2
B: Likely number of failures to be around 4
C: Likely number of failures to be around 8
D: Likely number of failures to be around 10

The next item of interest is the positioning of the failure modes. Immediately to the right of the ZBFR locations you will see three points showing the location for each of the modes we are interested in. Two scales for the Failure Mode are shown, the one on the left-hand side corresponds to an unmitigated situation, while that on the right corresponds to situations where some mitigating measures have been put in place. Examples of hazard mitigating measures are:

- Good communication of Process Safety Information (PSI)
- Training of response teams
- Availability of hot spares
- Availability of process buffer tanks, etc.

Immediately to the right of the failure mode locations is the transfer-line used to capture the combined effect of the ZBFR and failure mode for further processing.

Moving on further to the right from the transfer-line we see the positions for the types of safety impact we are interested in:

- No safety impact, indicated as NONE
- Injury, indicating a physical injury to a human being within the plant or the surrounding areas
- Disability, indicating a disability to a human being within the plant or the surrounding areas
- Disaster or a fatality. Disaster is indicated by a fatality or the potential for a group of people (more that 5) sustaining a disability or injury.

The last vertical line on the right hand side shows the projected value for the Safety Threat Index.

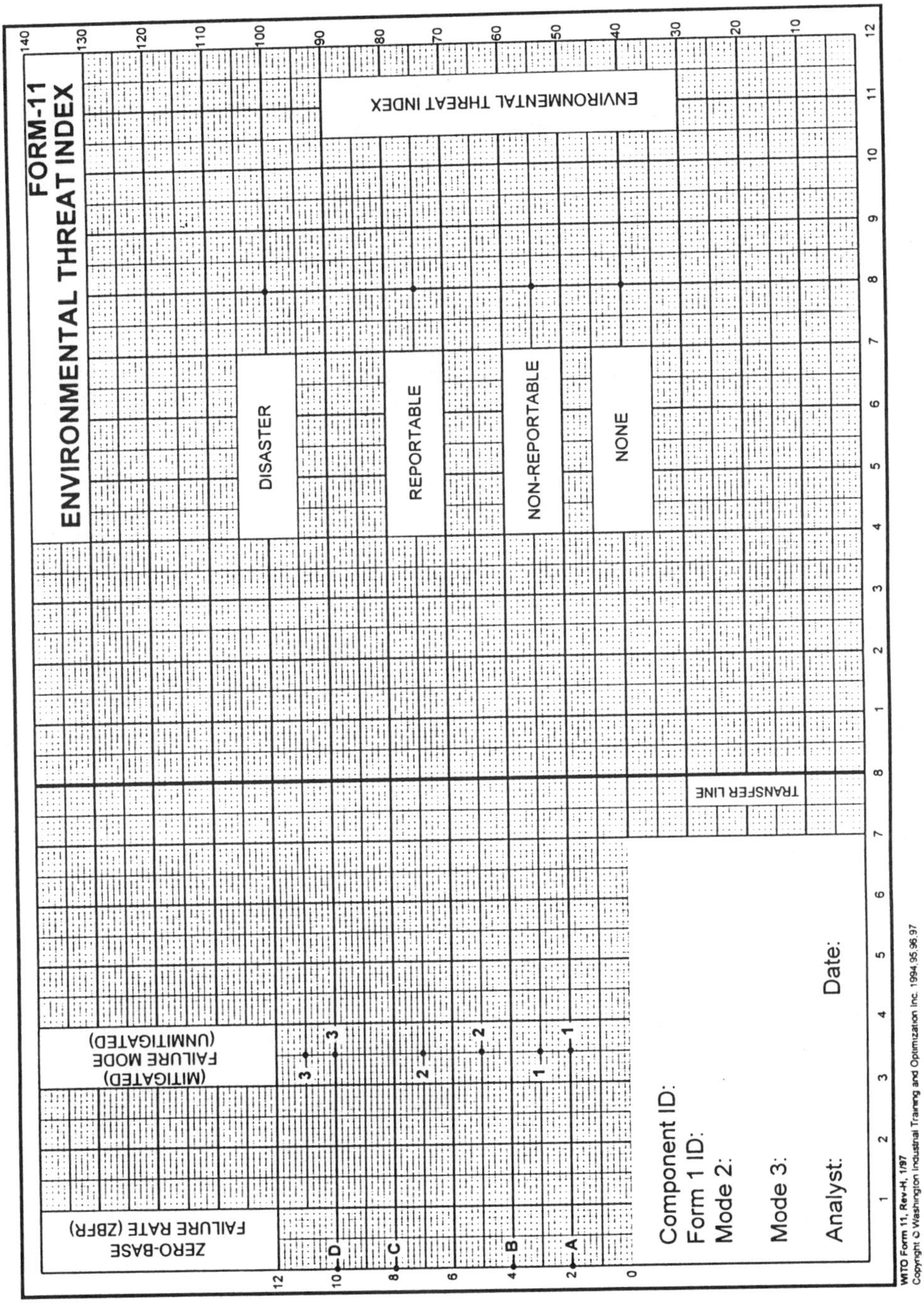
FORM-11
ENVIRONMENTAL THREAT INDEX
ZERO-BASE FAILURE RATE (ZBFR)
(MITIGATED) FAILURE MODE (UNMITIGATED)
DISASTER
REPORTABLE
NON-REPORTABLE
NONE
ENVIRONMENTAL THREAT INDEX
TRANSFER LINE
Component ID:
Form 1 ID:
Mode 2:
Mode 3:
Analyst:
Date:
WTO Form 11, Rev-H, 1/97
Copyright © Washington Industrial Training and Optimization Inc. 1994,95,96,97

WITO Form 11: Environmental Threat Index

This form is almost exactly the same as WITO Form 10, the only difference being the nature of impact under study. Instead of safety related items, four stages of environmental impact are given in the third column:

- No environmental impact, indicated as NONE
- A non-reportable incident, indicated as Non-Reportable
- A reportable incident, indicated as Reportable
- An environmental disaster, indicated as Disaster.

Note that the impact classification can easily be custom-fit to suit the specific needs of an organization.

The rest of the elements for this form having already been discussed.

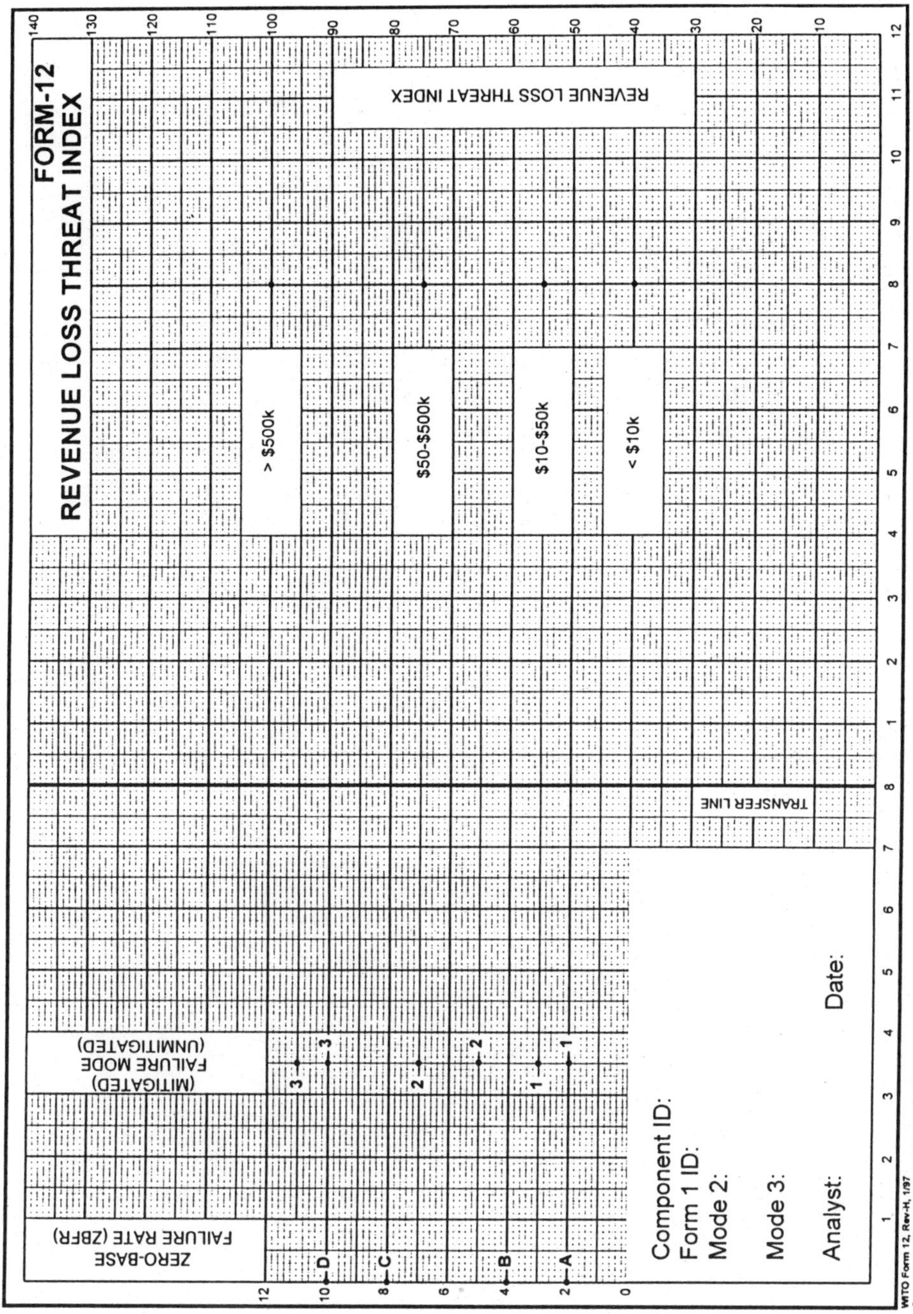
FORM-12
REVENUE LOSS THREAT INDEX
> $500k
$50-$500k
$10-$50k
< $10k
REVENUE LOSS THREAT INDEX
ZERO-BASE FAILURE RATE (ZBFR)
(MITIGATED) FAILURE MODE (UNMITIGATED)
TRANSFER LINE
Component ID:
Form 1 ID:
Mode 2:
Mode 3:
Analyst:
Date:
WITO Form 12, Rev-H, 1/97
Copyright © Washington Industrial Training and Optimization Inc. 1994,95,96,97

WITO Form 12: Revenue Loss Index

This form is also almost exactly the same as WITO Form 10, the only difference being the nature of impact under study. Instead of safety-related items, four stages of revenue loss impact are given in the third column:

- The magnitude of potential loss of revenue: less than 10K$
- The magnitude of potential loss of revenue: 10-50K$
- The magnitude of potential loss of revenue: 50-500K$
- The magnitude of potential loss of revenue: greater than $500K.

Note that the impact classification can easily be custom-fit to suit the specific needs of an organization.

The rest of the elements for this form having already been discussed.

BACK TO THE CRITICALITY DEFINITION

Having these tools at our disposal we are finally in a position to put the definition of the word "criticality" to bed. Remember earlier on, the best we could come up with was to say that the designation of a piece of equipment as "critical" implied that it was ***really really important***. We could not quantify it or differentiate between the magnitudes of criticality between two pieces of equipment deemed to be critical. We were also unable to tie the definition of criticality to catastrophic events.

Well, now we can take care of all of these problems.

Catastrophic-Criticality™

A piece of equipment is said to have Catastrophic-Criticality™ if the value for its ZBFR is 2 or less, and if it is likely to cause a catastrophic event when failing in Mode 1. We will shortly show that, in a standardized sense, this implies that any equipment with a threat index of greater than 125 will automatically be deemed to have a catastrophic criticality.

This definition is unambiguous and ties the failure rate to the likely impact. Furthermore it is quantified, which enables you to start taking care of equipment and systems with the highest indices.

Disaster-Criticality™

In a fashion similar to the above we can define the next lower level of criticality. A piece of equipment is said to have Disaster-Criticality™ if the value for its ZBFR is less than 2, and it is likely to cause a catastrophic event when failing in Mode 2. We will shortly show that equipment having a threat index between 88-125 belongs to this category.

For each piece of equipment there are four threat indices:

STI: which quantifies the threat to safety of personnel
ETI: which quantifies the threat to the environment
RTI: which quantifies the threat to revenue due to any reason
OTI: which gives a composite value for above three.

DETERMINATION OF THE FOUR INDICES

Step 1: Make a comprehensive list of all the equipment.
Step 2: Analyze the equipment for failure mode versus impact.
Step 3: Determine Zero-Base™ Failure Rate (ZBFR) for each piece of equipment.
Step 4: Apply the graphical tools to determine the Threat Index.
Step 5: Develop the requisite maintenance strategy.

In Appendix B a complete illustrative example is provided, here we'll cover the general ideas on how to go through these steps.

FAILURE-IMPACT-THREAT FORM **Form ID Number:** **Date:** 2/3/97 **FORM 1**

Main System: CRUDE; Topping **Subsystem:** Kero Tower **Ref:** 36-P-2

Component	ID No.	ZBFR	Failure Mode	Safety Impact						Environmental Impact						Revenue Impact						OTI
				None	Injury	Dis-ability	Fatal-ity	TI	STI	None	Non-Report-able	Report-able	Catas-trophic	TI	ETI	10K<	11-50K	51-100K	>100K	TI	RTI	
Pipe, PP-41, Suction	PP-6																					
Kero pump, PP-41	PMP-41																					
CHK V/V, PP Disch.	V-62																					
V/V on PP-41 Disch.	V-41																					
" "	V-42																					
" "	V-43																					
" "	V-44																					
Flow Control V/V	FCV-16																					
Flow Transmitter	FT-16																					
Flow controller	FIC-16																					
Pipe, Pmp 42 suction	PP-9																					
Kero Pump PMP-42	PMP-42																					
Pipe, purge steam	PP-27																					
Steam Temp Trans.	TT-62																					
Steam Temp Controller	TIC-62																					
Stm temp. Cont V/V	TCV-62																					
Naphtha Pipe	PP-3																					
Kero Bottoms Pump 1	Pmp-57																					
Kero Bottoms Pump 2	Pump-58																					
Pipe, Pmp-57, Suction	PP-69																					
Pipe, Pmp 58, Suction	PP-70																					
Bottoms Pump 57 Motor	M-3																					
Bottoms Pump 58 Motor	M-4																					

WITO-Form 1 Rev G, 04/97

STEP 1

Make a comprehensive list of all the equipment

This is done using the first two columns of Form 1. The sample on the left hand side shows how a list will look like.

FAILURE-IMPACT-THREAT FORM **Form ID Number:** **Date:** 2/3/97 **FORM 1**
Main System: CRUDE; Topping **Subsystem:** Kero Tower **Ref:** 36-P-2

Component	ID No.	ZBFR	Failure Mode	Safety Impact						Environmental Impact						Revenue Impact						OTI
				None	Injury	Dis-ability	Fatal-ity	TI	STI	None	Non-Report-able	Report-able	Catas-trophic	TI	ETI	10K<	11-50K	51-100K	>100K	TI	RTI	
Pipe, PP-41, Suction	PP-6	A	1,2,3	✓		✓	✓															
Kero pump, PP-41	PMP-41	C			✓	✓	✓															
CHK V/V, PP Disch.	V-62	B		✓✓✓																		
VV on PP-41 Disch.	V-41	B		✓✓✓																		
" "	V-42	B		✓✓✓																		
" "	V-43	A		✓✓✓																		
" "	V-44	A		✓✓✓																		
Flow Control V/V	FCV-16	C			✓	✓	✓															
Flow Transmitter	FT-16	A				✓✓	✓															
Flow Controller	FIC-16	B				✓✓	✓															
Pipe, Pmp 42 suction	PP-9	A			✓	✓✓																
Kero Pump PMP-42	PMP-42	A		✓✓✓																		
Pipe, Purge steam	PP-27	A		✓✓			✓															
Steam Temp Trans.	TT-62	C		✓✓	✓																	
Steam Temp Controller	TIC-62	C		✓✓	✓																	
Stm temp. Cont V/V	TCV-62	C			✓	✓✓																
Naphtha Pipe	PP-3	A		✓✓✓																		
Kero Bottoms Pump 1	PMP-57	A		✓	✓	✓																
Kero Bottoms Pump 2	Pump-58	C		✓	✓	✓																
Pipe, Pmp-57, Suction	PP-69	B			✓	✓	✓															
Pipe, Pmp 58, Suction	PP-70	B		✓✓✓																		
Bottoms Pump 57 Motor	M-3	A		✓✓✓																		
Bottoms Pump 58 Motor	M-4	A		✓✓✓																		

WITO-Form 1 Rev G, 04/97

STEP 2

Analyze the equipment for failure mode versus impact

To do this we continue on with the Form 1 shown earlier. This part of the exercise is conducted with a group of subject matter experts (SMEs). Each piece of equipment is considered for the three modes as described in earlier chapters.

Mode 1

To obtain information corresponding to Mode 1, you ask the SMEs:

If this equipment were to fail, while everything else operates normally, what impact will it have on safety, environment and the production loss (or loss of revenue in any way)?

The assumption here is that upon failure the technicians will notice the situation as they are supposed to do under normal circumstances, and immediately carry out the customary damage containment actions. If the operators are not properly trained to carry out such actions, it should be reflected in the answers–it serves little purpose to pretend that something will happen, while in real life the case is likely to be the opposite. This exercise will help determine the skills which the operators require.

The answer to this question is obtained in categories as shown in the form and the appropriate box is checked off.

Mode 2

To get information corresponding to Mode 2, you ask the SME's:

If this equipment were to fail in a fashion similar to Mode 1, but goes unnoticed by the technicians until something else happens which forcibly brings it to their attention, what impact will it have on safety, environment and the production loss (or loss of revenue in any way)?

Again, the answer to this question is obtained in categories as shown in the form and the appropriate box is checked off.

Mode 3

To get the information corresponding to Mode 3, you ask the SMEs:

For this mode, consider the operational conditions as outlined below:

- *The equipment under consideration fails while another piece of equipment is already in a failed position.*
- *The situation goes unnoticed by the technicians until something else happens which forcibly brings the situation to their attention, and they take appropriate responsive actions.*

What impact will this scenario have on safety, environment and the production loss (or loss of revenue in any way)?

The answer this question is also checked off in the form. In reference to this question, remind the SMEs that we are considering two events here and we are looking for the most damaging combination.

All of this may look cumbersome and like overkill. I've seen experienced SMEs go through this type of exercise very rapidly since these are the things they deal with all the time. Some of the knotty problems will need some discussion time or guidance from the engineering department.

FAILURE-IMPACT-THREAT FORM **Form ID Number:** **Date:** 2/3/97 **FORM 1**

Main System: CRUDE; Topping **Subsystem:** Kero Tower **Ref:** 36-P-2

Component	ID No.	ZBFR	Failure Mode	Safety Impact						Environmental Impact						Revenue Impact						OTI
				None	Injury	Dis-ability	Fatal-ity	TI	STI	None	Non-Report-able	Report-able	Catas-trophic	TI	ETI	10K<	11-50K	51-100K	>100K	TI	RTI	
Pipe, PP-41, Suction	PP-6	A	1,2,3	✓		✓	✓															
Kero pump, PP-41	PMP-41	C			✓	✓	✓															
CHK V/V, PP Disch.	V-62	B		✓✓✓																		
VV on PP-41 Disch.	V-41	B		✓✓✓																		
" "	V-42	B		✓✓✓																		
" "	V-43	A		✓✓✓																		
" "	V-44	A		✓✓✓																		
Flow Control V/V	FCV-16	C			✓	✓	✓															
Flow Transmitter	FT-16	A				✓✓	✓															
Flow controller	FIC-16	B				✓✓	✓															
Pipe, Pmp 42 suction	PP-9	A			✓	✓✓																
Kero Pump PMP-42	PMP-42	A		✓✓✓																		
Pipe, purge steam	PP-27	A		✓✓			✓															
Steam Temp Trans.	TT-62	C		✓✓	✓																	
Steam Temp Controller	TIC-62	C		✓✓	✓																	
Stm temp. cont V/V	TCV-62	C			✓	✓✓																
Naphtha Pipe	PP-3	A		✓✓✓																		
Kero Bottoms Pump 1	Pmp-57	A		✓	✓	✓																
Kero Bottoms Pump 2	Pump-58	C		✓	✓	✓																
Pipe, Pmp-57, Suction	PP-69	B			✓	✓	✓															
Pipe, Pmp 58, Suction	PP-70	B		✓✓✓																		
Bottoms Pump 57 Motor	M-3	A		✓✓✓																		
Bottoms Pump 58 Motor	M-4	A		✓✓✓																		

WITO-Form 1 Rev G, 04/97

Step 3

Determine Zero-Base™ Failure Rate (ZBFR) for each piece of equipment

This step has been dealt at length in Chapter 8: Zero-Base™ Failure Rate (ZBFR).

The form shown here shows the third column filled in with the ZBRF data.

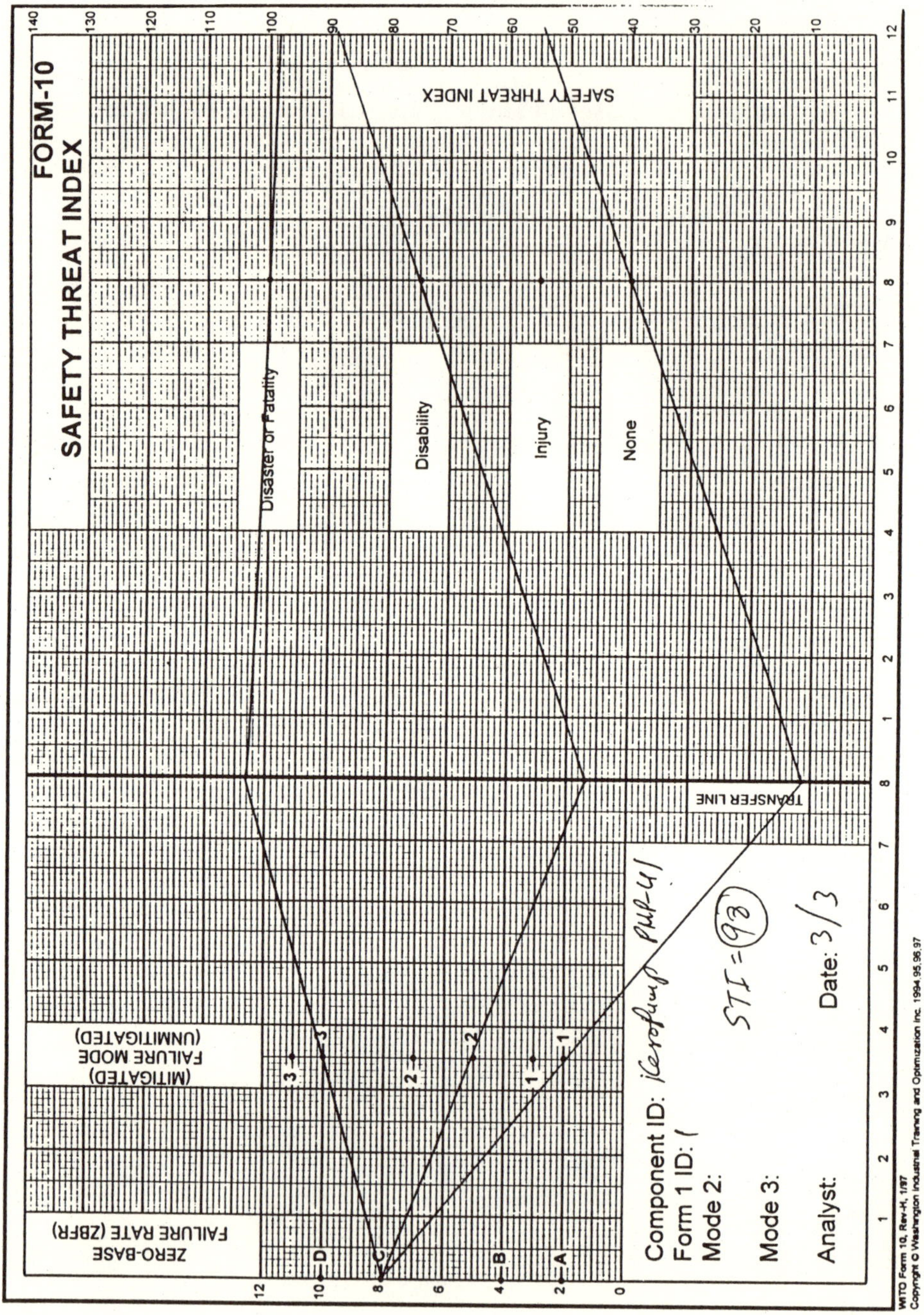
FORM-10
SAFETY THREAT INDEX
ZERO-BASE FAILURE RATE (ZBFR)
MITIGATED FAILURE MODE (UNMITIGATED)
TRANSFER LINE
Disaster or Fatality
Disability
Injury
None
SAFETY THREAT INDEX
Component ID:
Form 1 ID:
Mode 2:
Mode 3:
Analyst:
Date: 3/3
STI = 93
WITO Form 10, Rev-H, 1/97
Copyright © Washington Industrial Training and Optimization Inc. 1994,95,96,97

Step 4

Application of the graphical tools to determine the Threat Index

For this step we need to utilize the Form 10.

We use one form for each piece of equipment. After some practice, some find it more expedient to use one form for many identical pieces of equipment.

You start at the ZBFR located on the left hand side y-axis. At first you draw a line through the ZBFR and each of the modes of interest. The lines so drawn are extended to meet the transfer line. From the transfer line, each point of intersection is extended to go through the corresponding impact point, and is allowed to meet the y-axis on the right hand side. After that you simply read the Safety Threat Index™ as the point of intersection. To consolidate the data, transfer the indices on to the Form 1 as shown in Appendix C. Do this exercise for all pieces of equipment.

Step 5

Development of Requisite Maintenance Strategies

Once you have determined the threat indices for your equipment, the easiest thing in the world to do is to form maintenance strategies. If you take care of the equipment which threatens your operation the most, you'll achieve unprecedented levels of safety, compliance with the regulations, and productivity. To do all this you do not need to have unlimited funds. You can dial in the desired level of achievement commensurate with your specific needs, and have the confidence that you are getting the best bang for the buck.

We've already mentioned the equipment with a criticality index greater than 125 can cause a catastrophic event even in Mode 1 (the mode with highest probability of occurrence). Some would assume that if you took good care of equipment with threat indices higher than 125, you'd not need to do anything else, because there'd very little probability of a catastrophic event. Theoretically it would qualify as the minimum one would need to do to get the regulators off their backs, but it'd be highly imprudent and may not qualify as the due diligent response.

A RECOMMENDED PRUDENT APPROACH

Each industrial plant operates in circumstances unique to itself that are driven by:

- Toxicity and combustibility of the material being handled
- Age of the plant
- Design of the plant
- Proximity to population centers
- Competence and experience of the technicians and engineers
- Union/non-union status
- Management culture
- Cost of the material being handled
- Market value of the product.

This is a long list and probably does not even cover half of the variables. Staying cognizant of this list, it's not prudent to have a one-size-fits-all solution. However, general recommendations can be formed by classifying the plant equipment into three categories.

Class A

This category consists of equipment with threat indices of 85 or greater. While theoretical calculations lead us to look for numbers greater than 125, but prudence calls for a conservative approach.

Class B

The equipment with indices between 60 and 84 belong in this category.

Class C

The equipment which poses least threat to the operation, having a indices less than 60, belongs in this category.

At this time it should be pointed out the Zero-Base™ system is based on logic and experience, and cannot be deemed to be 100% accurate. It's probably 98% accurate. Therefore it's prudent for you to determine and add the following items to an appropriate classification:

- Items deemed by management decree, are to be handled in a certain way, irrespective of the results of the analysis. Some of these items are driven by agreements made between the regulators and the company. Also sometimes union/management agreements dictate the degree of care-taking for specific pieces of equipment.
- Items which your experienced people feel should have a higher degree of care-taking. It is important to do so, since it's possible that a few items will fall through the cracks in the analytical processes. However, such additions should be limited to approximately 1% of the total items, otherwise everyone will upgrade their favorite items and the purpose of the whole exercise will be lost.

The graphs shown in the following two pages are provided to give a general idea of how the equipment categorization may look like in some common industrial installations. At the end of this chapter equipment classification from two actual cases are given.

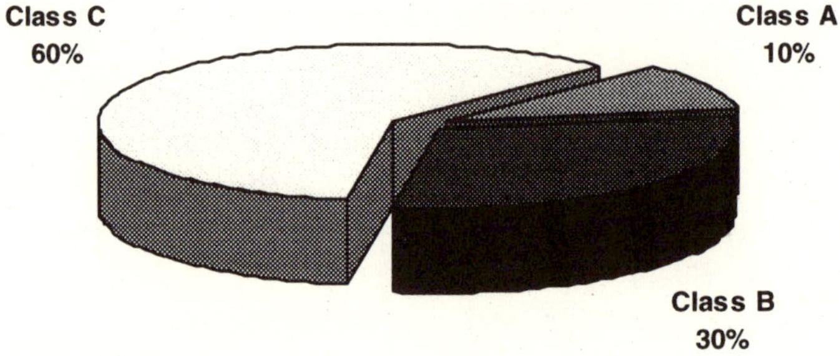

FIGURE 9	This figure shows a likely classification for an oil refinery equipment.

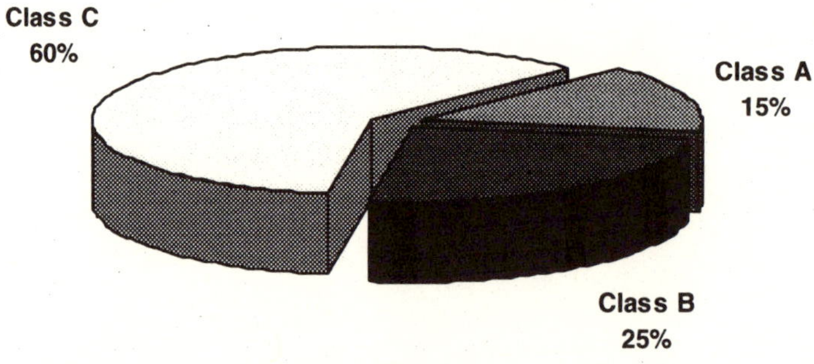

FIGURE 10	A chemical plant such as a chlorine manufacturing facility is likely to have a general classification for equipment as shown.

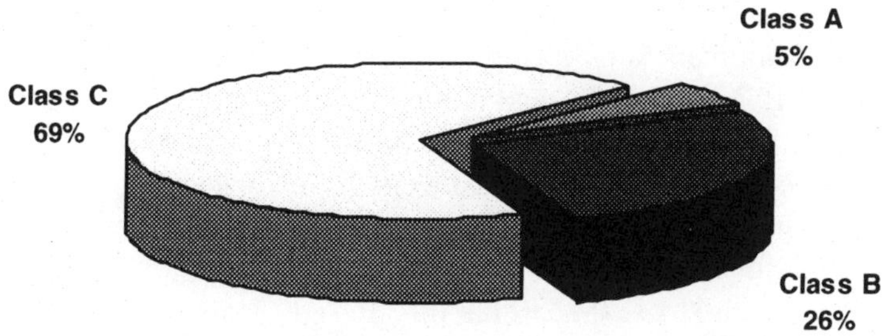

FIGURE 11	The equipment in a pulp mill is likely to have a classification similar to as shown here.

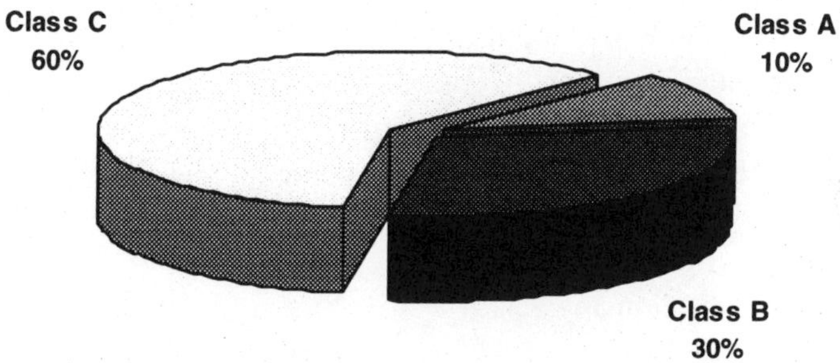

FIGURE 12	This figure shows a likely configuration for a thermal power plant.

MAINTENANCE STRATEGIES

Class A Equipment

This class of equipment should be given the highest level of maintenance attention. The PSM and EPA regulations must be followed to the letter and beyond. Since the number of pieces of equipment in this classification is rather small, it costs very little to go beyond what is required by the regulators. By definition, if you take care of this equipment you should end up with a highly safe and productive plant.

Many proponents of the Reliability-Based Maintenance (RBM) systems, want to apply their concepts to all of the plant equipment. And they usually fail, since the broad brush approach is too costly and misses many important systems and pieces of equipment. However, if the Zero-Base™ concepts are used as the overall strategy and the RBM concepts as the tactical end, the results can be truly wondrous. To be specific, most creative applications of the RBM notions should be targeted to the Class A and Class B equipment.

A case by case determination should be made and some or all of the following maintenance technologies should be applied:

- Gas detectors to pick up incipient faults
- Mass balance monitors to detect fluid loss/leakage
- Installation of local deluge systems
- Construction of drainage systems to contain and divert toxic and combustible substances
- Periodic vibration analysis
- On-line vibration analysis
- Installation of local and remote vibration alarms
- Lubrication system observation for froth and water
- Oil analysis
- Frequent wear-particles-in-oil analysis
- Thermography
- Motor load monitoring, each phase
- Motor current signature analysis
- Motor starter operation analysis
- Airborne ultrasonics
- Pulse echo ultrasonics

- Training of maintainers
- Ready availability of technical data and spare parts
- Ready availability of trained personnel to handle problems
- Clearly visible identification of equipment.

Class B Equipment

Again, the equipment and processes need to be looked at on a case by case basis and the requisite care-taking designed accordingly. In general the following technologies should be applied with much less rigor and frequency than that for the Class A equipment.

- Periodic vibration analysis
- On-line vibration analysis
- Installation of remote vibration alarms
- Lubrication system observation for froth and water
- Oil analysis
- In-frequent wear-particles-in-oil analysis
- In-freqent thermography
- Airborne ultrasonics
- Training of operators and maintainers
- Availability of technical data and spare parts.

Class B equipment also includes low-priority equipment (such as HVAC equipment driver belts) which simply has limited useful life. For such equipment manufacturer's recommendations should be followed.

Class C Equipment

Equipment belonging to this class should **not** be subjected to **any** automatic or routine maintenance attention. The operator route sheets should be designed so that they can routinely observe the function and integrity of the equipment and ask for maintenance help as necessary. To get additional benefits from this process, train the operators to carry out minor routine tasks such as taking care of pump packings, replacement of lubrication oil, etc.

MANAGEMENT STRATEGIES

Having the tools and maintenance strategies at your disposal, now you are ready to start looking at the overall strategies and selling of the same to the regulators and the shareholders.

After proper development, management strategies should be presented to the regulators as an action plan for diligent compliance to the regulations. The strategy should have the following phases.

Phase 1

Identification of Class A equipment and commissioning of appropriate maintenance strategies. This phase should include:

- An exercise to see how the index values for the top 5% of the equipment could be reduced
- Development of response plans
- High quality training of operators and maintainers vis a vis equipment in this classification.

By now you must have realized this strategy does wonders for your training plans. You really do not need to have mega-training programs, only focus on the high priority equipment.

Once you've taken care of this phase, you'll see a sharp drop in safety exposure and steep rise in productivity (if you'd decided to determine the revenue loss indices as well).

Phase 2

Identification of Class B equipment and commissioning of appropriate maintenance strategies. This phase should include:

- Development of response plans
- High quality training of operators and maintainers viz a viz equipment in this classification.

Once you've taken care of this phase, your safety and productivity problems should be almost eliminated.

Phase 3

This phase should consist of three components:

- Examine and re-do the operator route-sheets to ensure that all of the Class C equipment is included. Some equipment may need to be added to other special groups. For example, underground piping may need to be added to the inspection group to look at every five years or so

- You should ask your plant technicians and engineers to find innovative means to reduce the threat indices of high-end equipment. Each person or shift should be assigned particular items and given a few weeks to deliberate. This activity will turn out to be the best continuous (CI) program you ever saw. However, all this should be done as a part of regular work, there should be no special task forces or the like
- Make your case to the regulators and explain why your actions should be taken as a diligent response to compliance issues.

SOME ACTUAL EXAMPLES

In this section we'll briefly discuss some actual examples and see what role the basic engineering design plays in the safe operation and maintenance of a facility.

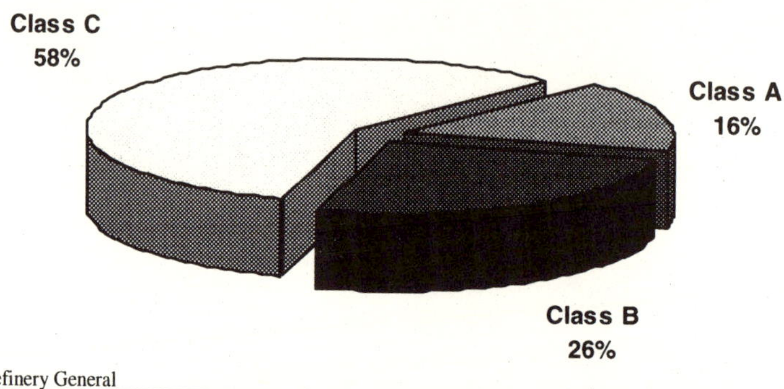

FIGURE 13 | **This figure shows the equipment classification for a chlorine dioxide manufacturing facility.**

This example corresponds to an actual chlorine dioxide generation facility which was constructed using standard design practices. You will notice the relative criticality of equipment for this facility is very similar to what we suggested earlier.

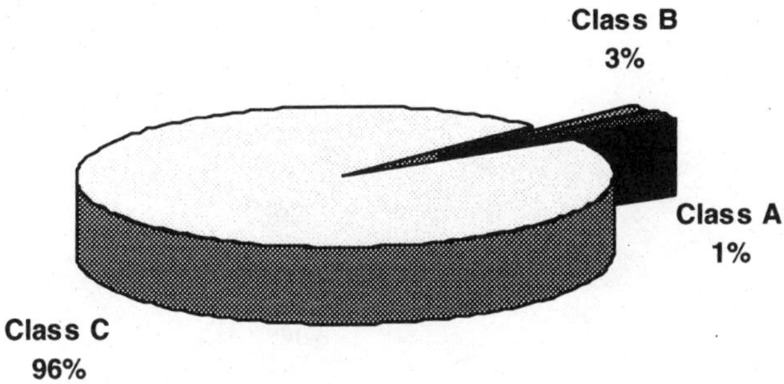

FIGURE 14	This figure shows the equipment classification for the electrical equipment for a crude oil handling facility.

This is a very interesting case study. This facility was constructed with little regard to money. Probably its remote location and intense regulator input played a big role in the design decisions.

Nevertheless, this facility has no dearth of redundant equipment and systems. All of that is reflected in the classification analysis, and as it turned out, very few pieces of equipment qualify to be considered as Class A material.

The new plant owners should really think about this. If you make your design robust you save a lot of money in the long run in operational and maintenance cost. If you don't, you should be ready to pay the piper after the first few years of operation.

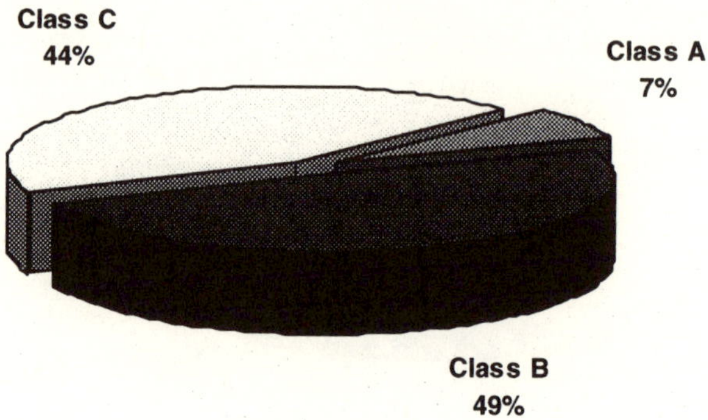

FIGURE 15	This figure shows the equipment classification for a mechanical oil tanker loading facility.

This is another interesting case study. This system is basically constructed with hydraulically operated mechanical equipment. Also there is not much room to construct redundant systems, even if you wanted to do so. This peculiarity is clearly reflected in the equipment classification. The number of Class B equipment is actually higher than that for the Class C equipment.

These examples are provided to highlight the fact that the attention which you need to give to a piece of equipment is not driven by its technological qualities or any such thing, but only by the business aspects –its relevance to the safety and productivity of your operation.

11

Pruning The Maintenance Work Down To Size

Stop the Insanity. Stop the Insanity.

THE DIET GURU SUSAN POWTER'S CHANT WHICH IS PROBABLY MORE APPLICABLE TO INDUSTRIAL MAINTENANCE.

Chapter Summary

This chapter deals with the following issues:

- ♦ How work is generated for the maintenance department
- ♦ Why the current practices cannot be sustained under the new legislative and competitive climate
- ♦ A logical way to prune the maintenance work to optimize reliability and compliance with regulations.

*T*he focus of this book is to find those activities which have the potential to do the most good for the operation. The supposition is that such activities are a small percentage of what can possibly be done. Thereby leading to the contention that you can achieve a lot while doing less. Working smart, not working hard.

In this chapter we review how, in general industrial facilities, work is really created for the maintainers. The intent is to demonstrate the randomness of work generation without careful thought.

THE FORMATION OF INDUSTRIAL MAINTENANCE WORK

There are numerous ways that are used to design and create the maintenance work. The principal among those are discussed below. The predominant modes among those listed differ from plant to plant. The key thing to remember here is that the maintenance resources are limited. If this were not the case, we'd have no problem. It would not matter how the resources were deployed as long some useful work was done. But that is not the case. Whenever you ask a maintainer to do something you are taking him away from something else–it is up to you make sure that whatever you have in mind is the most appropriate thing to be done at that time.

Dribble-Down Work

This mode of work generation usually applies to new equipment or large equipment which occasionally comes under the lime light for one reason or another. Perhaps an example will illustrate this the best. Consider the case where a company acquires a fairly large size pump and has it installed by its own maintenance department or a construction crew on contract. After the initial commissioning, which is sometimes done under the supervision of a vendor's field reps, the plant maintenance department takes over the unit. Within a few days the mechanical maintenance foreman will ask one of the planners to put the pump on the preventive maintenance (PDM) schedule. The foreman's instructions will be something like:

> *"Let's put this pump on the PM schedule along with the other pumps. We should sample the oil every six months and take vibration readings every six months or so. Put it down for a major every two years."*

You'll be surprised to know in how many plants oil samples are taken in this manner and sent out to labs for analysis. Nobody pays much attention to what the lab is supposed to be doing or what happens to the results. Usually the oil samples are collected by a junior mechanical technician known as the "oiler". There are two exceptions. First, sometimes the oiler, during the sampling process, notices abnormalities such as foam, sludge, water, etc., and raises the issue to his foreman. Second, for large pieces of rotating equipment, usually someone does pay attention – notice the emphasis is on "large", and not the criticality.

According to the PM plan, the pump is shut down and opened up for inspection every two years. For this pump, 70% of the failures occur within a week of the major PM.

In this example, we were considering a fairly large pump, which usually gets many people interested. Usually the foreman will mention his PM plan for the pump to one of the plant engineers, whose response will be something like:

> *"Taking vibration readings is really not very helpful. You need to know what you are looking at. You better start trending it to catch the problems before they occur. The alert value should be probably around 0.3 in/sec peak and shut down should be around 0.5 in/sec peak.*
> *For the first year, you should take an oil sample every month. Ask the lab to look for water and babbit. And let's open it up after a year for the first inspection."*

Well, this certainly is an improvement. Or so we think. What is wrong with this picture? An absence of a strategy! How do we know that what we are doing is the most appropriate thing. Clearly the intent is to take care of a piece of equipment and make it more reliable. Technically a case can be made that such PM plans have some merit. That being the case, why not do the same thing for all the existing equipment! If it makes sense for one of the pumps to be opened up (which, incidentally is considered to be a questionable idea, in spite of being practiced in many places) for inspection every two years, why not open every thing up? This would be a moot point if you had unlimited resources, but you do not.

Well, going back to our pump, since it is a fairly large installation, it catches the eye of one the reliability engineers from the corporate office. He suggests something like:

> *"Well, your plan is a good starting point. But you do need to customize your vibration numbers. You should get a baseline for this pump and generate your action numbers from that. Also a good oil analysis includes ferrography (wear particle analysis), emission spec analysis, viscosity, infrared analysis for oxidation, flash point and particle counting."*

Who can argue with that? So are you going to give this much attention to all the equipment? If not, why not? If yes, can you afford it?

Getting back to the point, the Dribble Down category includes work that is created by well-meaning internal and external people. You can't really blame them, they are doing their best. Remember, "management must manage", only applies to managers. If management does not manage, the technocrats will simply do what they think is the best for the plant. Remember, the technicians are trained to apply the best possible technology wherever they can. In this respect they are like doctors. But the subject of doctors' attention is one-of-a-kind equipment (our body) with very little redundancy, hence the application of the best technology makes sense. Getting back to the maintenance department, work created in this manner is really not controversial, but you simply do not have enough resources to do it all.

Some of such work loses lime light after a few months and fizzles out. The rest stays active for years. In one plant I saw oil samples being taken years after the pump was shut down. One pump was opened up and inspected annually for three years, while it sat totally idle during this period.

Breakdown Maintenance Work

Such work arises due to breakdown of the equipment. It automatically flows to maintenance for attention. Unfortunately, the predominant reason for such work is inadequate operator and maintainer training. The industrial equipment is designed not to fail, and it does take a lot of abuse before it fails. Proper training can cut such work to 10% of what it is today.

Many believe the main reason for the American leadership in the industrial world is the worker savvy and skills. I believe that to some degree, but I think there is a bigger reason lurking behind in the shadows. I think the main reason is the quality of our capital goods – equipment used to create wealth. I've seen workers in many countries, and I've noticed savvy coming out of their ears. But, unfortunately, (fortunately for us), they do not have good equipment to work with. No, we've not cornered the market in skills or savvy, which is actually a good thing. It indicates that we've a lot of room for upward growth in efficiency and we can potentially stay in the leadership role for decades to come. Additional comments on this aspect have been provided elsewhere in this chapter.

Planned Preventive Maintenance Work

The term "preventive maintenance" started coming to the forefront as a plant maintenance strategy in the early eighties. It was quickly supplemented by the term "predictive maintenance" and a few other lesser known terms. Now a days the phrase "Reliability Based Maintenance" is in vogue.

Such maintenance work involves on-line and shut-down inspection work as well as data gathering and testing. Some of the tests use the following technologies:

- Tribology (oil testing)
- Vibration analysis
- Thermography
- Insulation testing using surge and DC hipot testers.

In the next few years, as labor and industrial hardware costs keep on rising, this type of work will increasingly assume a central role in the maintenance activities.

At the present time this type of work and the associated technologies are applied in a rather ad hoc manner. This book, describes a methodology to apply the same with surgical precision to get the most out of the investment.

Maintenance Work created by the operators

Sometimes the work created by operators is controversial. Junior operators are notorious for dragging maintenance resources away from important jobs to some short term assignments which could have easily waited a few days. Most of the senior operators have a good appreciation of what is important and what is not.

A few decades ago, a lot of the routine maintenance was carried out by the plant operators. As a matter of fact in many places, there was no such thing as a maintenance department. As the maintenance departments start taking shape as separate entities, the role of the operators was chopped up in the turf battles, much to the detriment of the plant. When the operators had to maintain their own equipment they took pains to make sure it did not fail. Out of sheer necessity they learned basic trouble shooting skills and developed a keen sense for abnormal conditions. Granted, the time for such things has passed, but much needs to be said about demotivation of workers due to lack of meaningful work.

Today, in many plants, the operators have little idea about the condition of their equipment. They know, upon equipment failure, all they have to do is to write a work request for the maintenance. Smart operators still pass on some of the key symptoms to the maintenance, others don't. In a few plants the following were noted as the problem description:

- It don't pump
- NFG (which presumably stands for "NO #@& GOOD"
- Please fix.

In some plants they keep track of the percentage of resources diverted to short term (emergency) work generated by the operators. Sometimes this percentage is as high as 50%. In my estimation this work can be looked at as following:

- 10-15%: Essential. Under the best conditions it will be there
- 85-90%: Inappropriate work. Should be done later in a properly planned manner

This picture would not be complete if we didn't comment on the work the operators consider very important, and decide to put in a routine work request with importance clearly defined. Some of such work is never done. The evidence of this phenomenon is clearly visible if you take a walk through a large industrial plant. In the plants that suffer from this problem, you'll see many valves with blown gaskets, pressure indicators showing zero or off-the-scale pressure, bypassed controllers, etc. So the operators may have a point when they tend to declare everything an emergency.

Work Created Due to Inappropriate Operator and Maintainer Training

I encourage you to analyze all of the work done by your maintenance department during the last one year (excluding the construction work which sometimes lands in the lap of maintenance supervisors). Ask one of the senior industrial engineers to determine the root cause for the work. I guarantee that you'll be amazed at the findings. In my estimation, as much as 60% of the maintenance work is created by inadequate training of operators and maintainers. Sid Siddiqui, a senior mechanical engineer, once commented on the price ($18,000.00) of a centrifugal pump. He said, "For this much money you could easily buy a good car – which has over five hundred high precision components and lasts a long time. Notwithstanding the mass production components for this equation, the reason an industrial pump costs so much is because it is designed to give you reliable service for at least twenty years. It really takes a lot of ignorance and negligence to destroy such equipment in a few years." I've seen properly operated pumps and compressors to be in good working order after fifty or more years of service!

Regulatory Maintenance Work

This type of work is driven by safety and environmental regulations. At the present time it is usually limited to periodic or emergency calibration and testing of equipment. For example, pressure vessel safety codes may require annual testing and calibration of pressure relief devices. Environmental regulations may require periodic testing and calibration of some primary sensing elements or controllers (such as a pH meters). In the next section we look at the regulatory requirements in somewhat more detail.

Work Created By The Project Management Group

This type of work is essentially what is known as construction work. This book does not deal with this subject. It is strictly a matter of economics and logistics and has no bearing on the issues being discussed here.

PROCESS SAFETY AND RISK MANAGEMENT REGULATORY REQUIREMENTS

The preceding discussion primarily focused on the sources which create work for the maintenance group. The regulations not only demand delivery of certain goals but require that the manner in which the goals are delivered to acceptable as well.

Taking the present day regulations at face value, we are required to maintain the integrity of all equipment which is associated with the targeted processes. It certainly makes sense to do so. How else can one control or minimize the uncontrolled emissions.

Let's take an example and examine it. As mentioned elsewhere in this book, the term "equipment" includes a number of items, one of which is flow control valves. How does one maintain the integrity of a flow control valve? Surely by making sure that all of its components are reliable and operational, settings are appropriate, etc. Some of the components, say the pneumatic diaphragm, is critical for proper operation of the valve. Are we required to ensure that the diaphragm can provide a reliable service? Since the diaphragm has a direct impact on the integrity of the process, so according to the conventional wisdom, the answer is yes. Therefore, to meet the regulatory requirements, we need to do the following:

- Have a written procedure to maintain its on-going integrity
- Train each involved employee in maintaining the on-going integrity (give him an overview of the process and its hazards, and the requisite training in the procedures.)
- Inspect and test the diaphragm, using procedures based on generally accepted good engineering practices. Frequency of testing has to be consistent with the manufacturer's recommendations and good engineering practices. The testing frequency to be increased if so warranted. So we need to have an additional systems in place to determine if additional testing and inspection is warranted.
- The inspections need to be documented. The documentation must identify the date of inspection or test, the name of person who performed the test, the serial number or other identifier for the equipment, a description of the test or inspection, and the results of the test or inspection.

Let's refer to the above scope of work as Maintenance Work Scope Related to PSM (MWSR-PSM).

To do all of the above you need four or five properly written out procedures:

- how to remove it
- how to install it
- how to inspect it
- how to test it
- how to calibrate it (this one is probably not needed since the pneumatic diaphragms are not calibrated in the field. However you'll need to make sure that your supplier is using adequate quality control systems).

You will also need well planned and documented training of maintainers, and a record keeping system which provides excellent traceability of the associated activities. In addition to the pneumatic diaphragm, a control valve may have ten additional similar components – all of which require similar attention, because mal-operation of a component may render the valve unreliable. Are you prepared to do all of this for a control valve, and does it make sense?

Now let's consider another example. A very common piece of industrial equipment is a Limitorque valve operator. It is considered to be a very reliable piece of equipment and in some plants many models of this operator are in operation. We will consider only one model. If we limit ourselves to major maintenance items we come up with the following list of activities which need to be considered:

- Operator removal, standard method
- Actuator removal, (expedited method)
- Limit and torque switch removal
- Limit and torque switch installation
- Limit and torque switch inspection
- Limit and torque switch balancing
- Motor removal
- Motor installation
- Motor inspection
- Motor testing
- Motor calibration
- Handwheel removal
- Handwheel installation
- Handwheel inspection
- Handwheel testing
- Handwheel calibration
- Declutch removal
- Declutch installation
- Declutch inspection
- Declutch testing
- Declutch calibration
- Spring cartridge cap/worm spring pack removal
- Spring cartridge cap/worm spring pack installation
- Spring cartridge cap/worm spring pack inspection
- Spring cartridge cap/worm spring pack testing
- Spring cartridge cap/worm spring pack calibration
- Housing cover removal
- Housing cover installation
- Driver sleeve assembly removal

- Driver sleeve assembly installation
- Driver sleeve assembly inspection
- Lower quad ring removal
- Lower quad ring installation
- Lower quad ring inspection
- Clutch housing removal
- Clutch housing installation
- Clutch housing inspection
- Drive sleeve lower bearing cup removal
- Drive sleeve lower bearing cup installation
- Drive sleeve lower bearing cup inspection
- Worm and Belleville spring pack removal
- Worm and Belleville spring pack installation
- Worm and Belleville spring pack inspection
- Worm and Belleville spring pack testing
- Worm and Belleville spring pack calibration
- Worm-to worm gear removal
- Worm-to worm gear installation
- Worm-to worm gear inspection
- Worm-to worm gear testing
- Worm-to worm gear alignment
- Motor bearing and pinion removal
- Motor bearing and pinion installation
- Motor bearing and pinion inspection
- Motor bearing and pinion testing
- Limit switch finger base removal
- Limit switch finger base installation
- Limit switch finger base inspection
- Actuator lubrication
- Torque switch setting with load cell
- Torque switch setting for gate openers

In this list there are over 60 procedures. Note, for the sake of brevity, this list does not include dozens of minor, though necessary procedures.

If you were to show this list to a qualified technician and asked him how many of these procedures he thought were necessary to guarantee the operation of the valve-operator in a reliable order. The answer, invariably, would be "all". If you combine the above with MRWS-PSM, you have your work cut out for you. And don't forget that you may have to modify many of the above items, as soon as the manufacturer makes changes to the design.

Granted, a Limitorque assembly has far more components than most pieces of production equipment. Generally speaking, the required number of procedures for different pieces of equipment, using the same criteria, will vary between 3 and 150 – the average being close to 20.

Let's consider the case of an average size industrial plant which has about 5000 pieces of discrete equipment, of which about 2000 will have unique characteristics. Applying the required degree of rigor (to maintain the equipment integrity), you will need about 40,000 (20x2000) procedures and a fairly large bureaucracy to manage them. To put it in some perspective, an average procedure takes about three pages, and a 3-inch procedures manual can handle about 400 pages, you are looking at approximately 300 maintenance procedures manuals. For these manuals you will need 75 feet of shelve space.

Should you be doing all this work? Also don't forget, this is just the tip of the paperwork. To completely comply with the regulations you need to adhere to the earlier listed Maintenance Work Scope Related to PSM (MWSR-PSM).

If you decide to go ahead and do all of the above, you have to contend with the following issues:

- For an average size plant, just to develop the procedures you will need about four million dollars to develop the maintenance procedures.
- Once you do have the procedures developed, in my opinion, the safety of personnel and reliability of equipment will go down. The reason is very simple, human mind does not like to deal with 40,000 procedures and the associated paperwork. During the transition period (which may be as long as a few years), there will glitches, procedures will be misfiled in the computers, there will difficulties controlling amendments and versions etc. As soon as the transition period is over, you will find a large number of your procedures will be obsolete and will require amendments. The net result will be the tradesmen will largely ignore the procedures, and at times, incorrect version of procedures will cause safety hazards.
- The corporation's legal defensive position may become compromised in future litigation against public and injured employees. Many juries will listen compassionately to a maintainer (who did not follow the requisite procedures and got

hurt or caused an incident to take place), when he says that he did not do so because it is simply not a reasonable expectation to go through thousands of documents to find the right one. Under most circumstances, in a court of law, it is reasonably easy to demonstrate that the corporation really did not train the employee to find the right material in an expedient manner. It is also relatively easy to demonstrate a corporation's record retrieval system is not user friendly and is frequently in a disheveled mess. Remember the how the integrity of FBI labs was put in question by the Simpson lawyers. You see, the reality in the hands of lawyers takes new and sinister shapes.

So what do you really get? **Compliance to the letter of the law seems to go against the spirit of the law.**

I am sure the regulators did not intend for the regulations to compromise safety of personnel and process. In my opinion the spirit of the law is more important than the letter of the law. As a matter of fact you may not have much choice. It does not make sense to spend millions of dollars to end up in the situation where you compromise the safety of your personnel.

There is a better way. This is what this book is all about.

SITUATIONAL MAINTENANCE

The maintenance effort must depend upon the criticality of the piece of equipment under consideration. This concept is explored in-depth elsewhere in the book. However, the logic for limiting the maintenance effort to activities which make sense is discussed here.

Let's start off with the base case which calls for a need to develop 40,000 maintenance procedures under an unrestrained quest to comply, and having deep pockets to go with it.

First of all, we limit our procedure development work to Class A and B equipment. Using the Zero-Base™ methodology, you identify the equipment belonging to these two classes. Which should be about 15% of the total, hence 300, in our hypothetical case. You see we have already narrowed our sharpest focus to 15% of the field. If you did develop all of the possible maintenance procedures you will end up with a number close to 6,000 instead of 40,000. Which is still a large and unwieldy number.

Now we make another giant leap in logic and say that if we limited ourselves to only the following procedures, we will not end up compromising safety or environment or production:

- ♦ How to remove it
- ♦ How to install it (not how to construct – construction is not a true maintenance job)
- ♦ How to commission it in service after installation or major work
- ♦ How to calibrate it
- ♦ How to inspect it and test for proper operation

You see these procedures form a sieve through which all other work must flow through. If one messes up in any one of the other procedures, one of the above will catch the discrepancy or the shortcoming. Thus, as far as regulations or production issues are concerned you need to rigorously train your people only in these five types of procedures.

Applying the logic outlined above, the number of requisite procedures drops to about 1500 from 6000. So you need to apply your most intensive training and execution effort on these 1500 activities, which is about 3.75% of the unrestrained and no-holds barred work scope! Thus my contention that, ***through application of the Zero-Base methodology you not only achieve unprecedented levels of safety and productivity, you do so at huge cost savings.***

Let me hasten to make two points here before the above comments result in irrational exuberance.

First, the above comments do not mean that the remainder of the equipment is ignored. In the next chapter we discuss how to diligently handle the remainder of the equipment.

Secondly, the above limitation on procedures does not mean that you do not have to follow other procedures. For other activities worker trade knowledge and shop floor vendor supplied procedures should be used. Perhaps an example will illustrate this point. Consider a malfunctioning control valve. Your action plan will be something like the following:

1. Apply the authorized testing procedure to determine that the valve is malfunctioning and that something is wrong with its internals. You need to use the authorized procedure to protect the integrity of the process.

2. Apply the authorized removal procedure to remove the unit. Again, you need to use the authorized procedure to protect the integrity of the process.
3. Apply trade practices to move the unit to the shop. Any reasonable procedure may be used since this activity does not threaten the integrity of the procedure.
4. Apply generic vendor's procedures (available in manuals supplied by the vendor) to open up the unit, inspection and identification of faulty components. For bench testing of the unit, again using vendor's materials.
5. Install the unit using the authorized maintenance procedures. You need to use the authorized procedure to protect the integrity of the process.
6. Apply the authorized commissioning procedures to put the unit back in service. In this activity, you will probably need to work closely with the plant operators. You need to use the authorized procedure to protect the integrity of the process.
7. Apply the authorized function testing procedures to make sure the unit is operating appropriately. In this activity, you will again need to work closely with the plant operators. You need to use the authorized procedure to protect the integrity of the process. During this step you will catch any problems which may have crept in due to bad workmanship or application of inappropriate shop procedures.

I hope the above demonstrates the soundness of the logic which allows us to limit the regulation-driven rigorous maintenance work to a small fraction without sacrificing safety, environment or production.

12

The Bottom Line

What we anticipate seldom occurs; what we least expect generally happens.

–BENJAMIN DISRAELI, 1804-1881

Chapter Summary

The methodology presented in this book saves you money in many real and tangible ways. **You can start saving money immediately in a concrete and a measurable fashion.**

A. As far as methodology is concerned, the Zero Base™ Compliance method creates two major options for you:

- ♦ You can spend millions of dollars and hope to get results which are questionable to start with and may never materialize. This is what happens if you employ business as usual practices
- ♦ Or you can attain far superior results at a fraction of the cost. That is, if you employ the Zero Base™ concepts.

B. The Zero Base Compliance method gives you a highly focused tool to control your exposure to catastrophic events. Perhaps for the first time you will be able to convince yourself that your house is in order and you have done your job in a diligent manner.

C. Though presented here as an aid for effective compliance to safety regulations, this methodology is equally applicable to general maintenance and productivity management.

D. The Zero Base Compliance method, at a comparatively low cost, is likely to give you a high credibility with the regulators and shareholders.

E. You will be able to reduce your operator and maintenance training costs to a fraction of what you are doing right now and get far better results.

F. You can convert your maintenance department into a positive contributor with accomplishments which can be measured in easy and concrete terms. Not only it will enable you to have superior cost control systems, you'll see an enormous difference in the morale of your maintenance people.

G. Perhaps for the first time you will be able to sponsor meaningful Continuous Improvement initiatives.

I need to emphasize the tangible nature of the rate of return which accompanies the application of the Zero Base Compliance methodology. It must be done since I've seen hundreds of projects with extraordinary justifications on paper, where the ROIs simply evaporate into thin air as soon as the project is completed. In some industrial plants this problem is of an epidemic proportions. It is very easy to check that. All you need to do is to review the capital spending for the past five years, add the new projected revenue streams. Compare the actual revenue numbers for the two periods and see if the increase is comparable to the projected increases. You'll be surprised at the results.

Not so, for the ideas presented here. In the following sections, I'll describe where your savings will come from and how you can touch and feel them, and put your arms around them if need be. The Zero-Base™ methodology delineates the important from the not-so important. As soon as this is done you ask your technicians to cease doing work which has not been recommended. You'll be surprised how much inappropriate work is scheduled to be done every day. **Thus you start saving money the day you implement this system.**

Table-1: Comparative Cost For Criticality Assessment and Recommendation Generation

	Commonly Used Methods	Conventional Risk Analysis Systems	Zero-Based Compliance	Comments
Data Gathering, Making Equipment List, P&IDs, Etc.	20	160	100	The conventional system takes longer time since the effort is usually not focused. A considerable amount of time is lost in discussions, meetings and misdirected effort and rectification thereof. The ZBC methodology is highly focused and has very little dead time.
Assessment Of Probability Of Failure For Each Piece Of Eqpt.	20	1000	100	In spite of costing more, the conventional systems do not address each and every piece of equipment. The ZBC system addresses each and every piece of equipment.
Assessment Of Equipment Criticality	20	400	80	Most of the conventional systems use inconsistent and unrepresentative data to arrive at the equipment criticality. Again, all of the equipment is usually not covered. The ZBC methods use consistent plant-specific factors and address all equipment.
Recommendations Specific Actions	40	40	40	
Total Estimated Man-Hours Used In Assessment Of Equipment Criticality.	100	1600	320	The conventional systems can cost as must as four times the ZBC methodology while producing questionable results. If you were to force the conventional systems to yield the same degree of rigor, the cost is likely to be much more than what is shown here.
Estimated Effectiveness	40%	70%	90%	
Application To General Maintenance	No	No	Yes	Conventional risk assessment systems do not cover all the equipment, hence application is limited
Repeatability	No	Yes	Yes	
Defensibility To External Auditors	To a small extent	To a large extent	To a large extent	Nothing can be guaranteed against external auditors since these are not exact sciences or systems.

COST COMPARISON BETWEEN OPTIONS

A summary of cost comparison for a medium operation is given in Table 1. In this table the following three ways of doing business are compared:

- Business as usual, using commonly used hit-or-miss shop floor methods
- Rigorous methods based on quantitative risk analyses (using data from standard data vendors)
- Zero-Base™ techniques.

The actual numbers will probably differ somewhat, depending upon the availability of data, plant culture, process complexity, etc. However, in a comparative sense the picture will look close to what is presented here.

Note that the man-hours as shown in the table correspond to what it will take trained plant personnel to do this work. Incidentally, it is very easy to train the plant personnel to use the Zero Base™ concepts, since the system is heavily dependent upon the actual plant experience and common sense. This approach is designed to be used in-house by the plant people. On the other hand, for the conventional risk analysis, you need to acquire the services of very expensive external consultants.

Table-2: Comparative Implementation Schemes and Comparative Cost

	Usual Methods	Conventional Risk Analysis Systems	Zero-Based Compliance	Comments
Preparation of Operating Procedures. Man-hours.	2000	2000	650	If the ZBC methodology is not used, the only remaining option is a broad brush approach, which is very expensive.
Preparation of Maint. Procedures. Man-hours.	2000	2000	650	If the ZBC methodology is not used, the only remaining option is a broad brush approach, which is very expensive.
Operator Training on the new procedures. Training hours per person.	80	80	40	In reality, for approaches other than the ZBC approach one requires far more training hours than 80, but few organizations choose to train people for more than 80 hours for training of this or any other type. Hence, a conservative number of 80 is used.
Maintenance training on the new procedures. Training hours per person.	80	80	40	In reality, for approaches other than the ZBC approach one requires far more training hours than 80, but few organizations choose to train people for more than 80 hours for training of this or any other type. Hence, a conservative number of 80 is used.
Implementation of requisite maintenance. ZBC as the base case.	3X	3X	X	Maintenance effort resulting from the ZBC methodology is taken as the base case requiring X man-hours.
Estimated Effectiveness. Scale 1-10.	7	7	9	A broad brush approach causes dilution of knowledge retention and loss of focus.
Defensibility To External Auditors Scale 1-10.	7	7	9	Nothing can be guaranteed against external auditors since technician training and equipment maintenance is not an exact science.

COMPARATIVE COST FOR IMPLEMENTATION OF RECOMMENDATIONS

Due to the number of variables involved, it is not easy to prepare concrete comparative numbers. However, all things being equal, some numbers of indicative quality can be developed.

Table-2 provides such a comparison for a medium size system. Some elements of this table are discussed below.

Preparation of Operating Procedures

During the last few years many plants have undergone major operating procedure writing activities. In such plants you will see operating procedures by the yard. In some plants, unfortunately, some of these procedures have never been used by any of the operators. After a short flurry of interest the operators have gone back to using their little black books or no procedures at all. It is an unfortunate and sad situation. The primary reasons for this status are:

- Too many procedures
- Procedures too lengthy
- Management does not know the difference between a training procedure and an operating procedure
- Management does not know the difference between an abnormal condition and an emergency condition
- Inaccessibility of the printed material.

More details about this subject are beyond the scope of this book. However, I've covered this material in another book.

The application of Zero-Base™ methodology reduces the number of procedures to a very small number.

Preparation of Maintenance Procedures

This is even a tougher net to crack. In comparison to operations, the diversity of tasks handled by the maintainers is enormous. As far as the maintainers are concerned, technically speaking, some of the tasks are trivial and some are similar to rocket science. But management does not know that. So under the present tidal wave of procedure development, when maintenance procedures are developed, they usually miss the mark. In the industrial plants that I have visited since the early nineties, I am yet to see more than 5% of the recently developed procedures to be in use.

In the recent years an abundance of trivial procedures have been developed. Unfortunately, the tradesmen do not need any help for trivial work, and they resent being force-fed the trivial stuff. Complex tasks, where the maintainers really need help, are usually glossed over. Examples of such glossed over are:

- Trouble shooting the variable frequency drives
- Function testing of a pump
- Setting the mechanical overspeed trip for a steam turbine, etc.

The cornerstone for doing a good job starts off with a good problem definition, which not only defines what needs to be done, but puts boundaries around it. The absence of a defined scope results in enormous amount of wasted effort. The Zero-Base™ methodology takes care of this part of the problem for you. It clearly defines what you need to train your people for.

The procedures which are developed should be appropriately in-depth and address real problems. This aspect is outside the scope of this book and I've attempted to take care of it in another book.

Regarding training, the complaints which I have heard the most from the operators and maintainers are:

- Management does not have proper material to train us with
- Management does not really know our training problems. It occasionally makes training advisory committees and then ignores them (by not acting on the recommendations of the training committee)
- Management is more interested in training us in fads which come and go every year. Examples: Team building, sexual harassment, workplace diversity, etc. All of these programs are good, but what about training for our real job?

Implementation of the requisite maintenance

The table provides a set comparative numbers, using the maintenance effort needed if the department used the Zero-Base™ methodology as the base case requiring X man-hours.

The other options are simply not enough fine-tuned to be effective and hence it takes a lot more effort. The extra work results from the following reasons:

- Some of the work done is not necessary
- Due to lack of training some of the completed work creates additional work
- Some of the necessary work which is not done, creates additional work

The numbers quoted for efforts other than Zero-Base™ reflect my guestimates. In the years to come I hope to be able to quote some real shop floor numbers.

Estimated Effectiveness of the Implemented Schemes

You will notice that methods other than the Zero-Base™ methodology require a considerably larger amount of resources and money to be implemented. The main reason for this is the application of broad brush strategies. Examples: If they want to prepare technician procedures the call is – *we do not have enough or up to date operating or maintenance procedures, let's develop them.* Or. *"our technicians need better training, let's train them"*. However, while I advise against it, once you do incur such an expenditure, it has a positive effect on the regulators. Whether the approach is effective or not, the regulators are likely to consider this as a "due diligent" effort.

In the table I have rated the three options on a scale of 1 to 10. For approaches other than Zero-Base™ methodology,I've guessed the rating to be at 7 simply because the expenditure of money and resources is awe-inspiring, yet it leaves lingering questions in the minds of the regulators and the share holders. "But does it really work?" This is the question which never quite gets sorted out. On the other hand, since the Zero-Base™ methodology is fundamentally based on a quest for logic and effectiveness, it is likely to leave a better impression.

Defensibility To External Auditors

The reasons for selecting ratings for various options are same as those discussed above. The defense of your strategic approach depends upon how effective, practical and comprehensive it is.

The Zero-Base™ process, since it maintains strong ties to the real life, charges up the participants to high levels of enthusiasm. For the same reasons, it is likely to generate a wholesome case in the eyes of the regulators. However, it should be noticed the defense of your program depends upon the following factors:

- Rationality of your compliance process
- Your commitment
- Actual action plans being executed
- Your ability to communicate your compliance processes to the plant personnel, regulators and shareholders
- Your credibility in the eyes of the regulators (sometimes historical skeletons keep on rattling in the closets).

Some of these factors are very subjective in nature and do not lend themselves to be expressed in absolute terms. For this reason it is very difficult to determine what will positively yield a blessing from the regulators. Having said that, I've noticed that these days some regulators tend to take an advisory and helpful stance. Involving them at the beginning of the process and keeping them continuously informed will do wonders for your credibility.

CONVERSION OF THE MAINTENANCE DEPARTMENT INTO A TRULY PRODUCTIVE GROUP

At the present time the claim to fame most maintenance departments have has following elements:

- They work hard and put in long hours. In many places overtime runs over 20% for the field technicians and supervisors
- They are conscientious and spend many weekends at the plant
- Their response to forced shutdowns is getting better all the time
- They successfully find their way out of problems on equipment for which they have no training, and which sometimes utilizes cutting edge technology
- Their safety record is great
- In spite of manpower cutbacks they maintain the equipment uptime.

In ninety percent of the plants the above sums up what the maintainers do. But there is something missing in this picture. From the above criteria can you answer the question: ***Is their work efficient and productive?*** You really cannot answer this question. All you can say is: Every one is very busy and works hard. The actual question to be asked is: Are they effective? If yes, how so? This is a difficult question to answer, because to be effective you need to know what needs to be done and then measure your performance against it.

The Zero-Base™ methodology solves this problem by ferreting out the actions you need do to be considered effective. All you have to do is to get them executed in a safe and cost effective manner. The goals for the maintenance department should be something like:

- Maintain the reliability of the Class A equipment at 98% or higher
- Maintain the reliability of the Class B equipment at 90% or higher
- The backlog for Class C equipment should not be more than 4 weeks at any time
- The estimated cost of this service is X dollars, therefore the cost must be maintained at the budget numbers.

The characteristics of the above goals are:

- They are measurable
- They are limited in scope, hence practical. They are limited because the number of pieces of equipment belonging to Class A and B is very small
- You can dial the reliability numbers up or down.

This forms a great paradigm shift for the maintenance department. **Immediately it is transformed from a necessary evil to the givers of reliability.** Meeting of such goals creates a great sense of accomplishment, and the maintainers cease to be second class citizens.

BETTER UTILIZATION OF OPERATORS

In other chapters we have seen the best people to handle the immediate needs of the Class 3 equipment are the operators. Putting these jobs in the lap of operators will not only free up the maintainers but will add value and substance to what the operators do on a day to day basis. This is likely to create a new culture where equipment will work better due to improvement in the rigorous custodianship efforts. It stands to reason that if the operators understand their equipment better, they will operate it better. Another reason why the operators would like to take on the additional work is the opportunity for cross-training. During this day and age, the more cross-training one has, the better the chances at continuous gainful employment.

MEANINGFUL CONTINUOUS IMPROVEMENT PROGRAM

We have seen elsewhere in this book that by utilizing Zero-Base™ methodology you end up assigning a threat index to each piece of equipment. Actually you assign three different threat indices, one each for safety, environment and production. Obviously, the higher the threat index the greater your exposure to loss of the given category. You start your continuous improvement program by assigning the high threat index items to the experienced plant people with a request to think about reducing the threat through innovative and cost-effective means. Management can decide the area it is seeking the improvements in: employee safety, environmental protection or production enhancement.

Thus the Zero-Base™ methodology not only solves your immediate problems, but it gives you tools to continuously improve in all aspects of your core business.

LOWER INVENTORY OF SPARES

CNN reported on 3/18/97: Fifty percent of the items in the Pentagon's $70 billion dollar inventory are not necessary – *General Accounting Office*.

Unfortunately, similar stories can be written about many industrial plants. With Zero-Base™ methodology you have an opportunity to cut the inventory down to size.

SAFETY, ENVIRONMENTAL PROTECTION AND PRODUCTION

The *raison de etre* for the Zero-Base™ methodology is to provide you with a razor sharp focus as far as your activities regarding safety, environmental protection and productivity are concerned – which is practically every thing you do – or at least 95% of every thing you should do. In this methodology the search for effectiveness is at center stage. Therefore it stands to reason that you should expect, other than superior compliance with the regulations, higher levels of consistent production.

Appendix A

CONVENTIONAL FAILURE RATE DATA PROVIDERS

During the last fifty years an enormous amount of work has been done in the fields of quantitative and qualitative techniques to evaluate equipment reliability and potential for human injuries. At the forefront of this work are the following:

- American Institute of Chemical Engineers (AIChE)
- Center for Chemical Process Safety (CCPS)
- Electric Power Research Institute (EPRI)
- North American Electric Reliability Council
- Imperial Chemical Industry (ICI)
- Netherlands Organization for Applied Scientific Research
- United Kingdom Atomic Energy Authority

Two of the most common ways to characterize equipment failure data are:

- Number of equipment failures per 10^6 operating hours, or
- Failures per 10^3 demands.

Appendix B

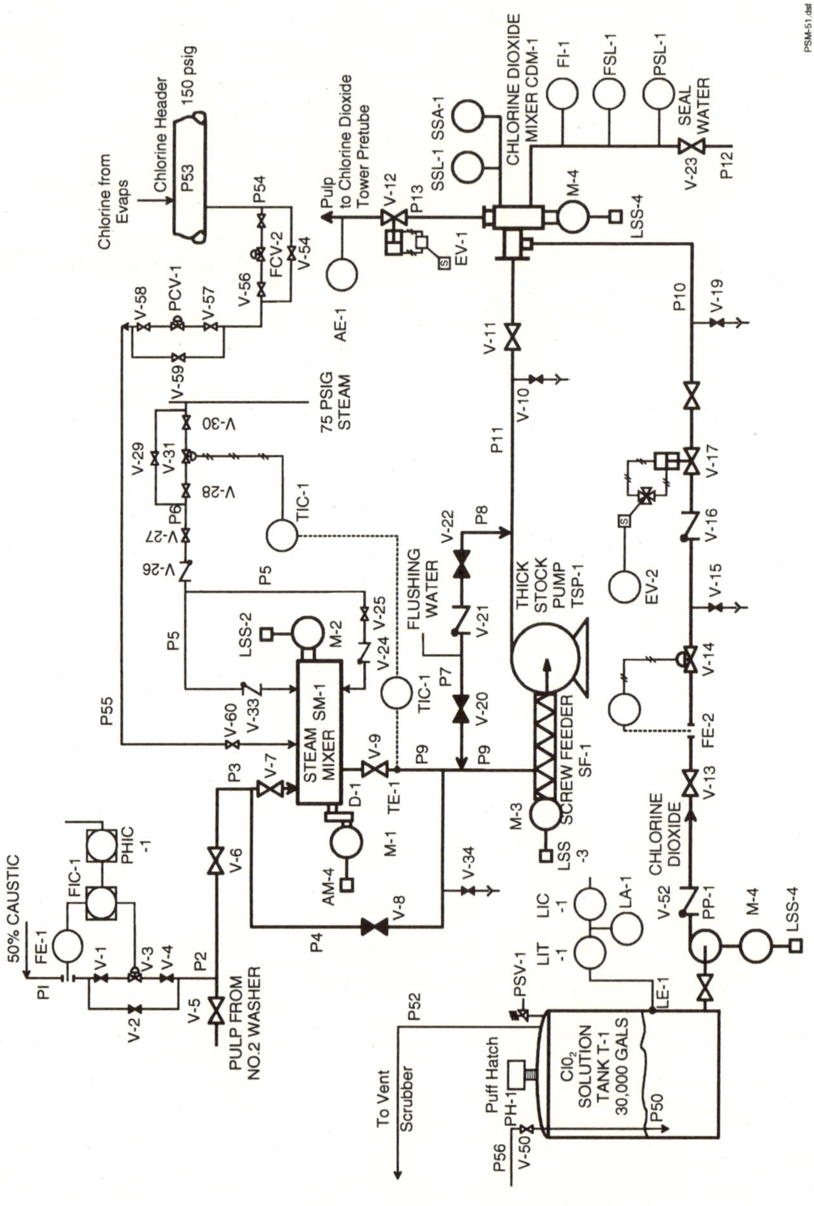
Chlorine from Evaps
Chlorine Header
P53
150 psig
P54
FCV-2
V-54
V-56
V-58
PCV-1
V-57
V-59
75 PSIG STEAM
V-30
V-29
V-31
V-28
P6
V-27
V-26
TIC-1
P5
P55
LSS-2
M-2
V-25
V-24
V-60
V-33
STEAM MIXER SM-1
P3
V-7
D-1
TE-1
V-9
P9
M-1
AM-4
V-6
V-8
P4
V-34
50% CAUSTIC
FE-1
FIC-1
PHIC -1
PI
V-1
V-2
V-3
V-4
P2
V-5
PULP FROM NO.2 WASHER
Pulp to Chlorine Dioxide Tower Pretube
AE-1
V-12
P13
EV-1
SSL-1
SSA-1
CHLORINE DIOXIDE MIXER CDM-1
FI-1
FSL-1
PSL-1
SEAL WATER
V-23
P12
M-4
LSS-4
V-11
V-10
P11
P10
V-19
FLUSHING WATER
V-22
P8
V-21
V-20
P7
THICK STOCK PUMP TSP-1
SCREW FEEDER SF-1
M-3
LSS -3
V-17
V-16
EV-2
V-15
V-14
FE-2
V-13
CHLORINE DIOXIDE
V-52
PP-1
LIT -1
LIC -1
LA-1
LE-1
PSV-1
P52
To Vent Scrubber
Puff Hatch
PH-1
P56
V-50
ClO2 SOLUTION TANK T-1 30,000 GALS
P50
PSM-51.dsf

B

An Illustrative Example For Zero-Base™ Technique Principles

In this section we discuss a part of a pulp mill production process to demonstrate a hands-on example of Zero-Base™ techniques. The diagram presented here shows a small portion of a bleach plant where chlorine dioxide (ClO_2) is mixed with the pulp.

This is a hypothetical system constructed with real components borrowed from a few plants. The system shown here provides some food for thought. It would have been far easier take a system which deals with hydrogen sulfide or some highly explosive substances where it is relatively easier to construct dangerous combination of circumstances.

In the system shown here, pulp is received from No. 2 Washer and is forwarded to the steam mixer SM-1. The system is equipped with an obsolete 50% caustic injection line which is still tied to the pulp transport piping leading to the steam mixer. The mixer is operated by two mixing screws each equipped with its own driver, one on each side of the mixer housing. The east screw is driven by an electric motor with a built-in gearbox, while the west unit has an external chain driven mechanism. Each of the electric drivers is equipped with a local start/stop station as well as access from a DCS station located in the control room.

The steam mixer is injected with 35 psig saturated steam supplied by an old 75 psig header located near the steam mixing station.

The steam mixer is also supplied with chlorine from a twenty year old 150 psig header. The chlorine flows to the steam mixer through a pressure control valve and a flow control valve.

From the steam mixer, chlorinated and heated pulp is routed to a screw feeder at the inlet of the thick stock pump. The screw feeder and the thick stock pump are operated by electric motors. The thick stock pump forwards the pulp to a motor-driven chlorine dioxide mixer which routes the pulp to the chlorine dioxide tower pretube. The mixer is furnished with seal water supplied through a well-instrumented line as shown.

The chlorine dioxide for the mixer is supplied from a storage tank having a capacity of 30,000 gallons. The tank is supplied with chlorine dioxide mixture (9 gm/l) through the pipe P56 and valve V-50. The chlorine dioxide is supplied to the tank via a line (P50) which is kept submerged in the fluid inside the tank. The tank is equipped with a puff hatch as well as a pressure safety valve. A vent from the top of the tank is tied to the scrubber or the chlorine dioxide generation system. The tank level is maintained by a level indicating controller (LIC-1) and is constantly monitored on the DCS. The chlorine dioxide pump (PP-1) takes suction from this tank and supplies the fluid to the ClO_2 mixer at a rate of approximately 300 gpm. A forced failure of this pump along with some other instrumentation failure would result in overflowing of the tank in about an hour – which is a very dangerous situation since chlorine dioxide is extremely explosive in air if its concentration exceeds 10%. To avoid such a situation the operators try to maintain the tank level at under 50%.

The system, as shown, has about one hundred elements. For the sake of simplicity and convenience, many minor system elements have not been shown and many have been altered. Fictitious model numbers are used in this analysis. Key features of this system are:

- It is located near two control rooms and some other locations that are heavily populated by plant personnel
- There are many confined spaces nearby
- The system is twenty years old and many of the components have never been tested or inspected.

HOW TO HANDLE THE SITUATION WITHOUT THE ZERO-BASE™ PRINCIPLES

The challenge in front of us is rather simple (or so we believe). We simply need to improve the mechanical integrity of the system so that it does not jeopardize the safety of personnel near the components or around the plant. I've talked about such a situation in many plants and asked how they'd proceed. Generally I'm told the following:

> The first business item is to determine what is regulated and what is not. This is handled by a team usually led by the Process Safety Managers. Usually they end up consulting with the regulators as well. Once they've delineated the areas of interest, they pass it on to maintenance managers to make sure the mechanical integrity aspects of the regulations are complied with. At this point maintenance managers do not know what to do with this problem which suddenly landed in their lap. Everyone means well and wants to help out, especially the engineers who, by default, have to assume the leadership role. But they have their own day to day responsibilities to handle along with anything else which is routed their way. First, they are swamped with other work (especially after the recent downsizing waves) and secondly they don't understand the regulations very well, as a consequence not much happens. In many places the engineers and maintenance people do use innovative measures to solve a part of the problem.

Let's try a similar experiment by placing a copy of the system presented here in front of a maintenance manager and say: "We've determined that this system is covered by the PSM and RMP regulations, please do whatever is necessary to comply with the mechanical integrity aspects of the regulations".

Now what'll a maintenance manager do? He doesn't know where to start. To be helpful, let's break down the challenge for him in the following components:

- Examine the mechanical integrity of the system and determine its strengths and weaknesses
- Identify the components which pose high risk due to inadequate mechanical integrity
- Propose specific recommendations to reduce the risk level or to mitigate its consequences.

Usually he'll ask his planners to prioritize the equipment and start improving the reliability of the important equipment. The planners would work with the tradesmen and operators and start assigning priority to the equipment. Over ninety percent of the time they'll identify the following equipment as having the highest priority:

- Chlorine Dioxide Mixer, CDM-1
- Seal water line to the mixer
- Steam Mixer, SM-1
- Screw Feeder, SF-1
- Thick Stock Pump, TSP-1.

All of the above equipment has a high profile in maintenance circles. Also some of the above items need constant maintenance attention and have a relatively low reliability. The priority designers will completely ignore the tank, because a tank is just a tank.

Guess what? **The above list is totally wrong.** Shortly we'll find out why.

Let's complicate the challenge a little further. Let's say to our maintainer friends: "Please note that what we gave you earlier was less than 1% of your plant, here are the remaining 150 sketches. Now tell us how you'll maintain equipment integrity if you have to consider all of the items simultaneously". Bafflement, all around. You see, you need to put the question in this manner since taking care of important items in one system is rather useless when far more critical pieces of equipment are left unattended to in other systems.

This is where the human mind is about at its limits and starts to look around for some aids. This is precisely what the Zero-Base™ methodology gives you: an aid to rationally analyze complex situations in a consistent manner, when handling large amounts of data.

NOW THE ZERO-BASE™ TECHNIQUE APPLICATION

In the Zero-Base™ methodology we use standardized vocabulary, therefore we modify the challenge in front of us to read as:

- Examine the mechanical integrity of the system and determine its strengths and weaknesses.
- Determine the safety threat indices for all pieces of equipment and list them in a descending order.
- Propose specific recommendations for items belonging to the following categories:
  - ⇒ Equipment with a threat index of 85 or higher
  - ⇒ Equipment with a threat index between 60 and 84
  - ⇒ Equipment with a threat index less than 60

To apply the Zero-Base™ methodology we'll apply the following steps:

Step 1

Make an equipment listing by filling out the *first three* columns of Form 1 as shown in seven filled in forms provided in Appendix C. You can do so by referring to the P&IDs (in this case the process sketch provided here).

Step 2

For each piece of equipment fill out a Form 2 (identical equipment can be added to one form to reduce the paperwork). Samples of some such filled out forms are provided in Appendix D.

The failure rate assessments, Zero-Base™ Failure Rate-(ZBFR), should be noted at the end of the forms as shown. Now these are your ZBFR numbers.

Step 3

Go back to Appendix C and insert the ZBFR numbers in the column provided for this purpose in Form 1.

Step 4

For each piece of equipment, analyze the failure modes and check off the likely impact in the appropriate columns in Form 1. In this respect, note the following.

We are interested in modes 1, 2 and 3. This should be noted on the form as shown.

For each mode the check mark is made in the appropriate impact column. Since the ascending mode number increases the severity of the impact, therefore from the three check marks, it is easy to correlate the marks and the impact.

In this analysis we only study the impact on safety, therefore we'll not worry about the Environmental or the Revenue impact.

Appendix C provides a sampling of such filled-in forms.

Step 5

For this step we need to utilize Form 10. We use one form for each piece of equipment. After some practice, some find it more expedient to use one form for many identical pieces of equipment.

You start at the ZBFR located on the left hand side y-axis. At first you draw a line through the ZBFR and each of the modes of interest. Note that we are only considering unmitigated circumstances. The lines so drawn are extended to meet the transfer line. From the transfer line, each point of intersection is extended to go through the corresponding impact point, and is allowed to meet the y-axis on the right hand side. After that you simply read the Safety Threat Index™ as the point of intersection.

A sampling of worked out Form 10 forms is included in Appendix E.

Step 6

Transfer the Safety Threat Index™ (STI) on to the Form 1 as shown in Appendix C. Do this exercise for all pieces of equipment.

Step 7

Review the results. In this case the distribution looks like the following:

	STI	
Class A	85-100	5
Class B	60-84	3
Class C	0-59	88

Going through the forms you'll find that the following pieces of equipment have an STI greater than 59:

- Chlorine Dioxide supply pipe P56
- Chlorine Dioxide storage tank T-1
- Chlorine Dioxide storage tank puff hatch PH-1
- Chlorine supply pipe P53
- Chlorine supply pipe P54
- Chlorine Dioxide storage tank instrument LIT-1
- Chlorine Dioxide storage tank instrument LE-1
- Chlorine Dioxide pump P-1.

Step 8

Having obtained the above fairly short list, it is very easy to develop specific recommendations to enhance the mechanical integrity of the equipment as far as preservation of human safety is concerned. For this short list, you can consider any or all of the following:

- Better training of operators and the maintainers
- Better and more frequent equipment testing, such as pressure or hydrostatic tests
- Better monitoring by the operators and the maintainers
- Better availability of drawings and spare parts
- Better response plans.

The equipment with STI numbers lower than 60, depending upon the individual STI values, can be added to the operator walk-through routes. For such equipment, maintenance help is provided on as-needed basis, rather than routine shutdowns and overhauls.

Step 9

If you do all of the above you'd guarantee yourself a safe plant and far better compliance with the regulations – all achieved very inexpensively. ***This is the magic of Zero-Base™ Strategy.***

SOME FINAL COMMENTARY

1. Did you notice that many of the high profile pieces of equipment which were identified by an ad-hoc approach to be critical, did not quite make the list? There is a profound message in all of this. Intuitively, we gravitate toward the exotic and the failure-prone pieces of equipment, especially those which are frequently on work orders. To make matters worse, the taste in "exotic" varies from person to person. Not so in the Zero-Base methodology, it does not matter how exotic or failure prone a piece of equipment is. What matters is a combination of reliability and the potential impact on safety, and its comparative relevance to the operation.

2. If we were considering the "Revenue Loss" impact, then some of the high profile equipment such as the steam or the chlorine dioxide mixer would play a far greater role and have a high value for Revenue Threat Index™.

3. In the example considered here, if a piece of equipment is determined to have "none" safety impact, then the STI numbers are meaningless. However, they've been determined and quoted, because for larger systems a computer program is used where instead of employing broad terminology as "none", finer cuts can be made, and most STI numbers do make sense.

4. Finally, as shown above, you need to focus on very few pieces of equipment to avoid catastrophic incidents, and, indeed, to improve the plant overall safety to exceptionally high levels.

Appendix C

Form-1: Failure-Impact-Threat Forms

FAILURE-IMPACT-THREAT FORM **Form ID Number:** 1 **Date:** 04/04/97 **FORM 1**
Main System: No.2 Bleach Plant **Subsystem:** ClO2 Supply **Ref:** PSM-51

Component	ID No.	ZBFR	Failure Mode	Safety Impact						Environmental Impact						Revenue Impact						OTI
				None	Injury	Disability	Fatality	TI	STI	None	Non-Reportable	Reportable	Catastrophic	TI	ETI	10K<	11-50K	51-100K	>100K	TI	RTI	
Pipe, ClO2 Supply	PS6	B	1,2,3		✓	✓	✓		87													
Pipe, ClO2 Supply	PS0	B	1,2,3	✓	✓✓				48													
VV, " "	V-50	A	1,2,3	✓✓	✓				35													
Tank, ClO2 storage	T-1	A	1,2,3			✓✓	✓		88													
Puff Hatch " "	PH-1	B	1,2,3	✓		✓	✓		87													
Pipe, " "	PS2	A	"	✓✓	✓				35													
PSV, " "	PSV-1	A	"	✓✓		✓			36													
LIT, " "	LIT-1	C		✓	✓	✓			62													
LE, " "	LE-1	C		✓	✓	✓			62													
LIC, " "	LIC-1	B		✓	✓	✓			48													
VV, " "	V-51	A		✓✓	✓				35													
Pump, ClO2	PP-1	C		✓	✓	✓			62													
Motor, "	M-4	A		✓	✓	✓			43													
STOP/START "	LSS-4	A		✓✓	✓				35													
CHK VV, "	V-52	A		✓	✓	✓			35													
VV, "	V-13	A		✓	✓	✓			35													
FE, "	FE-2	A		✓✓✓					35													
FIC, "	FIC-2	B		✓✓✓					42													
FCV, "	V-14	A		✓✓✓					35													
VV, "	V-15	A		✓✓✓					35													
CHK VV, "	V-16	A		✓✓✓					35													
POV, "	V-17	B		✓✓✓					45													
VV, "	V-18	A	↓	✓✓✓					35													

VV → Valve; PP → Pipe; pmp → Pump; POV → Piston Operated Valve
LSS → Local stop/start

FAILURE-IMPACT-THREAT FORM **Form ID Number:** 2 **Date:** 04/04/97 **FORM 1**
Main System: No. 2 Bleach Plant **Subsystem:** ClO_2 Supply **Ref:** PSM-51

Component	ID No.	ZBFR	Failure Mode	Safety Impact						Environmental Impact						Revenue Impact						OTI
				None	Injury	Dis-ability	Fatal-ity	TI	STI	None	Non-Report-able	Report-able	Catas-trophic	TI	ETI	10K<	11-50K	51-100K	>100K	TI	RTI	
PP, ClO_2 Supply	P10	A	1,2,3	✓	✓	✓			35													
VV, " "	V-19	A	1,2,3	✓✓✓					35													
LA, " "	LA-1	B	1,2,3	✓	✓	✓			48													

FAILURE-IMPACT-THREAT FORM **Form ID Number:** 3 **Date:** 04/04/97 **FORM 1**

Main System: No. 2 Bleach Plt **Subsystem:** Cl₂ Supply **Ref:** PSM-51

Component	ID No.	ZBFR	Failure Mode	Safety Impact						Environmental Impact						Revenue Impact						OTI
				None	Injury	Disability	Fatality	TI	STI	None	Non-Reportable	Reportable	Catastrophic	TI	ETI	10K<	11-50K	51-100K	>100K	TI	RTI	
PP, Chlorine Supply	P53	B		✓		✓	✓		86													
PP, "	P54	B		✓		✓	✓		86													
VV, "	V-53	A		✓✓✓					35													
VV, "	V-54	A		✓✓✓					35													
VV. "	V-56	A		✓✓✓					35													
FCV, "	FCV-2	B		✓✓✓					42													
VV, "	V-57	A		✓✓✓					35													
VV, "	V-58	A		✓✓✓					35													
VV, "	V-59	A		✓✓✓					35													
VV, "	V-60	A		✓✓✓					35													
PP, "	P-55	B		✓	✓	✓			48													
VV, "	PCV-1	B		✓✓✓					42													

WITO-Form 1 Rev G, 04/97

FAILURE-IMPACT-THREAT FORM | **Form ID Number:** 4 | **Date:** 4/4/97 | **FORM 1**

Main System: No. 2 Bleach Plt **Subsystem:** 50% Caustic Supply **Ref:** PSM-51

Component	ID No.	ZBFR	Failure Mode	Safety Impact						Environmental Impact						Revenue Impact						OTI
				None	Injury	Dis-ability	Fatal-ity	TI	STI	None	Non-Report-able	Report-able	Catas-trophic	TI	ETI	10K<	11-50K	51-100K	>100K	TI	RTI	
PP Caustic Supply	P1	A	1,2,3	√√	√				35													
FE, " "	FE-1	A		√√√					35													
FIC, " "	FIC-1	B		√√√					41													
PHIC, " "	PHIC-1	C		√√√					55													
FCV, " "	V-3	A		√√√					35													
VV, " "	V-1	A		√√√					35													
VV, " "	V-2	A		√√√					35													
VV, " "	V-4	A		√√√					35													
PP, " "	P2	A		√√	√				35													

WITO-Form 1 Rev G, 04/97

FAILURE-IMPACT-THREAT FORM Form ID Number: 5 Date: 04/04/97 **FORM 1**

Main System: No 2 Bleach Plt **Subsystem:** Steam supply (75 psig) **Ref:** PSM-51

Component	ID No.	ZBFR	Failure Mode	Safety Impact						Environmental Impact						Revenue Impact						OTI
				None	Injury	Disability	Fatality	TI	STI	None	Non-Reportable	Reportable	Catastrophic	TI	ETI	10K<	11-50K	51-100K	>100K	TI	RTI	
CHK VV, Steam Supply	V-24	A	1,2,3	✓✓✓					35													
VV, " "	V-25	A		✓✓✓					35													
CHK VV, " "	V-26	A		✓✓✓					35													
VV, " "	V-27	A		✓✓✓					35													
VV, " "	V-28	A		✓✓✓					35													
VV, " "	V-29	A		✓✓✓					35													
VV, " "	V-30	A		✓✓✓					35													
VV, " "	V-31	B		✓✓✓					42													
VV, " "	V-32	A		✓✓✓					35													
CHK VV, " "	V-33	A		✓✓✓					35													
PP, " "	P-5	A		✓	✓	✓			35													
PP, " "	P-6	A		✓	✓	✓			35													
TE, " "	TE-1	B		✓✓✓					42													
TIC, " "	TIC-1	C	✓	✓✓✓																		

WITO-Form 1 Rev G, 04/97

FAILURE-IMPACT-THREAT FORM | **Form ID Number:** 6 | **Date:** 04/04/97 | **FORM 1**

Main System: No.2 Bleach Plant **Subsystem:** ClO_2/Cl_2 Mixing | **Ref:** PSM-51

Component	ID No.	ZBFR	Failure Mode	Safety Impact						Environmental Impact						Revenue Impact						OTI
				None	Injury	Disability	Fatality	TI	STI	None	Non-Reportable	Reportable	Catastrophic	TI	ETI	10K<	11-50K	51-100K	>100K	TI	RTI	
VV, Pulp Flow	V-5	A	1,2,3	✓✓✓					35													
VV, " "	V-6	A		✓✓✓					35													
PP, " "	P3	A		✓✓	✓				35													
VV, " "	V-7	A		✓✓✓					35													
Steam Mixer	SM-1	C		✓✓✓					55													
" "	LSS-1	A		✓✓✓					35													
" "	M-1	A		✓✓✓					35													
" "	D-1	B		✓✓✓					35													
" "	M-2	A		✓✓✓					35													
" "	LSS-2	A		✓✓✓					35													
VV, " "	V-8	A		✓✓✓					35													
PP, " "	P-4	A		✓✓	✓				35													
PP, " "	P-9	A		✓✓	✓				35													
VV, Flushing Water	V-20	A		✓✓✓					35													
VV, " "	V-21	A		✓✓✓					35													
VV, " "	V-22	A		✓✓✓					35													
PP, " "	P-8	A		✓✓✓					35													
THICK STOCK PUMP	TSP-1	B		✓✓✓					42													
SCREW FEEDER	SF-1	B		✓✓✓					42													
" "	LSS-3	A		✓✓✓					35													
" "	M-3	A		✓✓✓					35													
VV, Pulp supply	V-10	A		✓✓✓					35													
VV, " "	V-11	A		✓✓✓					35													

Appendix D

Form-2: Zero-Base Failure Rate Forms

Zero-Base™ Failure Rate (ZBFR) **Form 2**

Raw Data Collection and Assessment

System:	NO. 2 Bleach Plant	Form 1 Identification No:	1
Subsystem:	ClO2 Supply		
Component	2" PIPE External to Storage Tank, PS6		
Model No.		Years in service: 20	
	Design maturity: ☐ Mature; ☐ New; ☐ Not sure	Manufacturer's reputation: ☐ Good; ☐ Not good; ☑ Not sure	
Ambient Conditions	☑ Located in open air ☐ Located indoors ☐ Clean, dry ambiance ☑ High humidity ☑ Presence of corrosive gases	☐ Occasional water and pollutant splashes ☐ Controlled temperature ☐ Frequent detrimental high temperatures ☐ Occasional freezing temperatures	
Application Severity	☐ Primary equipment, continuous service ☐ Usually on standby ☑ Steady continuous service ☐ Intermittent service, frequent stop/start	Inspection/Testing Information: Never tested or inspected, 20 yrs old	
Operational Conditions	☐ Always warmed up (pre-start) as required ☐ Usually warmed up (pre-start) as required ☐ Never warmed up (pre-start) as required ☐ Frequently overloaded ☐ Never overloaded N/A	☐ Frequent routine observation by technicians ☑ Infrequent routine observation by technicians ☐ No routine observation by technicians ☐ Always kept clean ☐ Sometimes kept clean ☐ Rarely cleaned	
Operator Competence: N/A	Formally trained to operate this component: ☐ Not formally trained to operate this component: ☐		
Maintainer Competence: N/A	Formally trained to maintain this component: ☐ Not formally trained to maintain this component: ☐		
Failure history–last 5 years	Actual Number: _____; ☑ None; ☐ 0-2; ☐ 3-10; ☐ >10		
Has the reason for these failures been positively eliminated	Yes; No; Not sure		
Published rate of failure: Units:	N/A	Data Bank:	

Assume that this piece of equipment is made fully operational by using your normal construction, maintenance and operational practices. **In your opinion, how many times is it likely to fail in the next five years, if it is operated without any maintenance activity, under *your* usual operational conditions and using your usual operating procedures?** To answer this question, ignore all maintenance including preventive maintenance–irrespective of who provides it. In making your assessment, consider all of the information provided above.

		Guidelines	
Maint. Tech.			
Area Operator:		A:	Less than 2
Field engineer:		B:	2-4
Selected value:	(B)	C:	4-6
		D:	6-10 or more

WITO Form 2 Rev D

Date:
Approved:

Zero-Base™ Failure Rate (ZBFR) **Form 2**

Raw Data Collection and Assessment

System:	No. 2 Bleach Plant	Form 1 Identification No:	1
Subsystem:	ClO2 Supply		
Component	ClO2 Supply Pipe Inside the tank, PSO		
Model No.		Years in service: 20	
	Design maturity: ☐ Mature; ☐ New; ☐ Not sure	Manufacturer's reputation: ☐ Good; ☐ Not good; ☑ Not sure	
Ambient Conditions	☐ Located in open air ☐ Located indoors ☐ Clean, dry ambiance ☐ High humidity ☐ Presence of corrosive gases	☐ Occasional water and pollutant splashes ☐ Controlled temperature ☐ Frequent detrimental high temperatures ☐ Occasional freezing temperatures	
Application Severity	☐ Primary equipment, continuous service ☐ Usually on standby ☑ Steady continuous service ☐ Intermittent service, frequent stop/start	Inspection/Testing Information: Never tested or inspected, 20 yr old	
Operational Conditions	☐ Always warmed up (pre-start) as required ☐ Usually warmed up (pre-start) as required ☐ Never warmed up (pre-start) as required ☐ Frequently overloaded ☐ Never overloaded NA	☐ Frequent routine observation by technicians ☐ Infrequent routine observation by technicians ☑ No routine observation by technicians ☐ Always kept clean ☐ Sometimes kept clean ☐ Rarely cleaned	
Operator Competence: N/A	Formally trained to operate this component: ☐ Not formally trained to operate this component: ☐		
Maintainer Competence: N/A	Formally trained to maintain this component: ☐ Not formally trained to maintain this component: ☐		
Failure history–last 5 years	Actual Number: ____; ☑ None; ☐ 0-2; ☐ 3-10; ☐ >10		
Has the reason for these failures been positively eliminated	Yes; No; Not sure		
Published rate of failure: Units:	N/A	Data Bank:	

Assume that this piece of equipment is made fully operational by using your normal construction, maintenance and operational practices. **In your opinion, how many times is it likely to fail in the next five years, if it is operated without any maintenance activity, under *your* usual operational conditions and using your usual operating procedures?** To answer this question, ignore all maintenance including preventive maintenance–irrespective of who provides it. In making your assessment, consider all of the information provided above.

			Guidelines	
	Maint. Tech.			
	Area Operator:		A:	Less than 2
	Field engineer:		B:	2-4
			C:	4-6
	Selected value:	B	D:	6-10 or more

Date:
Approved: ✓

Zero-Base™ Failure Rate (ZBFR) **Form 2**

Raw Data Collection and Assessment

System:	No. 2 Bleach Plant	Form 1 Identification No:	1
Subsystem:	ClO2 Supply		
Component	Valve V-50		
Model No.		Years in service: 20	
	Design maturity: ☐ Mature; ☐ New; ☐ Not sure	Manufacturer's reputation: ☒ Good; ☐ Not good; ☐ Not sure	
Ambient Conditions	☒ Located in open air ☐ Located indoors ☐ Clean, dry ambiance ☐ High humidity ☐ Presence of corrosive gases	☐ Occasional water and pollutant splashes ☐ Controlled temperature ☐ Frequent detrimental high temperatures ☐ Occasional freezing temperatures	
Application Severity	☐ Primary equipment, continuous service ☐ Usually on standby ☒ Steady continuous service ☐ Intermittent service, frequent stop/start	Inspection/Testing Information:	
Operational Conditions	☐ Always warmed up (pre-start) as required ☐ Usually warmed up (pre-start) as required ☐ Never warmed up (pre-start) as required ☐ Frequently overloaded ☐ Never overloaded NA	☐ Frequent routine observation by technicians ☐ Infrequent routine observation by technicians ☒ No routine observation by technicians ☐ Always kept clean ☐ Sometimes kept clean ☐ Rarely cleaned	
Operator Competence: NA	Formally trained to operate this component: ☐ Not formally trained to operate this component: ☐		
Maintainer Competence: NA	Formally trained to maintain this component: ☐ Not formally trained to maintain this component: ☐		
Failure history–last 5 years	Actual Number: ____; ☒ None; ☐ 0-2; ☐ 3-10; ☐ >10		
Has the reason for these failures been positively eliminated	Yes; No; Not sure		
Published rate of failure: Units:	NA	Data Bank:	

Assume that this piece of equipment is made fully operational by using your normal construction, maintenance and operational practices. **In your opinion, how many times is it likely to fail in the next five years, if it is operated without any maintenance activity, under *your* usual operational conditions and using your usual operating procedures?** To answer this question, ignore all maintenance including preventive maintenance–irrespective of who provides it. In making your assessment, consider all of the information provided above.

		Guidelines	
Maint. Tech.		A:	Less than 2
Area Operator:		B:	2-4
Field engineer:		C:	4-6
Selected value:	A	D:	6-10 or more

WITO Form 2 Rev D

Date:
Approved:

Zero-Base™ Failure Rate (ZBFR) **Form 2**

Raw Data Collection and Assessment

System:	No 2 Bleach Plant	Form 1 Identification No:	1
Subsystem:	ClO₂ Storage Tank		
Component	T-1		
Model No.		Years in service: 20	

	Design maturity: ☐ Mature; ☐ New; ☐ Not sure NA	Manufacturer's reputation: ☐ Good; ☐ Not good; ☑ Not sure
Ambient Conditions	☑ Located in open air ☐ Located indoors ☐ Clean, dry ambiance ☐ High humidity ☐ Presence of corrosive gases	☐ Occasional water and pollutant splashes ☐ Controlled temperature ☐ Frequent detrimental high temperatures ☐ Occasional freezing temperatures
Application Severity	☐ Primary equipment, continuous service ☐ Usually on standby ☑ Steady continuous service ☐ Intermittent service, frequent stop/start	Inspection/Testing Information: Tank shell inspected every six years
Operational Conditions	☐ Always warmed up (pre-start) as required ☐ Usually warmed up (pre-start) as required ☐ Never warmed up (pre-start) as required ☐ Frequently overloaded ☐ Never overloaded N/A	☐ Frequent routine observation by technicians ☐ Infrequent routine observation by technicians ☑ No routine observation by technicians ☐ Always kept clean ☐ Sometimes kept clean ☐ Rarely cleaned

Operator Competence:	Formally trained to operate this component: ☑ Not formally trained to operate this component: ☐
Maintainer Competence: N/A	Formally trained to maintain this component: ☐ Not formally trained to maintain this component: ☐
Failure history–last 5 years	Actual Number: _____; ☑ None; ☐ 0-2; ☐ 3-10; ☐ >10
Has the reason for these failures been positively eliminated	Yes; No; Not sure
Published rate of failure: Units:	N/A — Data Bank:

Assume that this piece of equipment is made fully operational by using your normal construction, maintenance and operational practices. **In your opinion, how many times is it likely to fail in the next five years, if it is operated without any maintenance activity, under *your* usual operational conditions and using your usual operating procedures?** To answer this question, ignore all maintenance including preventive maintenance–irrespective of who provides it. In making your assessment, consider all of the information provided above.

			Guidelines	
	Maint. Tech.		A:	Less than 2
	Area Operator:		B:	2-4
	Field engineer:		C:	4-6
	Selected value:	A	D:	6-10 or more

WITO Form 2 Rev D

Date:
Approved: u

Zero-Base™ Failure Rate (ZBFR) **Form 2**

Raw Data Collection and Assessment

System:	Bleach Plant No. 2	Form 1 Identification No:	1
Subsystem:	Puff Hatch on Tank T-1		
Component	PH-1		
Model No.		Years in service: 20	
	Design maturity: ☒ Mature; ☐ New; ☐ Not sure	Manufacturer's reputation: ☐ Good; ☐ Not good; ☒ Not sure	
Ambient Conditions	☒ Located in open air ☐ Located indoors ☐ Clean, dry ambiance ☐ High humidity ☐ Presence of corrosive gases	☐ Occasional water and pollutant splashes ☐ Controlled temperature ☐ Frequent detrimental high temperatures ☐ Occasional freezing temperatures	
Application Severity	☐ Primary equipment, continuous service ☐ Usually on standby ☒ Steady continuous service ☐ Intermittent service, frequent stop/start	Inspection/Testing Information: never inspected	
Operational Conditions	☐ Always warmed up (pre-start) as required ☐ Usually warmed up (pre-start) as required ☐ Never warmed up (pre-start) as required ☐ Frequently overloaded ☐ Never overloaded N/A	☐ Frequent routine observation by technicians ☐ Infrequent routine observation by technicians ☐ No routine observation by technicians ☐ Always kept clean ☐ Sometimes kept clean ☐ Rarely cleaned	
Operator Competence: N/A	Formally trained to operate this component: ☐ Not formally trained to operate this component: ☐		
Maintainer Competence:	Formally trained to maintain this component: ☐ Not formally trained to maintain this component: ☒		
Failure history–last 5 years	Actual Number: ____; ☐ None; ☒ 0-2; ☐ 3-10; ☐ >10		
Has the reason for these failures been positively eliminated	Yes; No; (Not sure)		
Published rate of failure: Units:	N/A	Data Bank:	

Assume that this piece of equipment is made fully operational by using your normal construction, maintenance and operational practices. **In your opinion, how many times is it likely to fail in the next five years, if it is operated without any maintenance activity, under *your* usual operational conditions and using your usual operating procedures?** To answer this question, ignore all maintenance including preventive maintenance–irrespective of who provides it. In making your assessment, consider all of the information provided above.

			Guidelines	
	Maint. Tech. Area Operator: Field engineer: Selected value:	B	A: B: C: D:	Less than 2 2-4 4-6 6-10 or more
© WITO Inc. 1994, 95, 96, 97 WITO Form 2 Rev D			Date: Approved:	S

Zero-Base™ Failure Rate (ZBFR) — Form 2

Raw Data Collection and Assessment

System:	No 2 Bleach Plant	Form 1 Identification No:	1
Subsystem:	ClO_2 Storage Tank Vent Pipe		
Component	PS2		
Model No.		Years in service: 20	
	Design maturity: ☐ Mature; ☐ New; ☐ Not sure N/A	Manufacturer's reputation: ☐ Good; ☐ Not good; ☐ Not sure NA	
Ambient Conditions	☑ Located in open air ☐ Located indoors ☐ Clean, dry ambiance ☐ High humidity ☐ Presence of corrosive gases	☐ Occasional water and pollutant splashes ☐ Controlled temperature ☐ Frequent detrimental high temperatures ☐ Occasional freezing temperatures	
Application Severity	☐ Primary equipment, continuous service ☐ Usually on standby ☑ Steady continuous service ☐ Intermittent service, frequent stop/start	Inspection/Testing Information: Not routinely inspected	
Operational Conditions	☐ Always warmed up (pre-start) as required ☐ Usually warmed up (pre-start) as required ☐ Never warmed up (pre-start) as required ☐ Frequently overloaded ☐ Never overloaded	☐ Frequent routine observation by technicians ☐ Infrequent routine observation by technicians ☑ No routine observation by technicians ☐ Always kept clean ☐ Sometimes kept clean ☐ Rarely cleaned	
Operator Competence: NA	Formally trained to operate this component: ☐ Not formally trained to operate this component: ☐		
Maintainer Competence: NA	Formally trained to maintain this component: ☐ Not formally trained to maintain this component: ☐		
Failure history–last 5 years	Actual Number: _____; ☐ None; ☑ 0-2; ☐ 3-10; ☐ >10		
Has the reason for these failures been positively eliminated	Yes; No; (Not sure)		
Published rate of failure: Units:	NA	Data Bank:	

Assume that this piece of equipment is made fully operational by using your normal construction, maintenance and operational practices. **In your opinion, how many times is it likely to fail in the next five years, if it is operated without any maintenance activity, under *your* usual operational conditions and using your usual operating procedures?** To answer this question, ignore all maintenance including preventive maintenance–irrespective of who provides it. In making your assessment, consider all of the information provided above.

			Guidelines	
	Maint. Tech. Area Operator: Field engineer: Selected value:	A	A: B: C: D:	Less than 2 2-4 4-6 6-10 or more

WITO Form 2 Rev D

Date:
Approved: 6

Appendix E

Form-10: The Graphical Tool

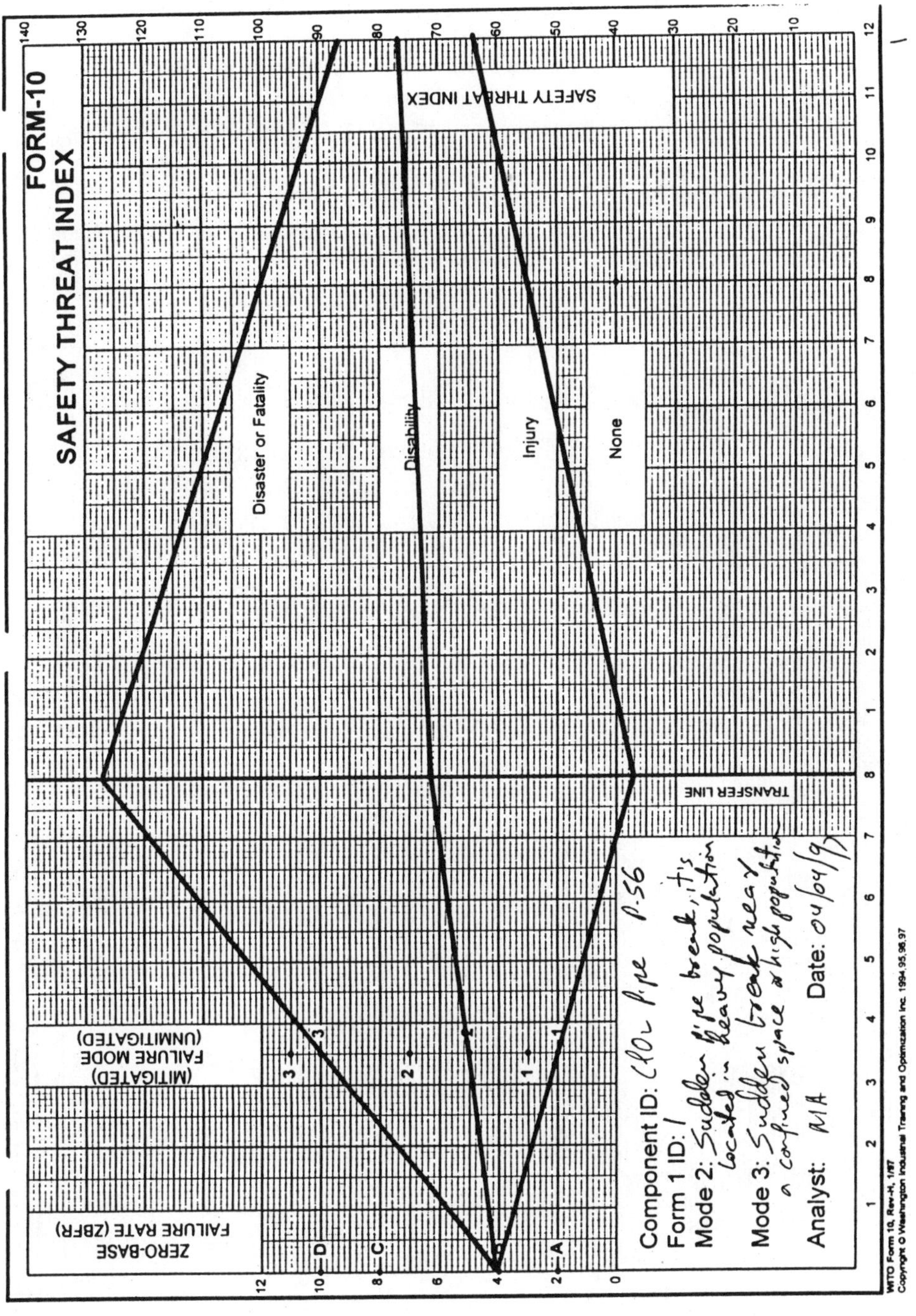
FORM-10
SAFETY THREAT INDEX
ZERO-BASE FAILURE RATE (ZBFR)
(MITIGATED) FAILURE MODE (UNMITIGATED)
Disaster or Fatality
Disability
Injury
None
SAFETY THREAT INDEX
TRANSFER LINE
Component ID: CROL Pipe P.56
Form 1 ID: 1
Mode 2:
Mode 3:
Analyst: MA
Date: 04/04/97
WITO Form 10, Rev-H, 1/97
Copyright © Washington Industrial Training and Optimization Inc. 1994,95,96,97

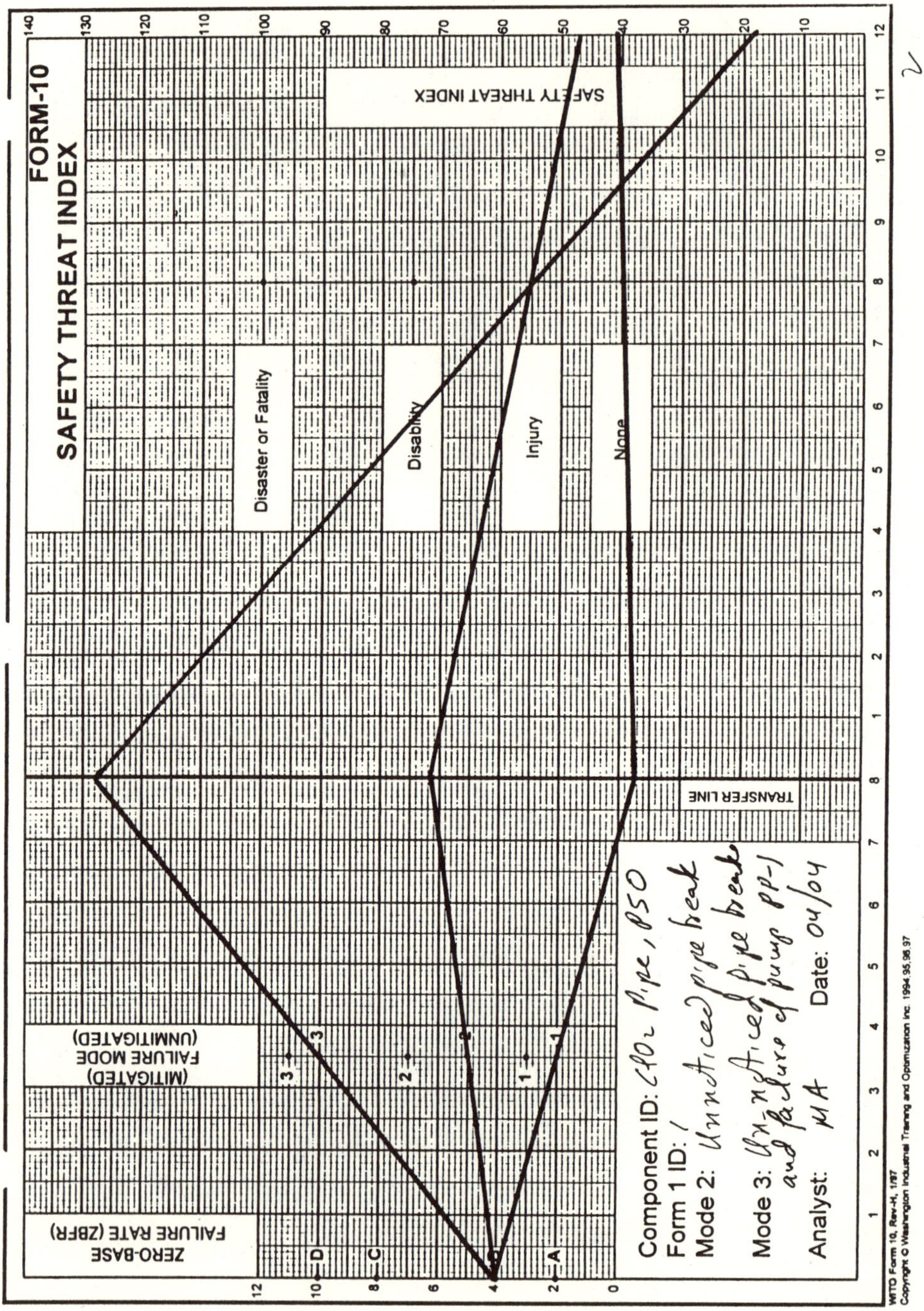
FORM-10
SAFETY THREAT INDEX
ZERO-BASE FAILURE RATE (ZBFR)
(MITIGATED) FAILURE MODE (UNMITIGATED)
TRANSFER LINE
Disaster or Fatality
Disability
Injury
None
Component ID:
Form 1 ID:
Mode 2:
Mode 3:
Analyst:
Date:
WITO Form 10, Rev-H, 1/97
Copyright © Washington Industrial Training and Optimization Inc. 1994,95,96,97

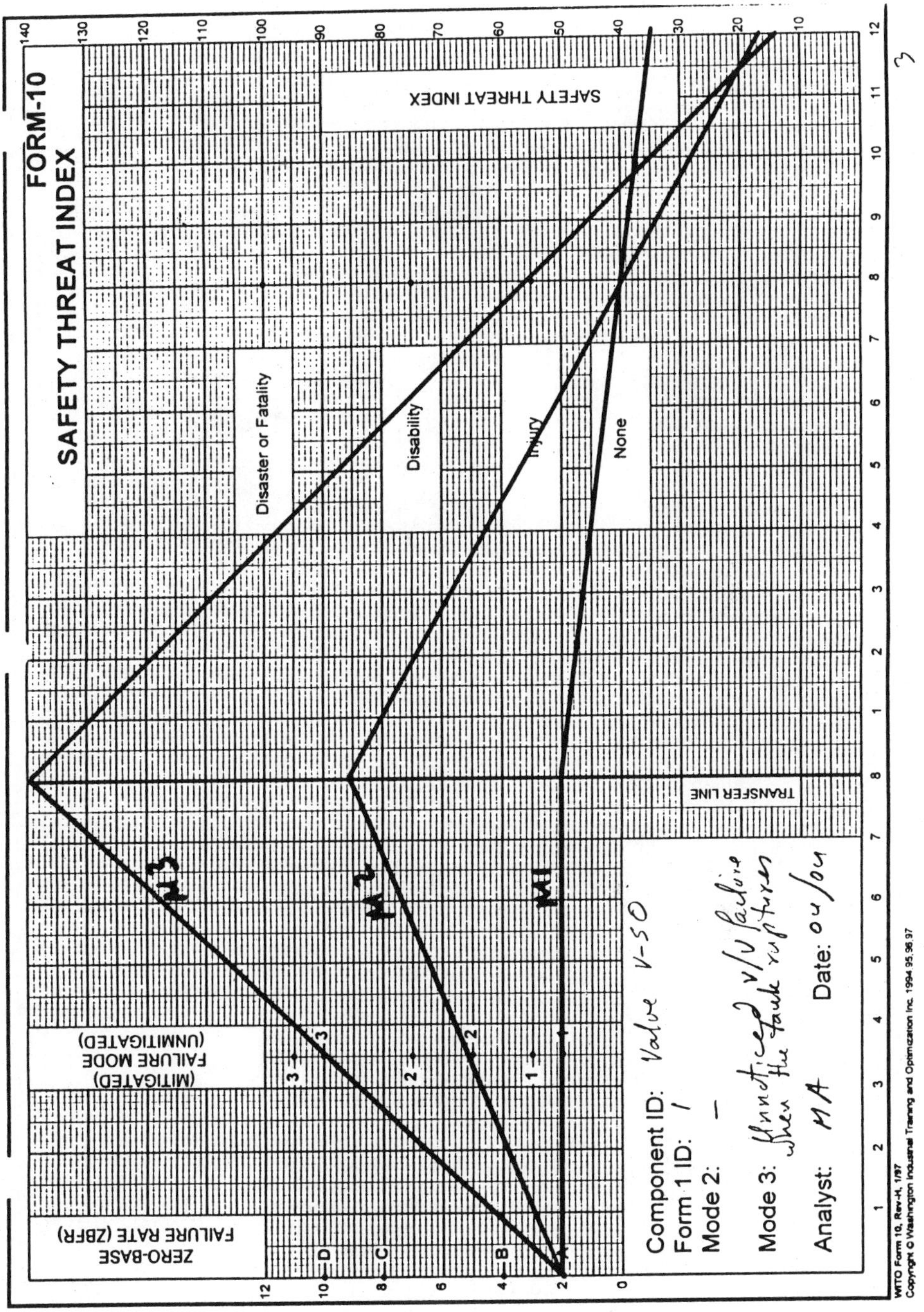
FORM-10
SAFETY THREAT INDEX
ZERO-BASE FAILURE RATE (ZBFR)
(MITIGATED) FAILURE MODE (UNMITIGATED)
Disaster or Fatality
Disability
Injury
None
SAFETY THREAT INDEX
TRANSFER LINE
Component ID:
Form 1 ID:
Mode 2:
Mode 3:
Analyst:
Date:
WITO Form 10, Rev-H, 1/97
Copyright © Washington Industrial Training and Optimization Inc. 1994 95,96,97

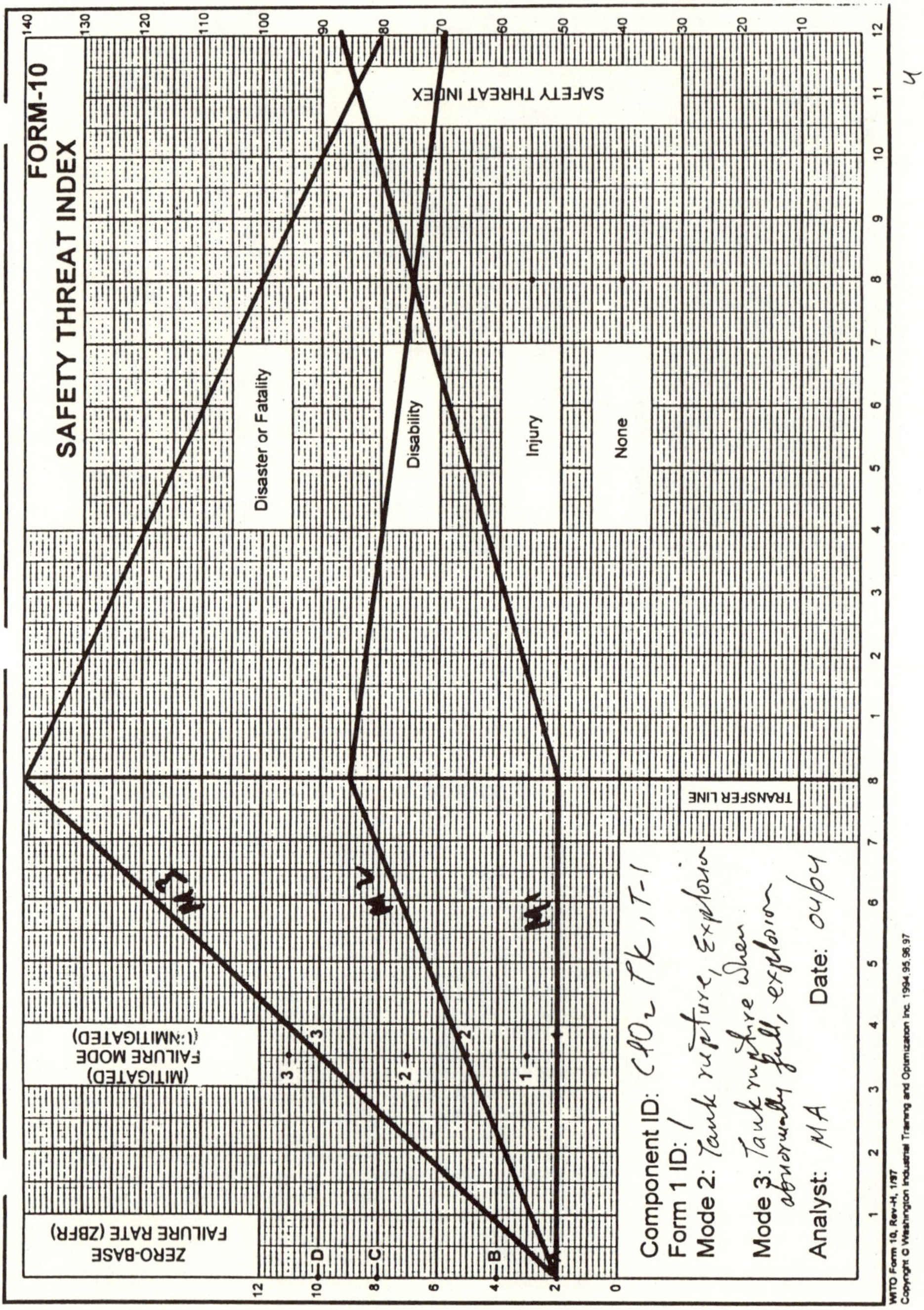

FORM-10
SAFETY THREAT INDEX
ZERO-BASE FAILURE RATE (ZBFR)
(MITIGATED) FAILURE MODE (UNMITIGATED)
TRANSFER LINE
SAFETY THREAT INDEX
Disaster or Fatality
Disability
Injury
None
M1
M2
M3
Component ID: ClO2 TK, T-1
Form 1 ID: 1
Mode 2: Tank rupture, Explosion
Mode 3: Tank rupture when abnormally full, explosion
Analyst: MA
Date: 04/04
WITO Form 10, Rev-H, 1/97
Copyright © Washington Industrial Training and Optimization Inc. 1994,95,96,97

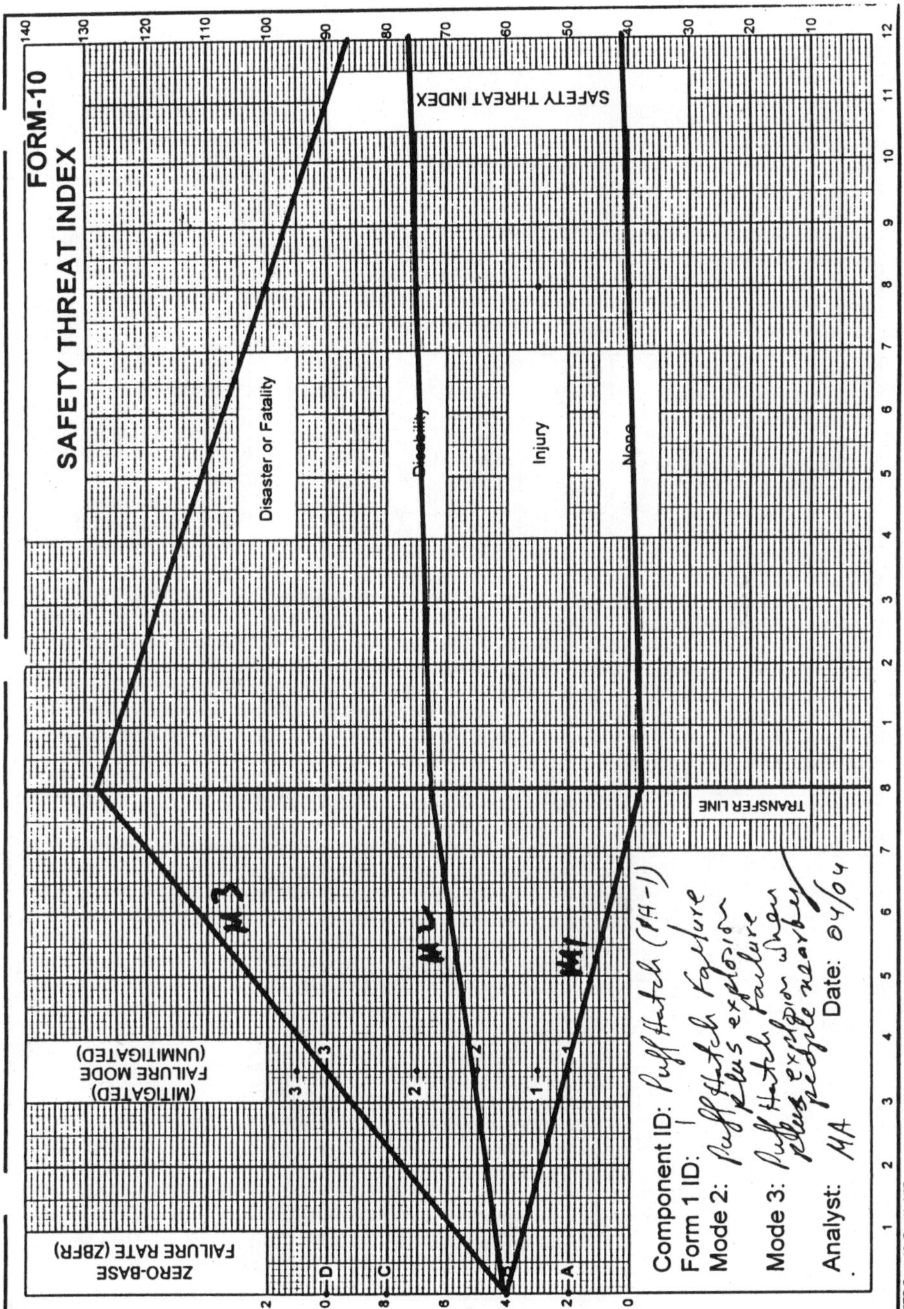
FORM-10
SAFETY THREAT INDEX
ZERO-BASE FAILURE RATE (ZBFR)
(MITIGATED) FAILURE MODE (UNMITIGATED)
Disaster or Fatality
Disability
Injury
None
TRANSFER LINE
SAFETY THREAT INDEX
Component ID:
Form 1 ID:
Mode 2:
Mode 3:
Analyst:
Date:
WITO Form 10, Rev-H, 1/97
Copyright © Washington Industrial Training and Optimization Inc. 1994,95,96,97

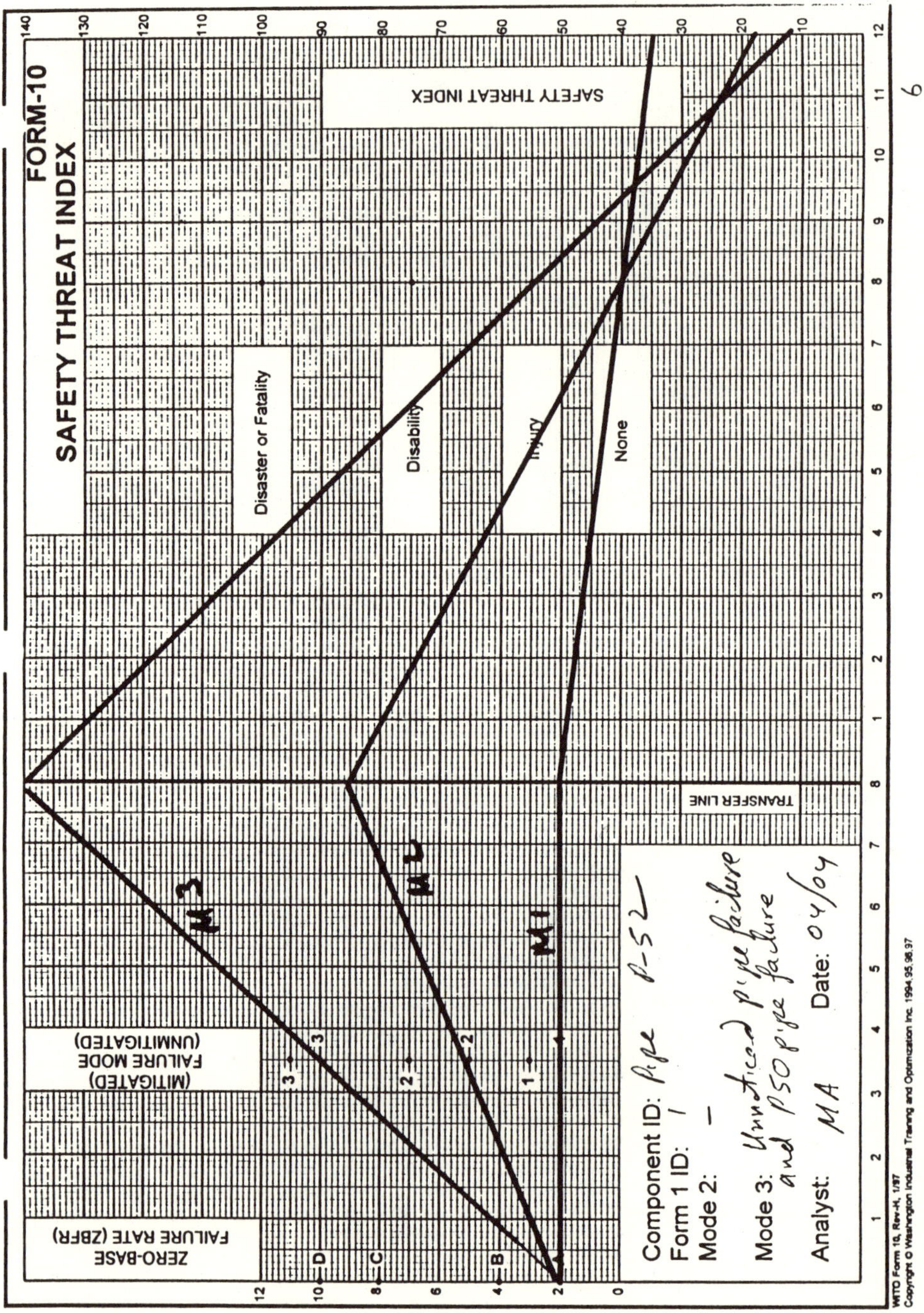
SAFETY THREAT INDEX
FORM-10
ZERO-BASE FAILURE RATE (ZBFR)
(MITIGATED) FAILURE MODE (UNMITIGATED)
TRANSFER LINE
SAFETY THREAT INDEX
Disaster or Fatality
Disability
Injury
None
M1
M2
M3
Component ID: Pipe P-52
Form 1 ID: 1
Mode 2: —
Mode 3: Unmitigated pipe failure and P50 pipe failure
Analyst: MA
Date: 04/04
WITO Form 10, Rev-H, 1/97
Copyright © Washington Industrial Training and Optimization Inc. 1994,95,96,97

Appendix F
Glossary

*I*n the arts and sciences of risk assessment some terminology is commonly used:

Availability
The time when a system is fully operational divided by the total calendar time in question.

Calendar Time
The actual period which is being studied. All such periods should add up to a full year and should include normal operation, shutdowns and non-operation periods.

Catastrophic-Criticality
A piece of equipment is said to have Catastrophic-Criticality if the value for its ZBFR is 2 or less, and if it is likely to cause a catastrophic event when failing in Mode 1.

CPQRA
Chemical Process Quantitative Risk Analysis.

Confidence
A statistical measure of uncertainty.

Confidence Bounds or Limits
The points defining the boundaries of a confidence interval.

Disaster-Criticality

A piece of equipment is said to have Disaster-Criticality if the value for its ZBFR is less than 2, and it is likely to cause a catastrophic event when failing in Mode 2.

Environmental Threat Index (ETI)

This is a standardized measure which gives the value of the threat posed by a piece of equipment or process to the environment.

Event Tree Analysis (ETA)

A method encompassing the intermediate and final outcomes originating from a single initiating incident.

Failure Frequency

This parameter is given in one of two ways. Firstly, generally for continuous operations such as operation of pump, it is given by the number of failures during a given period. Secondly, for discrete events such as operation of a relay, it is given by number of failures for a given number of demands.

Failure Mode and Effect Analysis (FMEA)

This is failure analysis technique which, for a given system, is based on analyses of different modes of failure and the associated effects.

Failure Probability

The probability (a number between 0 and 1) that a component or system will fail on demand or will fail in a given time period.

Failure Rate
This number is given by dividing the number of failures by the time period in consideration or the total number of demands.

Fault Tree Analysis (FTA)
An analytical method which is based on analyses of contributing components to an undesired event.

HAZOP
Hazard and Operability Study

Mean
This number is given by the arithmetic average of series of numbers.

MTBF
Mean Time Between Failure

MTBR
Mean Time Between Repair

MTBM
Mean Time Between Maintenance Actions

Operational Criticality Index (OCI)
This is a standardized measure which quantifies the overall level of threat posed by a given piece of equipment or process. This factor consists of three components: STI, ETI and RTI. This factor is also known as Operational Threat Index (OTI).

Operational Threat Index (OTI)
This is a standardized measure which quantifies the overall level of threat posed by a given piece of equipment or process. This factor consists of three components: STI, ETI and RTI. This factor is also known as Operational Criticality Index (OCI

PRA
Probabilistic Risk Assessment.

Probability
The probability (a number between 0 and 1) that an event will occur on demand or during a given time period.

Revenue Threat Index (RTI)
This is a standardized measure which gives the value of the threat posed by a piece of equipment or process to the revenue stream or monetary loss in any form.

Risk
An expression which, in composite form, describes the probability of an event along with associated consequences.

Safety Threat Index (STI)
This is a standardized measure which gives the value of the threat posed by a piece of equipment or process to the safety of personnel.

Zero Base Failure Rate (ZBFR)
The expected rate of failure for a piece of equipment while operating in a specific location and under a given set of operational conditions. To determine this factor all maintenance effort is zeroed out–only the inherent and operational characteristics are considered.

Appendix G
Bibliography

A Guide to Hazard and Operability Studies. Chemical Industries Association, 1977.

Amalberti, Rene. *Safety in Process-Control: An Operator-Centered Point of View.* Reliability Engineering and System Safety, 1992.

Ansoff, H. Igor. *Implementing Strategic Management.* Englewood Cliffs, NJ: Prentice-Hall, 1984.

Anthony, Robert N. *Management Control Systems.* Homewood, IL: Richard D. Irwin, Inc., 1984.

Anthony, Robert N. *The Management Control Function.* Boston: Harvard Business School Press, 1988.

Asbjornsen, 0. A. Technical management: A major challenge in industrial competition. *Chem. Eng. Prog.,* Nov. 1988, pp.27-32.

Baybutt, P. Communicating risk step by step. *Hydrocarbon Processing,* 68(6), 1989, p.85.

Buchner, H. et. al. *Comparative Evaluation of Active vs Passive System Designs.* Reliability Engineering and System Safety, 1994.

Burk, A. F. Managing process safety to prevent catastrophes. *Industrial Hygiene Management.* New York: Wiley, 1988.

Camillus, John C. *Strategic Planning and Management Control,* Lexington, MA: Lexington Books, 1986.

CCPS Guidelines for Process Equipment Reliability Data, with Data Tables. New York AIChE/CCPS, 1989.

Chemical Plant and Petroleum Refinery Piping-ANSI/ASME B31.3. New York: American Society of Mechanical Engineers, 1984.

Chhibber, S. et. al. *A Taxonomy of Issues Related to the use of Expert Judgments in Pobabilistic Safety Studies.* Reliability Engineering and System Safety, 1992.

Coolen, F. P. A., et. al. *A Bayes-Computing Risk Model for the use of Expert Judgment in Reliability Estimation.* Reliability Engineering and System Safety, 1992.

Crosby, Philip B. *Quality without Tears.* New York: McGraw-Hill, 1984.

Davoudian, K. *Incorporating Organizational Factors Into Risk Assessment Through the Analysis of Work Processes.* Reliability Engineering and System Safety, 1994.

Dekker, R. *Applications of Maintenance Optimization Models: A Review and Analysis.* Reliability Engineering and System Safety, 1996.

Deming, W. Edwards. *Out of the Crisis.* Cambridge, MA: MIT Center for Advanced Engineering Studies, 1986.

Dermer, Jerry, *Management Planning and Control Systems.* Homewood, IL: 1977

Eilon, Samuel. *Management Control.* London: Macmillan, 1971.

Electrical Transmission and Distribution Reference Book, Westinghouse Electric Corporation, 1977.

Feigenbaum, Armand V. *Total Quality Control,* 3rd Edition. New York:

Guide for Inspection of Refinery Equipment. Washington, DC: American Petroleum Institute, 1957.

Guidelines for Chemical Process Quantitative Risk Analysis. New York: AIChE/CCPS, 1989.

Guidelines for Hazard Evaluation Procedures. New York: AIChE/CCPS, 1985.

Guidelines for Human Reliability in Process Safety. New York: AIChE/CCPS,

Hollnagel, E. *Reliability Analysis and Operator Modelling.* Reliability Engineering and System Safety, 1996.

Hudoklin, A. et. al. *Reliability of Railway Traffic Personnel.* Reliability Engineering and System Safety, 1996.

Ishikawa, Kaoru. *Guide to Quality Control.* Tokyo: Unipub, 1982.

Kafka, Peter. *Important Issues Using PSA Technology for Design of New Systems and Plants.* Reliability Engineering and System Safety, 1994.

Kaplan, Stan. *"Expert Information" versus "Expert Opinions." Another Approach to the Problem of Eliciting/Combining/Using Expert Knowledge in PRA.* Reliability Engineering and System Safety, 1992.

Kemp, R. V. *Risk Tolerance and Safety Management.* Reliability Engineering and System Safety, 1991.

Kletz, Trevor A. *Cheaper, Safer Plants or Wealth and Safety at Work.* Rugby, England: The Institution of Chemical Engineers, 1984.

Kletz, Trevor A. *HA ZOP & HAZAN, Notes on the Identification and Assessment of Hazards.* Rugby, England: The Institution of Chemical Engineers.

Kletz, Trevor A. *What Went Wrong? Case Histories of Process Plant Disasters.* Houston, TX: Gulf Publishing, 1985.

LeVine, R. *Guidelines for Safe Storage and Handling of High Toxic Hazard Materials.* New York: AIChE/CCPS, 1988.

Macwan, A. et. al. *A Methodology for Modeling Operator Errors of Commission in Probabilistic Risk Assessment.* Reliability Engineering and System Safety, 1994.

Martinott, R. T. Maintenance management systems. *Chemical Week,* March 9, 1988, pp.20-24.

Montmayeul, R. et. al. *The Managerial Dilemma Between the Prescribed Task and the Real Activitiy of Operators: Some Trends for Research on Human Factors.* Reliability Engineering and System Safety, 1994.

Overview-A Total Management Program for Loss Prevention and Control. Hartford, CT: Industrial Risk Insurers, 1986.

Process Safety Management (Control of Acute Hazards). Washington, DC: Chemical Manufacturers Association, May 1985.

Pulkkinen, Urho. *Methods for Combination of Expert Judgments.* Reliability Engineering and System Safety, 1993.

Rasmussen, Brigitte. *Chemical Process Hazard Identification.* Reliability Engineering and System Safety, 1989.

Reinertsen R. *Risk Measures in Practical Use: Risk Reduction Has Its Price: But is it known?* Reliability Engineering and System Safety, 1995.

Rouhiainen, Veikko. *Importance of the Quality Management of Safety Analysis.* Reliability Engineering and System Safety, 1993.

Svenson, Ola. *On Expert Judgments in Safety Analyses in the Process Industries.* Reliability Engineering and System Safety, 1989.

Tait, N. R. S. *The use of Probability in Engineering Design–An Historic Survey.* Reliability Engineering and System Safety, 1993.

Watson, P. R. *The Meaning of Probability in Probabilistic Safety Analysis.* Reliability Engineering and System Safety, 1994.

Woods, D. D. *Risk and Human Performance.* Reliability Engineering and System Safety, 1990.

Index